Pork Chop Hill

Other Books by S.L.A. Marshall

On Tactics and Leading

Men Against Fire
The Soldier's Load
Vietnam Primer

The Armed Forces Officer
The Officer as a Leader

On War

Crimsoned Prairie
The War to Free Cuba
Armies on Wheels
World War II Story
Swift Sword

Blitzkrieg
World War I
Military History of the Korean War

On Battle

Battle at Best
Battles in the Monsoon
Island Victory
Night Drop
Bird: The Christmastide Battle
The River and the Gauntlet

Bastogne: The First Eight Days
Sinai Victory
Makin
West to Cambodia
Ambush

On Operations

Hill 400
Critique of Infantry Weapons and Tactics in Korea
Problems of the Defense in Atomic War
Guide to the Use of Information Materials

Memoir

Bringing Up the Rear

PORK CHOP HILL

The American Fighting Man in Action
Korea, Spring, 1953

by
S.L.A. MARSHALL

Infantry Operations Analyst, ORO, G3, Eighth Army
Chief Historian, European Theater
Correspondent, *The Detroit News*

Maps and Drawings by

H. GARVER MILLER, ORO

THE BATTERY PRESS
NASHVILLE

© by S.L.A. Marshall

THE BATTERY PRESS, INC.
P.O. Box 3107, Uptown Station
Nashville, Tennessee 37219

Twelfth in The Combat Arms Series
1986
ISBN: 0-89839-090-7
Printed in The United States of America

This book is affectionately dedicated to the United States Navy because it won the love of my wife, Cate, when she served it as a Specialist S.

Contents

List of Maps

Preface

Duration the spring of 1953 I returned to Korea to work for the first time as a war correspondent with American forces. Shortly, at Army request, I found myself doing essentially the same kind of field work in which I had pioneered in Central Pacific operations during World War II, then carried to Europe during the Normandy invasion and continued in Korea in 1950-51.

The task: to analyze our infantry line and its methods under pressure, to estimate whether troops are good or bad, to see what is wrong or right in our tactics and to recommend such corrections as are indicated.

On the two earlier occasions I was on loan from *The Detroit News*, and my family. In the big war, I went as a soldier, subject to orders. Later in Korea I worked as a "research scientist," still subject to orders and charged as a committee-of-one with analyzing infantry operations. The first task given me in the hour when we were defeated in the Battle of the Chongchon and beaten back from North Korea was to define the fighting methods of our "surprise" adversary, the Red Chinese.

What's in a name? Neither job entailed anything more complex than interrogation, fact-gathering, straight reporting and some deduction, which are supposed to be the *abcd* of news work. In 1953, for reasons which had to do with my personal life rather than with my professional obligations, I was present only as *The News* correspondent.

It made no difference in the work. I was given the same help and the same unlimited backing. The same willing and candid response came from the troops. The change in hats seemed to bother no one except a few minor functionaries.

To my mind this has always been one of the better things about the United States Army. In the field, status becomes of relatively little importance, provided one gets essential work done and can develop information which is of general benefit. I was afforded that opportunity, and the resources put at my disposal to take advantage of it were proof of the interest and support of the higher command.

Upon arriving in the Theater I began to hear pessimistic reports about how gravely our musical chairs rotation policy had down-graded the fighting spirit of the average young American in the combat line. Worried senior officers expressed the view that if the war's pace changed and the pressure rose suddenly, troops might be found lacking in the old drive and guts. Line captains told me that morale had so far deteriorated that when units came under full attack more men died from taking refuge in the bunkers than from fighting their weapons in the trenches.

Quickly, the occasion arose for systematic inquiry. The 7th Infantry Division was brought to battle in a determined three-day attempt by the Red Chinese to smash its vital outpost line. In that year it was the only United States division to know major fighting. Compared to Gettysburg or the Ardennes, Pork Chop Hill was hardly more than a skirmish. But within the force that engaged, losses were unusually heavy. Maj. Gen. Trudeau's command acquitted itself with the highest credit.

But because Operation Little Switch was going on coincidentally at Freedom Village, and every correspondent rushed to that spot as if all life depended upon it, all that happened, all of the heroism and all of the sacrifice, went unreported. So the very fine victory of Pork Chop Hill deserves the description of the Won-Lost Battle. It was won by the troops and lost to sight by the people who had sent them forth.

I felt strongly that the ignoring of the fight by the press and the people only made it more important that some day the story should be told. The neglect was worse because in preceding weeks this same division—the 7th—had been lambasted for the loss of Old Baldy and the staging of Operation Smack. They had been described as weary, slipshod, demoralized troops, and, while the Pork Chop Hill fight was on, this caustic criticism from home was repeated over Red Chinese loud-speakers to the American fighters. Then when the moment came that their brave deeds refuted all disparagement of them, there were no witnesses to sing their praises. It was terribly unfair.

Certainly the prisoner exchange was sensationally interesting and possibly highly significant. It was the big news and deserved the big spotlight. But as the song says, the fundamental things apply as time goes by. One fundamental question in Korea, 1953, and now, is how the American character continues to meet the test of great events. It would have been possible for the correspondents to keep shuttling between Freedom Village and Pork Chop Hill which were less than seventy miles apart. Under pressure from their home offices they had to stick fast to the Panmunjom story. I kept mobile for reason which had little to do with the requirements of my newspaper. In the middle of the Pork Chop fight, which I had already under study, I was called to Freedom Village as an adviser to Gen. Mark W. Clark on the problems of censorship. So the decision was made for me. It was necessary to keep shuttling between the two points.

One at a time, we formed the companies which had taken the main blows on Pork Chop, Dale and Arsenal. The assemblies were held immediately. Already, units which were 200 strong when the fight began were down to 40 or 50 men. Some of the platoons mustered not more than five or six men. These little bands were still chins up.

If the company happened to be holding a sector of the front line, we brought it back to the reverse slope to hold the group interview, leaving the main trench outposted, since there was no shelter or space along the ridge crest ample enough to accommodate the assembly. Where the company was in a so-called "blocking position," blocking a valley or other avenue which bisected the main line, the work was done on the spot where the troops bivouacked.

The average length of the question-and-answer session with each company was seven and one-half hours, during which we worked steadily together, except for two or three short breaks for coffee and to uncramp my fingers.

But when we had finished, we knew practically everything that had happened to these units during the fight, the determining events were in almost exact chronological order, and we could account for the manner in which most of the men had been killed or wounded as well as how effectively the weapons had been used.

The method was the same as I had first used during the invasion of the Gilbert Islands ten years earlier. In working with a group to reconstruct a confused action, clarification becomes possible, indeed almost inevitable, if one starts at the beginning and thereafter develops each incident in its proper sequence. All of the participants in the fight appear as witnesses. The memory of each man is refreshed by what he hears others say. At these formations all rank is put aside. The greenest private may contradict his colonel if he believes that his colonel's statement is in error. Testimony is weighed according to its obvious validity and pertinence to the course taken by the operation. There are several surprising things about the process which in itself is elementary and requires little more than patient concentration. Blank spots rarely occur. In the average critique, once work starts, there is almost no disagreement between the witnesses.

By the time I was through on Pork Chop Hill, my notebook contained more than 50,000 words on this one fight. It was evident that its great human values could not be compressed into newspaper space. Some of the incidents were synopsized and sent home. Later, when there was leisure, I began to read back through the cold notes. As they warmed again, what had been written on the distant ridges seemed clearly to point to several general conclusions.

The in-fighting which took place in the entrenched works of the outposts was as hard-pressed and bloody as Cold Harbor, Attu or the Argonne. The Americans won, not simply by the superior weight of their artillery, but because the infantry, man for man in the hand-to-hand battle, outgamed the Red Chinese.

In two vital particulars these Americans outshone any of our troops with whom I have ever dealt: there was a superior command presence in their young officers, and a higher ratio of enlisted men exercised strong initiative in the most dangerous moments.

The one manifest weakness in our youngsters was in their leg muscles and not in their fighting spirit; the former the Army, in the time allotted it, can do little to correct; it should rejoice that they are not deficient in the latter. Their officers were wrong in suspecting that when the Red tide moved in, too many young Americans took refuge inside the bunker walls, neglecting to use their weapons. But it was unmistakably true that an inordinate percentage of ROK soldiers behaved that way, and I so reported.

But in more ways than one, the show remained an enigma. Being a book soldier, I could not believe in the policy of individual rotation then in use by the United States. To my mind, it was ruinous to morale and to good administrative order within an armed force. Whatever it gave the soldier, it sacrificed most of the traditional values, such as earned promotion and citation, pride in unit and close comradeship, which are supposed to keep troops steadfast. Yet in the crucible the metal still looked like gold. Maybe the truth is that we haven't begun to understand the potential of young Americans for meeting the great challenge.

Shortly after Pork Chop Hill I attended a memorial service for the battle dead of one battalion. It did honor to 73 men. But they had been given no other honor by their country for the victory which they had helped win; it drew no headlines, nor did the voices on the national radio give adequate testimony. There is a great deal of iron in war. There is also irony.

My work with the patrols was of a slightly different order because of a sharply defined objective. For nearly two years, Eighth Army had fought an almost stationary war, and patrolling was its main combat activity. In that time, there had been no uniformly regulated system of patrol reporting or "debriefing" and there was much slack in these operations because the records were not clear. It was quite possible for a patrol to fake a probe and get away with it if only a few hands wished to avoid an embarrassing exposure. So the work had the threefold purpose of demonstrating the weakness in the old hit-or-miss method, substituting a system which could be centrally controlled, and last, starting a school for the training of people who could extend the system. Had the war lasted, it might have proved more than a novel, local experiment.

I dealt with the patrols as rapidly as I could get to them by jeep or helicopter, starting as soon as the word came through that a patrol had been hit. We did our work in the early morning before the survivors had been given rest or a chance to clean up. The average debriefing session lasted four hours and we forgathered in whatever bunker was handiest to their point of return. The curious thing was that the work, instead of further straining men already near exhaustion, seemed to have a therapeutic effect and provide a spiritual purge. They were burdened and brooding over a feeling of failure at the beginning. As they talked things out, and all that had happened for good or bad came clear to them, they freshened. The recuperative powers in the young American fighter in this situation are absolutely amazing. Even if only a half dozen have survived out of twenty, they go at the problem with almost uniform interest and professional exactitude.

The lessons in these night operations should be clear to all who study the detail of what happened. For my own part, I was impressed most strongly by the almost invariable collapse of communications and the showing that disarrangements in night fighting usually come of some freak happening which no one could have anticipated. With all the emphasis that is put upon control, there is still room to search for improved safeguards.

Of the enlisted men who appear in this book, I recommended 73 for decoration, the awards ranging from Bronze Star to the Congressional Medal. In Korea, uniquely, I had time to talk to a large group of honor men about their background. Not one of the 73 came of a family which could have afforded to send him to college. Most of them came from families with three children or more. Not one of them was an only child. The majority spoke voluntarily of their home folks with enthusiasm, recognizing that the love given them was a vital force in their lives. Of the 73, 52 expressed warm admiration for their fathers, most often with high regard for their masculine qualities. Several of these tributes are an integral part of the battle narrative. The sample is not large enough to be highly significant. It is reported only as it bears on the character of the young men whose deeds carried this particular fight for the United States. In the words of Elliot Paul: "It was a privilege to be associated with such courageous, high-minded men, and their enemies will do well to be afraid of them so long as they are above ground."

What of the enemy? In this book, both during the main fight and in the patrol actions, he appears as hardly more than a fleeting shadow in his brief forays across the surface before he returns to earth. That was the nature of Red Chinese operations during the last year of the war. If an attempt were made in this book to materialize this force, to make the intangible comprehensible, it would be unreal. Red Chinese operations were a vanishing act on the grand scale. Their defensive works were engineered for maximum concealment and deception; ours were not. In the attack, their individuals were furtive, light of foot and highly elusive; ours were not. The essential difference between the two sides did not come of any natural traits which made one light, the other ponderous. After fighting operations were relatively stabilized by the truce negotiations, the Red Chinese kept men and units in line. The longer they stayed, the craftier they became. On the American side, men moved in and out as if the fighting line operated on a conveyer belt. No one stayed long enough to graduate in the fine art of deception. "Even so was wisdom proven blind, so courage failed, so strength was chained."

In 1950, the Red Chinese were a crude lot, given more to pell-mell attacks and diehard stands than to deception and protection. But they stayed and they learned as they went along. When they entered the war, apart from their exceptional skill and persistence with the machine gun, they were not accurate users of hand weapons in pressing the attack home. Until the end, that general weakness was evident. Otherwise, by 1953 few of the old signs remained. They had become as tenacious and as earth-seeking as ants, and in that lay a great part of their success. Two and one-half years of war in Korea were a bonanza for Communist China. On that training ground her armies became as skilled as any in the world in the techniques of hitting, evading and surviving.

Much of the warfare that is described in this book becomes comprehensible only when it is examined against the background of the two opposing defensive systems.

The enfilading of our trenches occurred almost invariably when the Red Chinese got inside our works. It could hardly be prevented. The profiles of the American bunkers stood so high above the trench that the enemy was able to use their sandbagged walls as breastworks from which to fire along the trench. Once he became so placed, it was almost impossible to dislodge him with counter grenade and automatic fire. The only tactic which availed was for one or two hardy spirits to crawl along the high ground behind the parados and try to blast him from the flank.

Downhill communications trenches from the main line to the outpost subridges were frequently dug so deep that it would have been impossible to fire any weapon from within them so as to cover the ridge slopes. Yet in many instances they were suitably placed for the putting of flanking fire against an enemy force attacking upslope toward the outpost. The main object of entrenchments, judging by their depth, was to provide the fullest possible cover against enemy artillery bursts rather than to afford the garrison a reasonable protection without limiting its employment of its own weapons.

Bunkers had been built without particular regard to the slopes which they were supposed to cover or the weapons which would be fired from within them. So many times the height and outlook of the embrasure made the siting of the weapon excessively high. It could not be turned against the immediate downslope unless the firer leaned out and beyond the aperture. Thus, in effect, the weapon was aimed at ground along the flat beyond the ridge foot where its automatic fires overlapped the fires of the mortars and artillery. Often the rifleman in the trench was similarly interdicted by the depth of the cut and the height of the parapet. To put fire on the immediate downslope, he had to get out of the trench.

Roads leading to the main line, under full observation by the enemy, many times running parallel to his lines, often within less than 1,000 yards of his gun positions, were at best only superficially screened. At many points the screening had been either weathered down or flattened by the enemy fire. Its appearance suggested it had been in that condition for weeks, though there had been no effort to replace it. Where the screening was up, the one layer could not have been sufficient to conceal vehicular movement along the main supply route.

The placement of main-line fire trenches seemed to be arbitrary and according to the whim of local commanders rather than standardized according to accepted fire principles. Sometimes the line followed the military crest. Sometimes it was along the topographical crest. Along still other ridges, it was somewhere between the two. But these variations did not appear to be governed by the dominant terrain conditions, for example, the topographical crest being too sheer for entrenchment, or the military crest being rejected because it was too far downslope. In fact, there was no discernible pattern.

Most bunkers, particularly those on reverse slopes used for sleeping and warming, were too heavily built. The surplus of sandbags on the roofs weakened the timbers and tended to break the bunker down under artillery fire. Then, because the over-all weight of the structure was often much too heavy for its insecure moorings, the run-off of only a little rain from the bunker, washing away a few inches of soil from the downslope, would collapse the bunker.

Many of the sleeping bunkers, of no use for anything except shelter in the hour of engagement, were distributed along the fighting trench on that side of the hill which faced the enemy. They were therefore on direct line of sight to the enemy artillery. They contributed little or nothing to the defense of the hill to make up for this additional jeopardy to troops, since the reverse slope, as to contour and structure, was just as useful for the purpose and provided more defilade. The works of the outpost positions were usually more soundly engineered than those of the main line, with better placement and greater thickness of defensive wire and less straight alignment of the trenches.

These were the conditions in the system of fortifications during the spring, 1953. The field army had already been sitting on approximately this same ground for almost two years. Many of the newly arrived commanders, particularly those with engineering training, were appalled to discover that it was so badly prepared, and that "the impregnable line, strongly organized in depth" did not, in fact, exist. Conspicuously, within the forward defense zone, the one tier which was most vulnerable either to conventional or atomic attack from the air was the front line proper. It presented a continuous and wholly obvious target to vertical attack in any form, and its troops were poorly insulated against any of the effects of atomic missiles.

Though the works of the Red Chinese were in some ways short of ideal, they were not similarly vulnerable. The enemy had toiled over his fortified belt for almost two years, handicapped by material shortages, lack of an adequate motorization and the retracted position of his air defenses, but favored by the muscle power in his hard-driven masses. The salient characteristics of the system that had evolved were thoroughly impressive.

Behind the most forward firing posts of the Red Chinese, the ridges were entrenched to an average depth of approximately fourteen miles. This was not in all respects a perfectly reticulated system. But the enemy could have fallen back upon successive prepared positions for all that distance.

Their trenches were a maze which presented few profitable targets to the opposing air and artillery at any time. There were no easily identifiable gun positions, dumps, CPs, OPs, communications centers, etc. There were few observable signs of human life or activity even during the after-dark periods of engagement. The American air could always batter down sections of the trench system. But no real advantage came of so doing. Getting at any target more important than a line of unoccupied trench was largely in the nature of a guessing game.

Rarely, indeed, were groups of personnel in any size to be seen within the trenches of the enemy side. I recall one 24-hour period in May, 1953, when only 37 persons were observed along the enemy front by the whole Eighth Army. Normally, the trench system seemed to be manned only by occasional outposts and lookouts whose mission was to alert the garrison in the event of an attack.

The garrisons lived under the protection of the ridge mass. Tunnels were put into the ridge from the rear. The tunnels led to chambers large enough to house a company or battalion. Air bombs striking the ridge crests scarcely shook these subterranean shelters and shelling by the artillery was without effect. The tunnel entrances were too well camouflaged to be detected through air photography.

Enemy artillery pieces were fought from other tunnels put through the ridge near the crest. The guns were manhandled to the top after completion of the tunnel. When fired, they would be run to the forward aperture, and then drawn back into the tunnel when the firing was completed. Entrances to these shafts were so well concealed that it was all but impossible to observe them directly.

Enemy antiaircraft guns were fired from deep pits usually dug adjacent to the foot of the ridge. The top of the pit was screened with material which blended quite well into the surrounding terrain. The pits sometimes appeared as a dimple-like spot on an air photo but could scarcely be distinguished from other common features of the landscape. The guns proper were rarely seen, even when engaging.

Though this description has been put down with a broad stroke, these were the main features of the system. By reason of the great extension of their diggings, their diligent use of camouflage and their recourse to ground cover, the Red Chinese had better protection against any type of missile, conventional or fantastic, than did the Eighth Army.

The two systems were quite unlike, though each line was immobolized by the conditions which it had accepted. Among the Red Chinese, the infantry advance was slowed to a tortoise pace by its cave-anchored guns. When the Communist infantry broke through the opposing crust, as happened in the offensive against the ROK divisions in the 1953 summer, its assault waves immediately moved beyond the reach of the supporting artillery.

The Eighth Army became immobile because it was under-divisioned for defending from a trench system while still retaining forward offensive power. By military theory, trenches are dug for the purpose of reducing the numbers of men required for the defensive, thereby adding to the general reserve or striking force.

Field armies are supposed to resort to trench systems only to enable the resumption of the offensive from them. Since trench warfare adds little to individual skill, unit training and general mobility, it is axiomatic that every effort should be made to reduce the number of men employed in defense so that greater numbers can be trained for offensive action.

During its two years of position warfare, however, the Eighth Army had only enough men to garrison its trenches. Not only was the line exceedingly thin, but its people were always at least 50 per cent deficient in fighting experience. Therein lay the contradiction. As to equipment, the Eighth was a mobile army, but for lack of manpower, it was compelled to use the implements of mobility simply to sit and survive.

So on both sides in 1953 there were general conditions which radically limited opportunity in any local engagement. The fighting which resulted seemed like a deadly form of shadow boxing. It may well be that when armies are thus bound, the paralysis of the general force is reflected in the slowed reaction of the average individual. The pace at times becomes retarded until it seems as unreal as a picture in slow motion. The energy and fire spent by both sides is all out of proportion to the meagerness of the stakes and the numbers of men who are actively fighting to seize or hold ground. It is as if both sides are at grips with something they can neither let go of nor hold.

The helpers in the field work which led to this book were legion. Simply to acknowledge the great debt I owe them must fall far short of payment. In my journeyings along the front and about the theater I had the advantage of the support and advice of many distinguished commanders. To these, many of them dearly cherished old friends, I give my warmest gratitude. I only refrain from the pleasure of listing their names because I hesitate to involve eminent professional men in any responsibility for a work which in some parts represents an independent exercise of my personal judgment. *The Marine Gazette, Cavalier* and *Army* magazine earlier published some of the patrol stories, thereby stimulating the larger effort and graciously agreeing to the use herein made of the material. Last, I thank James B. O'Connell who goaded me into making the start, failing which I would still be saying, "Some day I'll get on it."

S.L.A. MARSHALL

Birmingham, Michigan

Book 1 ❧ Pork Chop Hill

On Arsenal Hill

T HE TWIN OUTPOST HILLS OF ERIE AND ARSENAL THRUST FAR OUT INTO the Yokkokchon Valley like a side spur of Eighth Army's main line across the higher ridges. On those hills, men were expecting an attack that night.

For almost a week the word had been out. No mere rumor, it was spread to the squads on the authority of Division G2 that the Communist enemy would make a "main effort" at Hour 2300 on 16 April.

The word had leaked from the other side and that was a good reason to believe it. The reason lay in a contradiction within the fighting system of this peculiar Chinese enemy. Though his tactics—his movement of forces on the battlefield—reflected the extreme rigidity of an autocratic state, his manner of handling vital information was democratic to the point of recklessness.

When a battle plan was decided by the high command, its essentials were passed down the line until finally even the rifle squads were permitted to chew them over. The theory was that the troops got a "good feeling" from knowing the secret. It made them think that the plan was the best possible one. At least, that was the American explanation of the Chinese reasoning.

So when any agent or other line-crosser brought word that a Communist attack was imminent, it didn't lessen his credibility that he specified the hour and place.

This time the men on Erie and Arsenal were told that the main blow would land against the 2nd ROK's sector on White Horse Hill which lay within rifle shot distance to the right. Because it was nearby, they expected to become engaged. Easy Company of the 32nd Regiment did not view that prospect as a special privilege or feel superior to the rest of the 7th Infantry Division, which, being extended to the left and westward of the company sector, would probably miss the show.

The company strength was quite evenly divided into two garrisons, one covering Arsenal Hill, the other guarding the rearward outpost, Erie. The airline distance between the two perimeters, CP to CP, was 440 yards. The crowns of both hills wore ringed entrenchments and were stoutly fortified with heavily timbered, thickly sandbagged, artillery-resistant bunkers. Also, they were oversupplied with thrice as much ammunition as they were likely to need under any circumstance.

On Arsenal Hill were First and Second Platoons, 94 men altogether, under 2nd Lieuts. Donald P. Murphy and Ralph R. Drake, two sturdy characters. The other two platoons of Easy garrisoned Erie Hill under Lieut. Jack K. Thun, the company commander. But there the garrison had been re-enforced through the attachment of one rifle platoon from George Company, and the 81-mm mortar platoon and one heavy machine-gun section out of How Company. So, when it came to the balance of fighting power between the two hills, Arsenal was but the outpost of an outpost.

Positions of this kind, isolated, engineered for all-around defense, encircled by broad wire entanglements and capping the lower ridges, formed an outwork all along the Eighth Army front in 1953. Of this reticulation came the only real justification for the claim that the defensive line of the United Nations forces was organized "in depth." It was otherwise a very shallow and undermanned front. Lying at varying distances from the main-line trench, though always within artillery and 4.2 mortar reach, the outposts were kept supplied by motor carriers operating over dirt roads in broad daylight. Then, the enemy artillery usually slept.

Tactically, the great value of the outposts came from the fact that they looked temptingly weak. They were the cheese in the trap. The grand object was to confront the Communist enemy with a soft touch and thereby lure his forces out of their underground galleries and into the open where they might be brayed to bits by the superior power of the United States artillery. The defending infantry was hardly more than a pawn in this game; decision was dictated by the guns. Compared with the sedentary state of the general front during the truce-talk period, it was extraordinarily hazardous duty and men and units stood it in five-day stretches or less.

Easy Company had been nesting on its two hills for 48 hours and was feeling quite at home when it started. In late afternoon, starting at 1730, Arsenal and Erie were shelled. For 72 minutes mortar and artillery fell with about equal weight on both hills. When the first rounds hit, the men were already in the strong-walled bunkers, most of them catching a few winks after the evening meal. Even so, on Erie Hill, one artillery shell exploded through a bunker door, killing three men and wounding seven. Arsenal had better luck. Thirty yards of its trench were caved in and one bunker crushed by the fire. But after the barrage lifted, Murphy checked all squads and reported to Thun that he had lost no skin.

Through the early dark there was random shellfire against Arsenal. Also a recoilless gun, speaking accurately and persistently from a tunnel somewhere on Hill 200, cut two clean avenues through the belt of wire which protected the hill. There was no chance to repair the breach.

One other incident deserves mention. Just before the afternoon bombardment began, there arrived on Arsenal Hill a grass-green artillery forward observer, lately graduated from Fort Sill, fresh from the United States and still awaiting his baptism of fire. He had been sent forward to "look around" and to learn by easy stages how the artillery party already present did its work. After 48 hours in this finishing school, he would be ready for his turn in line.

2nd Lieut. William W. DeWitt, 23 years old, had the build of a miniature Jack Dempsey and even looked like the Old Champ. His home town was Vinita, Oklahoma. His ambition was to return there as soon as possible and join his dad in selling farm machinery. He explained that to Drake and Murphy soon after meeting them. They liked the frankness with which he said, "You see, Dad and I have been like partners since I was a baby, though he'll always be twice the man I am."

DeWitt was impressed though not awed by the promptness with which the thunder began rolling just seven minutes after he joined the fighting front. In one hour he counted 73 shells as they exploded atop the hill. He was impressed still more by the cool way in which the infantrymen took the pounding. After the heavy shelling ceased and while a few sparks were still flying, he moved out of the artillery OP and along the bunker line "to get the feel of troops." What he saw and heard gave him assurance that he was among strong companions.

The three hours of silence that followed was to DeWitt, as well as the others, more unnerving than the shellfire.

The clock ticked on. As the minute hand moved toward 2340, the situation on Arsenal Hill was absolutely quiet, the attitude of the garrison relatively normal. Though their ground was already invaded, the men of Easy remained for the moment unaware of it. Then the curtain rose, the lights went on, the action started and the play rushed to its climax. It was all compressed within a few seconds of time.

Lieutenant Drake was on his bunk in the CP trying to read a copy of *The Stars and Stripes*. But the light was bad and he dozed. At arm's length from him was Sgt. F. C. Vance, working the phone which connected the CP with the squads and the outguards manning alarm posts on the lower slopes of the hill.

In the artillery OP, which was an anteroom joined to the Arsenal CP by a 35-foot revetted tunnel, Lieutenant DeWitt, the green hand, was getting some coaching from Lieut. Edward Haley, the old hand, while the artillery reconnaissance sergeant and the private who worked as wire man stood by.

Lieutenant Murphy's men at the starting moment were all either standing in the trenches, attending the automatic weapons in the bunkers or sitting at their outguard posts on the lower slopes.

One of the outguards, Private Ramey, happened to glance back over his left shoulder. He had heard nothing; it just chanced that way. Not more than 20 yards away, he saw the figure of a man standing in the clear. Over the phone he whispered, "There's a man behind me. Shall I fire?"

Sergeant Vance awakened Drake. He said, "Ramey's calling from No. 32. He says he sees a man inside his position. He wants to know if he should fire."

Drake grabbed the phone. Talking to Private Martinez on Outguard No. 33, he said, "You must have heard Ramey. Do you see anyone from where you sit? Anything moving out there?" Martinez answered, "I don't see a thing. There's nothing stirring. Ramey must be wrong."

Drake deliberated for a split second, then, handing the phone to Sergeant Johns, he said, "We got to clear it up. I think we ought to put a flare out there."

Before Johns had time to order the flare, three amber lights split the sky above Chinese-held Hill 200, followed at once by two green flares from the hill called Pokkae.

Drake, Johns and Vance saw these signals, as did Murphy, and Lieutenant Thun, back on Erie. Though so far the two hills were quiet, they knew at once that the battle was starting, twenty minutes ahead of schedule.

Johns yelled over the phone, "All outguards withdraw!" Already developments had made the order superfluous.

Murphy was on the sound power giving Thun on Erie a blow-by-blow description of what he saw at ringside. "They have put up four yellow flares over 200 . . . no, it's three, and right together . . . now over Pokkae I see two green lights." Thun answered, "Yes, I see the lights." Murphy broke off the conversation.

Thun called out over the Erie hot loop, "All outguards withdraw!"

Sgt. William MacBrien, who was standing next Murphy, shouted over the Arsenal loop, "All squads stand ready!"

Twice the artillery got on the phone to Murphy, asking him, "Do you want Flash Arsenal?" Twice he replied, "No! No! Hold off! I'll tell you when I want it."

Murphy was still nursing a doubt about his situation. He didn't want artillery fires unless Arsenal was under direct assault by the Communist infantry. Proof of that was still lacking. So for a brief interval he delayed decision. Only about forty seconds had passed since he got the first warning.

Even so, the defense had not reacted swiftly enough to assure all-around collection. Having gained entry by stealth, the Chinese followed through with extraordinary vigor.

Private Ramey, having called the first warning, put down his phone and again looked at the spot. Now, instead of a lone man, he saw at least ten skirmishers in line across his rear. They were bounding upslope between him and the platoon trench. He might have fired at them with his carbine. But he was too surprised to think of it; besides, there had been no shooting on the hill and the lack of it puzzled him. Too late, he realized that these were enemy, that they had gone on, that a battle was beginning and that he was already cut off. Ramey went flat and stayed motionless, his telephone forgotten. That put him fully exposed on the foot of the forward slope of Arsenal just as the opposing artilleries made ready to concentrate their fires toward his plot of ground. He hugged earth and prayed.

Four other outguards had not waited to hear Johns' order. They sprinted for the trench on hearing Ramey report that he had sighted a Chinese. By so doing, they gained security though they missed seeing any sign of the enemy. Had they tarried longer, they might have learned more, yet not have lived to tell it.

On No. 33, Private Martinez learned a split-second too late that he had given Lieutenant Drake bad information. As he dropped the phone after saying the words, "Ramey must be wrong," a squad of Chinese—at least eight men—arose among the rocks not more than twelve paces below his post and charged him. Martinez fired a quick burst from his carbine and, already on his way dashing for the trench, saw one man stagger and fall. Silently, the Chinese came on behind him, running hard. Gaining the trench, Martinez veered toward the CP. The Chinese went the opposite way, turning toward the frontal bunkers. Only one man on top the hill, Haley, the forward observer, witnessed their entry, and he saw them only as a few fleeting shadows.

For local security on that particular night, the Arsenal garrison had arranged a special challenge, the earthy four-letter word "———" to be answered by "you." Johns heard someone scratching at the poncho which was draped over the CP door and bellowed, "———!" In his excitement, Martinez couldn't think of the countersign, and he narrowly escaped death at Johns' hands. Martinez gasped, "I saw a pile of dead men outside the trench." But that was hallucination.

Followed by the artillery sergeant, Haley jumped to the fire port of the OP and began pumping his carbine in the direction taken by the enemy group. Neither of them yelled a warning to the men in the CP. However,

MacBrien and Johns saw them firing their weapons like grim death and guessed that the works were already penetrated. Haley's oversight didn't matter for there wasn't time to pass the word around.

In a bunker near the front of Arsenal Hill, an attached squad from How Company, warned by Johns' call, tried to get ready. But the crew on the Browning .30 heavy was in difficulty. From too great haste, the belt webbing had become snagged. Someone yelled, "The gun's jammed!" Then all hands clustered around it; what should have been in these vital seconds an all-around deployment became a tight knot of men. No one covered the door or stood to the embrasure. There had scarcely been time to think of it. And the Chinese who had followed Martinez into the trench were headed straight for this bunker.

That group, as well as the skirmishers who had gotten past Ramey, had made an almost perfect score. Only three men had seen them; only one had fired on them. They were now inside the defense. Combined, the two groups counted not more than twenty men. By speed and stealth, they had achieved a limited surprise. Whether it would bear full fruit would depend, from this point on, on the swiftness of the follow-up by the first Chinese assault wave.

For Arsenal Hill had now come to the fire. In Fourth Squad's bunker, which overlooked the main finger descending westward from the ridge, Cpl. C. H. Kinder and his men were in position to see and report any further movement developing along the same line. And Kinder was playing his part heads up. Over the phone he was saying to Drake, "I can't see anything yet. It's too dark. But they're bound to come this way and we're waiting for them. I'm going to open fire now." Kinder personally was handling the light machine gun. His two BAR men already were out in the trench, set either to fire along it or down the slope from both ends of the bunker. Corporal Norman, assistant squad leader, was passing out grenades and checking the ammunition.

At the rear of Second Platoon's sector, on top of Arsenal's reverse slope where its defenders could see any movement on the face of Erie Outpost, Pvt. John Wolzeak, toting a light machine gun, had taken position on the rampart, hugging a bunker wall. So situated, Wolzeak's weapon commanded the paddy flats on Arsenal's rear. A mellow glow suffused this hollow, bounced from a searchlight on the battalion ridge. Wolzeak was a bleak and lonely spirit. Thirty yards to Wolzeak's right was Private Crane, a newly arrived replacement, armed with a BAR. It was not a promising combination. Said Murphy, "Wolzeak had been until that moment the platoon's prize eight ball. I counted him an unwilling soldier, a man incapable of turning tiger."

Elsewhere along the bunker line, other men stood ready, shouted warn-

Arsenal was at the extreme end of the sub-ridge, and the other fortified outpost, Erie, was close enough to give it comfort.

ing, nervously checked their weapons and strained to see any movement amid the rocks of the darkened slope. But with a few minor exceptions, the rest of the 94 men on Arsenal Hill were the supernumeraries of the unfolding action. The drama was made and played by the artillery, plus the few infantrymen who have already been mentioned here.

Less than two minutes had passed since MacBrien had ordered the squads to stand ready. Martinez had just arrived at the CP, not carrying the word that the Chinese had followed him into the trench, since he had not looked back to see. Haley and the artillery sergeant were firing their carbines. Out in the trench the 81 and 4.2 mortar observers were moving among the bunkers warning the riflemen that a flash fire was probably coming. Murphy was again on the phone talking to Thun.

Right then the first salvo from the Chinese artillery dropped onto Arsenal. So close was the explosion that the CP bunker rocked.

Murphy said to Thun, "You heard that one. Now I can hear small arms. Rifles and burp guns. They're hitting the sandbags just outside me. I'm engaged by an unknown number of enemy. [It was, in fact, about two companies.] I'd say they're not more than 100 yards in front of me."

Murphy was about to add, "Fire Flash Arsenal!"

His words were stopped in his throat by an explosion which almost tore the CP apart while setting its beams and sandbags afire. It snapped Murphy's connection with Thun and severed every other telephone line on the hill except the one wire linking the CP with Fourth Squad. Corporal Kinder was trying to raise the CP at that moment. He wanted to say, "We see them now. We've got them in the open and we're giving them hell!" But at the other end, there was no one to listen. During those seconds the CP was totally absorbed in its own problems.

One round of enemy artillery, size unknown, had come directly through the window of the OP, hit the artillery sergeant in the head, decapitating him and, exploding from the contact, had wrecked the rest of the artillery party. The four men, Haley, DeWitt, the sergeant and the private, had been standing close together. While Haley and the sergeant had been working their carbines, DeWitt, for lack of anything better to do, had been scoring enemy artillery hits in the CP vicinity. He had counted to 33 just as the blast went off.

After exploding, the blast picked up the three others and blew them 35 feet back through the tunnel and to the far wall of the CP. DeWitt struck the wall with such violence that he knocked down Johns and Vance. DeWitt was unconscious and bleeding from several superficial wounds. A steel fragment had drilled Haley in the head. The artillery private had several slugs in his legs and one in his belly.

For the moment, there was no chance for the stunned infantrymen to attend the wounded gunners. The OP was fully ablaze and the flames were sweeping along the tunnel toward the CP. Two of the bunks were afire. All lights were out and only the fire illumined the scene against the heavy smoke from the burning gunny.

By the glare, Johns could see the legs of the fourth man projecting from the OP into the passageway. He could see that the clothing was afire. Johns crawled to the figure and beat out the fire with his hands. Then he crawled back through the passageway dragging the body. Not until he had completed the rescue did he see that the sergeant was headless.

Drake, Vance, MacBrien and the others beat at the flames with blankets, ponchos and whatever lay at hand. Their promptness saved the situation for a few precious minutes, but against the fire they could not do more than hold their own; the draft from the wide-open OP was working as a bellows. All of them came out of the ordeal badly singed. Both Haley and DeWitt had been set afire. Later, no one could remember who had saved them.

Murphy, steady as a rock, ignored the fire to sweat over his communications. Now, having waited a few seconds too long, he felt a desperate need to get through to the artillery and order, "Flash Arsenal." Finding that his telephone lines were out, he tried to raise Thun on the platoon radio. But the instrument, though still undamaged, wouldn't cut through. It was a helpless feeling, heightening his fear of what was happening to the men on the bunker line.

On Erie Hill, Lieutenant Thun was trying to see Arsenal's plight through the eyes of his subordinate. He knew nothing about the holocaust in the CP. He knew that Murphy had asked that the artillery "hold off." But the last interrupted message from Murphy had indicated that the fight was coming to a crisis. From the height of Erie, he could hear the crescendo of small arms fire around the Arsenal rampart. That was enough for him. He called the fire direction center and said, "Fire Flash Arsenal," then added as an afterthought, "Fire Flash Erie, also."

Murphy reckoned that his commander would give the order which he was not in position to relay. Jumping into the trench and running to the nearest bunker, he grabbed three men and said, "Move down the bunker line. See all of the men. Tell them I think a flash fire is coming. They are to return all fires but stay under cover. They are to pass back to the CP any information they have. Our lines are out and so they will do it by runner." The men moved out and Murphy returned to the CP.

By the time Lieut. Col. Joseph S. Kimmitt, commanding the 48th Battalion, got Thun's request for the two fires, what had happened to Erie and Arsenal had become but one segment in an all-encompassing problem. The Chinese artillery was now falling with total weight on the Alligator Jaws,

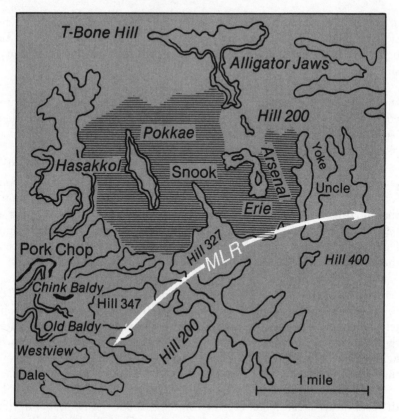

Pork Chop Hill and vicinity. The American-held ridges are shown in outline.
Enemy-held hills are shown in double line.

White Horse, Hill 327 and the other approximate main ridges. His battalion that night would get off 6,452 rounds of counterfire, a mark nearing the
all-time ceiling for any of the children of Saint Barbara, patron saint of all
gunners. Fortunately, Kimmitt had a habit of working physically as close to
infantry as a gunner can get. Only a swinging door separated him from the
S3 (operations section) of the 32nd Regiment. When a fight was on, he and
Colonel Van Way of the infantry, in effect, shared one office. Within a few
seconds, he had called Lieut. Col. Royall Taylor, the battalion commander
on Hill 327, and gotten approval for the shoot on Arsenal and Erie.

In the burning CP, DeWitt had regained consciousness after four or five
minutes. Johns told him to move a few feet because he was too close to the
flames. DeWitt said, "I can hear the fire but I can't see it; I guess I must be
blind." Johns was busy dressing Haley's wound and merely glanced up to
note from DeWitt's fumbling motions that he must be speaking the truth.

Then DeWitt said to Johns, "Give me your .45 and guide me to the door; if any Chinks come, I'll let them have it." Johns handed him the pistol and seated him on an ammo case at the CP entrance. Sightless and still reeling from dizziness, DeWitt sat there while the others beat at the flames. Afterward the infantrymen paid tribute to the effect on their spirits from the sight of his raised pistol. Said Johns, "The guts of that guy steadied us all."

Meanwhile a minor hell had been popping all around the Arsenal perimeter.

The first party of Chinese had gone straight for the bunker where the How Company squad was preoccupied with the balky machine gun. Before the How men could fire a weapon, they were caught in a crossfire of burp guns poked through the door and embrasure. All eight of them were cut down. They stayed where they had fallen, and moments later an artillery shell broke down the roof. Though one man lost a leg, all eight ultimately survived the fight. After gunning the bunker, the Chinese failed to grenade it. It is likely that they were partly destroyed, or at least interrupted, by their own artillery.

In front of Fourth Squad's bunker, the Chinese assault wave had broken through the wire barricade via the avenues cut by the recoilless gun fired from Hill 200 in the late evening. But Corporal Kinder had seen them in time. He sat at the light machine gun, blasting the slope where the Chinese came through. From the bunker ends, his two BAR men centered fire on the same target. Kinder could not see how much execution he was working because the Chinese stayed low. But he knew that no one was getting to the top of the slope and that satisfied him. He got Drake on the phone and said, "We're going strong and I think we're stopping them." Still, the bullet swarm against Kinder's bunker continued to thicken. One slug caught Kinder in the shoulder and put him out of action. The gun was taken over and kept going by Pfc. Ramon Angel, a Puerto Rican, while Kinder, though down, continued to direct the squad.

Whether deflected by their own artillery where it beat against the crest and forward slope of the hill, or diverted by the hope of staying inside the counter fire from the American batteries, the greater part of the enemy infantry body flowed around the hill to the rice paddies at the base of Arsenal's rear slope. Several machine guns took position behind the paddy embankments, and under their covering fire, an irregular line of grenadiers and riflemen started the climb. It was the moment for which Private Wolzeak had been waiting and the glow from the searchlight made the climbing figures stand out clear against the silvered surface of the paddies. He yelled to Crane, "Now's the time!" Together the two men, Wolzeak with the LMG, Crane with the BAR, opened fire, though they maintained distance from each other to get a better spread over the uneven slope.

Their two weapons checked the rush from the rear at the crisis of the fight. Still, they kept shooting. By the end of action Wolzeak had emptied seventeen ammunition boxes and Crane had fired eleven clips.

In these same seconds when Wolzeak made the astonishing discovery that he was a born infantry fighter, Flash Arsenal closed around the hill. It was maintained for four minutes. Differing little from the curtain barrage of World War I days, the "flash fire" of Korean operations was an on-call, tightly sown artillery (plus 4.2 mortar) barrage, usually horseshoe-shaped and so dropped that it would close around the front and sides of an outpost ridge. The main idea of a flash fire was to freeze enemy infantry movement, blocking out the enemy force on the low ground while locking in such skirmishers as had gained the heights. In effect, one battery fired on each concentration, 120 rounds per minute, two shells breaking into the ground every second. High explosive and proximity fuse shells were both used in this blast, the balance varying according to terrain conditions. While a flash fire lasted, infantrymen stayed in their fighting positions.

In the usual procedure, a flash fire was delivered with maximum power for three minutes, the howitzers then cutting back from twelve to six rounds per tube per minute while maintaining the fire six minutes. In the Arsenal-Erie action, the 48th Field fired the maximum rate for four minutes, then suspended briefly.

The immediate effect on the garrison was tremendous. In Murphy's words, "It was like a silver shield thrust between us and the enemy." But as the horseshoe of hot steel exploded into the earth around the hill, the dust cloud rose 50 to 60 feet in air, killing all chance for observation and quickly dulling any appreciation of the spectacle. While the bombardment lasted, the defenders could hear no small-arms fire and that gave them an illusion of total deliverance. No sooner had the shells ceased coming than the clatter of the in-fighting resumed and swelled.

As the flash ended, Murphy returned to the trench, accompanied by SFC Kenneth McDaniel, to make a quick round of the bunkers and see how things were going. They found Wolzeak, Crane and Kinder's squad still fighting like champs. But it was amazing how much destruction had been wrought by the enemy guns in the brief interval.

At least half the trench was now caved in. Four main weapons positions had been destroyed. One BAR man, Cpl. Angel Seggara, had been blown bodily out of his fire pit and slammed against a munitions pile; knocked cold, he was otherwise unhurt. There were five wounded in the wrecked positions. Pvt. Jim Richards, the medic, was already attending them. Another BAR man, Private Meadows, had escaped unscathed when the embankments of his pit were crushed by an exploding shell which half-buried him. Twenty yards down the trench from Meadows, two mortar rounds had smashed the emplacement and light machine gun serving Private Shiveley, though Shiveley, covered by his guardian angel, was still unscratched. Meadows had rolled over and was now firing with his BAR from the site where Shiveley had fought, and Shiveley was assisting him. A third BAR man, Corporal Sharpe, had been hit in the eyes and wounded in one arm by a round from the enemy's recoilless gun.

More than this Murphy and McDaniel did not get time to see in their snap survey of the lines. The situation was again changing. In the burning CP another hand was reaching for the stick.

DeWitt, though still blind, was thinking the harder because of it. He had never given an order in war. He had not been authorized to take over from Haley. But one thing prompted him to act.

He said to Drake, "I hear grenades outside."

Drake listened and replied, "You're right."

"They're coming closer," said DeWitt, "and there are more of them."

Filled with self-doubt, he reached for the PRC-10. The radio worked; he was talking to Kimmitt, his battalion commander. Uncertainty filled him as he said it, "Give us VT fire—lots of it—right on the position." What followed is proof of the magic which lies in the right words spoken at a crucial moment; they have power to change the course of a life. Back came Kimmitt's voice, "Very good, very good, very good, son." It was like a light suddenly shining on DeWitt. Then Kimmitt added this bit of information, "Re-enforcements are coming from Erie."

In a matter of seconds—43 of them—the killing shell was breaking over Arsenal directly above DeWitt's head. He said of it, "When the VT came in and splashed against our bunker, it sounded as merciful as falling rain. I have never heard anything sweeter. We could hear it beating on the sand-bags and trenches. During the five minutes I kept wondering if it would work. That question made it seem like an eternity."

It did work. The night was now bright with flares; all the ground of Arsenal stood revealed as by a spotlight. From his bunker Corporal Kinder could see plainly the groupings of Chinese on the lower slopes. He stayed on the phone, and as he reported to Drake what he saw, DeWitt kept shifting the fire. When at last DeWitt closed off the VT, he could no longer hear the popping of grenades or the chatter of the burp guns. The Chinese had pulled out. So he called for another flash fire in the hope of overtaking some of the enemy on the road home.

But by then he and the CP group were working from a different bunker. In the end, the flames had outlasted wind and muscle and they had lost the fight to save the old CP in the same minutes that they won the fight to save the hill. When at last the re-enforcement from Erie arrived, the stress was past.

Later in the night DeWitt's eyesight returned and he spent his time helping to regroup Arsenal's infantry garrison and setting up new positions along the heights of that much-mauled hill. Every bunker on Arsenal had been either smashed in or had at least one corner down. All of the wreckage had come of the Chinese mortar and artillery fire, the defending guns having been no less accurate than effective.

In this highly compressed action, which had more the nature of an explosion than of a trial by fire-and-movement, ending before it was well begun, Arsenal Hill suffered eight dead and seventeen wounded.

Private Ramey, who had been seated at dead center of the conflicting barrage fires, was not among them. When the din quieted, Murphy and Drake were again in the open inspecting their ruined works. Coming to a tunneled section of trench which was partly collapsed, they started crawling. There came a sudden noise as of someone moving to them over the rubble. Murphy called, "Who's there?" A voice answered, "Private Ramey. I just got back to the hill. But I've already checked Third Squad position. Don't worry about them. They're O.K. I was just coming to tell you."

What hurts had been suffered by the Communist enemy remained unknown. All bodies had been removed from the works. But the visitors had dropped one interesting souvenir—a chart of Arsenal, showing every main position and trench with blueprint accuracy, including two bunkers which had been set up within the preceding 48 hours.

Now that Arsenal was cooling, its leaders could look westward and see fire in the sky beyond the ridged horizon. Hour 2300 had come and passed. The fight begun on their ground, and carried off by the defenders as if it were a purely local affair, was spreading now to Dale and Pork Chop Hills. There the results would be more frustrating and the sweat more prolonged.

But after Arsenal had called Erie and reported the number of "Red Sox" (casualties) to be evacuated, it was through with bloodletting for a time. The Chinese had tried that door, found it closed, and would not try again.

The mood of the hill when morning came fairly matched the exultant words of young DeWitt: "I got the worst of it my first time out; now all the rest of war should be ice cream."

Loss of an Outpost

W<small>HERE FIRST BATTALION OF 31ST REGIMENT SAT THAT NIGHT, THE</small> main line looped across three ridges each roughly U-shaped. The right and center opened toward the enemy, while the left-hand ridge was reversed.

Forward of the center ridge 330 yards was Dale Outpost, an unimpressive bump at the terminus of the big ridge's farthest extended finger. It rose not more than 220 feet above the valley floor and was connected with the main line by a commo trench slotted along the straight-running crest line of the finger. So cramped was the position that Ringling's big show tent, closed down around Dale, would have concealed the whole perimeter.

No other friendly ground was closer to enemy country. Crisscrossed by Communist trenches, Hill 190-Able stood 20 feet higher than Dale and only 370 yards distant. The massive ridge beyond it, Hill 222, was garrisoned by a Chinese company, or so it was estimated. Day and night nothing was seen to move on 222's entrenched surface. Its people were said to live in a great chamber cut into the ridge from the rear.

Between Dale and 190-Able was a narrow valley pitted by shells and studded with blasted tree stumps. Under the full moon they shone like silver sentinels. Nervous outposts sometimes mistook them for marching men, which led to the wasting of much artillery.

Hill 222 dominates the valley, being sheerer than the other ridges. In easy sight to northeast of it is that loathsome hill, Old Baldy. Opposite Old Baldy, the battalion manned another outpost named Westview, an aerie of machine gun and rifle posts atop a sheer-walled limerock battlement. Its crown had barely room for one log-walled bunker too small to cover one full squad.

Pork Chop was still farther east. One end of it could be seen from the cap of Westview, which was the extreme shank of the battalion position.

Old Baldy, scabrous after months of battle, a mountain looking like a refuse dump, more cheated by nature than abused by man, was unsuited to the mounting of an attack. While its superior heights outflanked Pork Chop and made the manning of Westview seem like wanton defiance, it was much too naked to afford a concealed approach. The companion peak, Chink Baldy, was more suitable. Tree growth, rock outcroppings and conveniently spread fingers which descended evenly to the low ground gave it tactical privacy. So it was to this platform that troops looked, wondering if an attack would come.

For all hands in Baker Company it was watch night. Third Platoon garrisoned Dale. Beyond Dale, twelve of its men rode even closer to the danger, being paired in six foxholed listening posts which formed a rough crescent around the lower forward slopes. If the Chinese approached, the listeners were charged to phone the alarm and then run to the platoon trench. This echeloning of force—a squad covering a platoon, covering a company—materialized what the Eighth Army called "organization in depth."

Behind the 12 men nearest the enemy was deployed a relatively strong company. Of the 144 men under Lieut. Jack M. Patteson, 40 were newly arrived Korean replacements. Manning the outpost was 2nd Lieut. Ryan A. Bressler and 42 men. Besides personal weapons, his platoon had six light machine guns, one heavy, seven BARs and two rocket launchers. Where Patteson ran the company show on the big hill were 11 LMGs, two heavy .30s, one .50 machine gun, three 57-mm recoilless rifles, three 60-mm mortars and 15 BARs. If the fight started, air, artillery and armor would support them. But the integrity of the line came from these few men and their weapons.

Until 2300 the night was without incident. Anxiety kept the greener men wakeful. The more seasoned hands, made skeptical by frequent experiences with false alarms, sweated less. Some slept. Others kidded the replacements about the storm soon to come.

Their calm was broken and their vigil mocked without warning. No opening barrage was fired. Not one bullet droned. One moment there was no enemy. The next, he was already past the listening posts, invading the main trench or closing on the knob inside the redoubt. The infestation came in utter silence. Chinese had swarmed over the ground without either firing or alerting Bressler's men to the need of it.

So it is not strange that when later the survivors were drawn together to determine how the thing had happened, each man saw the start differently. The completeness of the surprise and the closeness of the embrace, by narrowing each fighter's vision, robbed the defense of unity.

Though Pfc. Joseph E. Smith, a 20-year-old fighter from Claxton, Ga., may not have been the first witness, he gave the alarm which rang all the way back to regiment. He had been with the company but five days and it

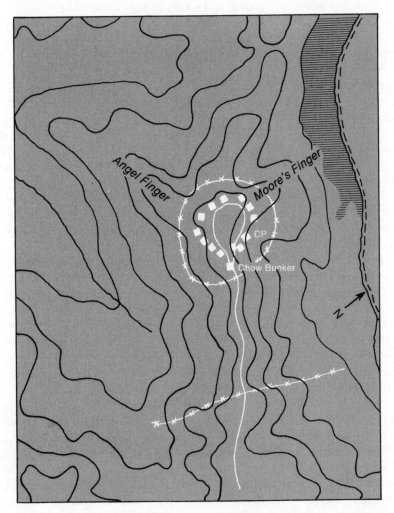

The fortifications at Dale Outpost.

was mere chance that put him that night in Listening Post 21, the station nearest the enemy.

That fact did not particularly concern him, though he wondered, as good men are ever prone to do, whether if an attack came, he could play a strong part. At 2302, he just happened to glance flankward toward Listening Post 20 on the next ridge finger. And then he saw it: a "whole mob of Chinese" were past the LP and scrambling upward toward the main trench.

Many things happened during those next few seconds.

Smith grabbed the phone connecting him with Bressler and said, "The Chinks are on the hill in great numbers; they've gone past LP 20." Bressler asked, "Are you sure?" At that moment, Smith's teammate in the LP fired a quick burst downslope with his M1. Smith said, "Now they're in front of me," and Bressler answered, "Run for the hill!" Smith emptied a clip downslope, turned and sprinted for the rampart. By then the air around him buzzed with bullet fire.

From his squad position on the left-hand switch of Dale's main trench, Pvt. Duane C. Pfaff saw men moving between the two LPs. But the silence nonplused him; if these were enemy, someone should be shooting. He put carbine to shoulder but still hesitated to fire.

To Cpl. John H. Droney in the main trench 30 yards from Pfaff, the first word came when Pvt. Lee Chang Woo jumped from the parapet yelling, "Chinks coming up the finger." Woo had been posted in LP 17 at the base of Dale's rear slope. Droney ran for a machine-gun bunker to start the action. As he reached for the ammunition, he glanced over his shoulder uphill and saw twenty or so Chinese standing atop the knob in the center of the outpost. Still, not a shot had been fired. Droney tried to swing the gun around, and in his excitement wedged the barrel in the bunker door-casement. He ran toward the CP crying, "They're in the trenches!"

In the same bunker sat the platoon sergeant, SFC Robert C. Reasor. Bressler had put him there with instructions that if an attack came, he was to get on the sound power and adjust mortar fire on the approach via Moore's Finger, which ran like a ramp from the valley to the CP. Half-dozing, Reasor had watched Droney's struggle with the machine gun without realizing it signaled danger. When Droney cried, "They're in the trenches!" Reasor came awake.

Pfc. Nathaniel Williams saw the Chinese as they charged up Moore's Finger, at least forty men rushing him from a distance of not more than 40 yards. He said to Pfc. Eddie Sales, "Look there! Chinks!" At that moment the enemy pack entered the beam of a searchlight which flooded part of Dale's slopes. Sales looked and answered, "Yeh, Chinks," then reached for the sound power to call Bressler. Perfectly highlighted, the Chinese came on. Yet neither man thought to use his weapon.

Seen from above and forward, Dale Outpost seemed stout enough, such were the steepness of its slopes and the commanding line taken by its bunkers and partly roofed trenches.

As Reasor got to the bunker door, Cpl. Chung Kyung Moon and Pvt. Joe Dawson jumped into the trench, completing their run from one of the LPs. Moon cried, "They're right behind us!" Reasor jumped for a phone to call Bressler and ask for VT fire. The line was already dead. So Reasor ran toward the CP. Halfway, he met Dawson again who laughed and said, "Look! They're still behind us." But this time he pointed uphill toward an enemy group inside the position.

There had as yet been no real fighting. But the best part of two Communist platoons had already penetrated the position from opposite directions. On right of the hill, one enemy force was gaining the trench atop Moore's Finger, and on left of the hill, another swarm was headed up Angel Finger. At least eight men had seen the enemy advance. But only Private Smith's warning had gotten through to Bressler.

Also, Smith's shooting from the LP launched the fire fight. Thereafter, the following things occurred more or less coincidentally.

Worrying about Smith, who was one of his men, Pfaff picked up his phone which was on a "hot loop" connecting Bressler with all of his squads and the six listening posts. It was just in time to hear Bressler tell Smith to run for the hill. Pfaff ducked from out the bunker and looked downslope. Smith was already running for the trench, and half-carrying Pvt. Felipe Rodriguez who was screaming, "My arm! My arm!" A burst of tommy-gun fire had shredded it from shoulder to elbow. Pfaff reached for the wounded Puerto Rican, eased him into the trench and yelled, "Get to the CP for first aid!" There was no need to say anything to Private Smith. He had seen that the squad's machine-gun bunker was silent, and he sprang to it. Seconds after hitting the trench, he was pouring fire down Angel Finger. The kid from Georgia had an instinct for fighting; in crisis he was incapable of doing things the wrong way.

From somewhere down the trench toward the front of the hill, Pfaff heard a yell, "Get VT fire!" It was clear as a bugle call. Without waiting to determine who had yelled, Pfaff again got on the phone to Bressler, saying, "We must have VT fire." Here was a startling example of assumption of responsibility by a 20-year-old private, his first time in battle, taken by surprise and burdened by the knowledge that for the first time in his life he was responsible for the lives of other men. Under rotation conditions, the average combat unit of the United States Army often had less than half the officer and NCO grades specified by the tables of organization. Pfaff had only that morning been named a squad leader, normally a sergeant's job.

The shout heard by Pfaff had come from Sgt. Robert L. Smith whose squad, extended rightward from Pfaff's sector, covered the left side of the nose of Dale Outpost. A 22-year-old farmer from Phillipsburg, Kansas, "Big" Smith, as the company later nicknamed him (to distinguish him from "Little" Smith, the private), was physically the giant of the company. Big Smith's first knowledge that the hill was beset came from the blaze of automatic fire which followed Little Smith's exit from his LP. He was sitting at a machine gun. With one hand he opened fire down Angel Finger while with the other he reached for the telephone to call Bressler. There was no response and he realized the line was dead. So he cried aloud what he had intended to say to Bressler. But he was scarcely aware he had said it and he didn't know that Pfaff had heard. So he yelled to the first aid man, Private First Class Scully, "Take over the gun!" It was in his mind that he must run to Pfaff's position and tell him to phone for VT fire as quickly as it could be delivered.

In the interim, Bressler had relayed both Private Smith's warning and Pfaff's request to Lieutenant Patteson on the big hill. Patteson ran for his observation point from where he could look directly down on Dale Outpost. His eyes confirmed the story. He could see, under the searchlight, a mob of Chinese milling around on the knob of Dale Outpost. But there were no signs of reaction from his own Third Platoon.

The first Chinese had been sighted by LP 20 and reported to Bressler at 2302. At 2305, Patteson, taking his reckoning in the CP, and getting the second message relayed from Pfaff, called Maj. Clifford W. Morrow, the battalion executive, and requested flash fires on Dale Outpost. As he put down the phone, he changed his mind, called again and asked that flares first be fired to warn the garrison, followed by VT. By his *first* estimate, the situation was already so desperate as to warrant the risk of killing his own men. Instinctive caution made him modify it.

When the two requests hit the fire control center almost together, it temporarily flummoxed the artillery. There was long argument about whether to shoot VT without first putting lights over the hill. When the decision went the other way, the flares burned so far to the right of Dale that Patteson knew his own men wouldn't be warned by them.

In the end that mattered very little. Patteson's one-eyed view of the fight, seen through a glass from 450 yards behind the outpost, was only slightly distorted. His estimate of where the balance lay was accurate. But he was wrong in thinking that his own people weren't fighting back. A few big men were still going strong on the little hill.

That their supreme individual efforts went uncollected and uncommanded was no one's fault in particular. The rush of events had tied Bressler to his phone in the CP bunker. Like the others who had started in that direction, Sergeant Reasor, his second in command, became accidentally diverted, never completing his journey. As he stopped to talk to Dawson, a bullet through the shoulder knocked Dawson flat in the trench. Reasor picked him up and carried him to Droney's bunker, forgetting his intention to see Bressler. Corporal Moon was inside with a bullet through his groin. Eight other men were either loafing inside the bunker or idling outside the door. Reasor formed them along the trench and stayed with them, worried now that if he left the others, they would quit. They fought as a block, the four in the middle firing alternately downhill and upslope while the end pairs fired along the trenches. Reasor used Moon's carbine until it was shot from his hands. Then he got Dawson's M1 and continued fighting. It was the one solid piece of defensive resistance within the platoon.

Not until he jumped from his bunker to seek Pfaff did Big Smith know that the Chinese were already inside the outpost and possessing the high ground. He saw at least twenty of them scrambling up the slope above his head. They grenaded back at him, and as he ran toward Pfaff, one grenade bounced off his shoulder and exploded harmlessly among the sandbags. So when Pfaff first saw him, Big Smith was pointing to the crest and yelling, "Watch out! They're coming over from behind you."

Pfaff understood him immediately and started down the trench to turn the fire of his squad from downslope to upslope. He yelled back to Big Smith, "I'll try to stop them." But that was the last that Big Smith saw of him during the fight. He was already doubling back to see what his own men were doing, clean forgetting that he had run to Pfaff to ask him to message Bressler. There were only six men in Smith's squad. He would have to leave it to Pfaff's six men to handle the penetration. Unless his own six could halt the uprush to the big trench, the position was gone. One thing comforted him as he ran: the LMG in Pfaff's squad bunker was burning up the slope of Angel Finger. At least one man was giving the Chinese a hard fight. He didn't know it was Private Smith, and the name in any case would have meant nothing, for they had not yet met. But their introduction was coming.

By then the clock had ticked seven minutes since the fight began. The first VT shell from the American guns broke over the outpost as Big Smith returned to his squad sector. It had taken Lieutenant Patteson until 2309 to get the fire adjusted so that the hot steel rained down exactly where he wanted it. The artillery FOs had been telling him that it was right on target. But they were looking at it from a different angle, and his eyes told him that the first fires were 150 yards too far to the right. When at last it came good, he was in despair, certain that at least a full Chinese company was inside his forward works and that his own platoon, if not dead, was wholly down.

The close-up view, as seen by Big Smith, wouldn't have solaced him. One of his Korean riflemen had already fled the position and wasn't seen again. Privates Small and Faria were down, Small with a bullet through his belly and Faria with a shattered hand. Faria, least hurt of the two, was screaming, "My God help me!" Big Smith couldn't stand the noise. He told Small to take Faria to the CP for first aid. There was no way of knowing that already the CP was beyond helping anyone.

Private Serpa jumped into the trench. The enemy rush had trapped him in an LP, but he had kept his nerve and managed an escape in the darkness. Without saying a word to Smith, he grabbed some grenades and began throwing upslope. Smith got the point. It was useless with the forces at hand to attempt a fight in both directions; he would have to depend on the VT fire to purge the lower slope. He jumped for the machine-gun bunker. As he made the door, a white phosphorus grenade exploded in air and showered his clothing. He shook off the pellets and turned toward the gun, yelling, "Scully! Scully!" In the darkness, he couldn't see that the aid man was already dead and lying on the far side of the Browning heavy .30. Thinking that Scully must have quit the gun, Big Smith swung it around and fired upslope. But the weight, the angle and the obtrusion of the trench wall made the fire unsatisfactory.

Then looking for, but missing, Serpa, Big Smith experienced that most wretched of moments when an infantryman finds himself utterly alone in a fire fight. He ran toward Pfaff's sector where he had seen the LMG firing. Little Smith in the interim had had his weapon shot out of his hands by a burst of tommy-gun fire through the embrasure. He was already in the trench and grenading uphill when Big Smith saw him for the first time.

He said, "My name's Smith."

Answered Private Smith, "So's mine. Watch me, I'm just getting started."

From where they stood, they could grenade both uphill and down. Flankward in either direction, it was a good 25 yards to a turn in the trench line. Little Smith had brought to the spot a full case of grenades and an ammo can filled with loose grenades. He had already thrown nineteen grenades against the Chinese on the upper slope. So with his work cut out for him, Big Smith conformed. Surrounded, they stood back to back, grenading all around the clock.

Their last stand was maintained in this manner for approximately ten minutes. Big Smith still had his carbine and Little Smith his M1. But because of the lack of clear sightings and defined targets, there was no payoff in these weapons. During this stage Private Serpa came back to them wriggling along the parapet. But he didn't join the fight. His M1 had jammed and a grenade explosion had numbed his right arm.

They got down to their last two grenades. They had thrown about forty and had drawn a little blood as they knew from the flashes and the screaming. At least a dozen enemy bombs had exploded within a 10-yard circle of where they stood but fast footwork had kept them unhurt.

Until Big Smith yelled, "Hold the grenade!" they had fought without a word. He signaled his intentions by fitting carbine to shoulder. They had cleared the immediate slope and the surviving Chinese had crowded down into the main trench. Then for perhaps another five minutes, they held the enemy at bay, Little Smith firing one way down the trench with his M1, Big Smith spraying carbine fire in the opposite direction. In the same split second they ran out of bullets: during those minutes Big Smith had fired a full belt and Little Smith had fired at least six clips. From Little Smith's end of the trench, a squad of Chinese charged toward them as the rifles went silent. They had already pulled the grenade pins.

Big Smith yelled, "Throw!" Both grenades landed and exploded right amid the enemy pack. Several Chinese went down and the others recoiled.

Little Smith asked, "What do we do now?"

Big Smith said, "Over the side! Give me your foot!"

He threw the smaller man over the parapet. (Little Smith is 5 feet 10 inches and weighs 172 pounds.) With a vault, Big Smith landed right behind him. Together they rolled about 15 yards downhill. There, Big Smith grabbed his partner by the leg and held him. Serpa had rolled with them and was already flattened.

"What do we do now?" asked Little Smith.

Said Big Smith, "You're dead. No matter what happens, don't move. It's the only chance."

The new game was improvised on the spur of the moment. The three of them were to play it for the next four and one-half hours on a spotlighted field rocked by shellfire from the ridges held by friend and enemy. In those hours, by their own account, they thought of little or nothing. An infantryman may play dead until by self-hypnosis he rejects thoughts of past and future, and minutes become contracted to seconds. It is not quite true that mortal man may not look directly either at death or the sun. The big flares fired by the American 155s already made their lost hill bright as day. But this they did not see as they lay with faces down and eyes closed not even turning to look at each other.

Back at Regiment, Colonel Kern was sweating out two reports, one from the artillery that the fires on Dale were now satisfactory, the other from Patteson that the guns were still doing but half a job. The VT fire was at last coming in where it should be, but there was no volume. Patteson wanted saturation fire, not merely a few occasional rounds. He counted his men lost and was thinking only about how to kill the enemy. It took him another quarter-hour to get what he wanted.

Dale's defense was already disintegrated, though Pfaff, Reasor and the few other diehards didn't know it. The platoon became lost in the few minutes when the Communists had passed the big trench and mounted the knob on scaling ladders. It mattered very little that, combined with the American VT fire, their own artillery came in on the Chinese, killing many of them in the open before they could strike a blow with their hand-carried weapons. The sufficient number remained quick and moving to abet the shellfire in its work of destroying the defense. From the enemy platoon which had won the high ground, one squad peeled off and, running down-slope, entered the main trench between Pfaff's squad and the platoon CP.

Of this entry Pfaff was unaware as he ran in that direction trying to pry his men from the bunkers so that they would fight for the trench. Sergeant Reasor and his scratch squad had already been driven back from the CP area by an enemy wave which swept up Moore's Finger and into the trench, thereby completing their envelopment. But even Reasor's situation remained unknown to Pfc. Frank Minor and Pvt. Randolph Mott who together were defending a fighting bunker just 10 yards from the CP, and not more than 35 yards down the trench from Reasor's group. Both men were having their first bath of fire. Mott, who was to win two Silver Stars within 30 days, is a country boy from Maine. Tall, angular, stoop-shouldered, slow of step, deliberate of speech, he habitually wears a good-natured grin. Hollywood would never pick him as a fighter type and in his first minutes of battle he didn't react like one.

So swiftly had come the on-fall that it seemed unreal to Mott. He wasn't dazed, he felt no fear, but he saw no reason to get excited. When his rifle jammed from a ruptured cartridge after he had fired a few rounds down Moore's Finger, he dropped the weapon and fell in beside Minor to serve as BAR loader. Minor was shaky but doing his best. Mott figured a little close assistance would steady him. Neither man knew the Chinese already held the height above the bunker since no one came to tell them.

Mott was shocked out of his lethargy by a heavy explosion from the direction of the CP. Mott's own bunker shook from the impact. After the action, platoon survivors said, "Two artillery shells hit the CP roof right together." But there was really no way of knowing this; the blast that hit the CP may have come from a hand-thrown satchel charge. Next Mott heard a man screaming in pain. It roused him as nothing else had done. He knew his leader hardly at all. But something told him that the cry came from Bressler and that the lieutenant was mortally wounded.

He went for the bunker door and looked down the trench. The CP was in ruins, its roof caved in and its nearest wall half-down. A Chinese stood at the broken entrance shining a flashlight inward. Mott saw at least five other Chinese with him. Oddly then, instead of grabbing the BAR, he yelled to Minor, "Hand me a cleaning rod!" The Chinese holding the flashlight heard the shout and turned the beam on Mott. He ducked within the bunker and with one violent thrust cleared his weapon. As he made the door again, he saw the enemy group still bunched outside the CP. He emptied the weapon and saw three men fall. Two others ran directly past him before he could pull again. The sixth Chinese jumped for cover behind the sandbag superstructure of Mott's own bunker. Like most other works of the kind along this grotesquely engineered American front, the bunker loomed so high above the outwork that an enemy gaining the wall was in perfect position to enfilade the trench.

This boarder had no such aim. Mott nipped into the trench trying to catch his silhouette against the skyline. But the man was already over the roof and flattened. Leaning down the face of the bunker, he tossed two grenades in the embrasure. They exploded under Minor and shattered his legs. An engineer sergeant, who until then had been sitting quietly in a corner, bestirred himself to help Mott lift Minor into a bunk.

Reaching for the BAR, Mott found it dry of ammunition. So doing, he stumbled across a pile of filled sandbags. He yelled to the engineer, "Help me fill the window!" While they heaved at the bags and stuffed the embrasure, three more grenades came through. Mott fielded them with a quick pitch through the bunker door. As he clutched the third one on the darkened floor, touch told him it was American issue. He scooped it up and outward in one motion. It exploded just beyond the door frame in the faces of a second Chinese party rushing the bunker.

That inspired him to search the bunker for more grenades. He found a full case. Then he stood at the bunker door grenading toward the mouth of the chogi trench which led back to the main line. Targets were plentiful. By that time the Chinese in large numbers had climbed the saddle at the rear of Dale Outpost and the back door was bending to their weight. While his grenade supply lasted, Mott would fight. When it ended, he would plug the bunker door from the inside, as he had done the embrasure, and try to stay the night.

Private Pfaff's sortie down the trench line, made to rally the other men in the same minutes when Mott started functioning in the fight, proved futile. In the first bunker were five of the platoon's Koreans. Each was armed with a BAR. None was firing. Their inertia was robbing the defense of a great part of its most useful fire power.

Pfaff yelled, "Come out and fight!" Not a man stirred. He tried it again, "Come out or I'll kill you!" They pulled back to the far wall and became lost in the darkness. Two ideas blocked his impulse. He wasn't sure he had authority, and if he spent bullets there, he'd disarm himself. So he walked on down the trench. Within a few minutes the five Koreans were grenaded to death in the bunker where Pfaff left them, paralyzed by their own fear.

At the next bunker, Pfaff saw a Chinese setting up a heavy machine gun on the roof. He fired once with his carbine and the man pitched backward down the slope. A second Chinese took his place and a second bullet got him.

Passing the CP bunker, and seeing that the roof was down, Pfaff sang out, "Anybody in there?" No answer came back. Possibly his voice was drowned by battle sound. Pfaff simply took it that Bressler and his assistants had moved elsewhere on the outpost. At the fifth bunker he joined Pfc. Dwight Marlowe who sat nonchalantly on the roof firing a machine gun down Angel Finger as if he enjoyed the work. For two minutes they sat back to back. There was no conversation. Uphill 30 feet away, three Chinese, armed with burp guns, were trying to dust Marlowe from the roof. The fire was going high overhead. Pfaff fired his carbine just long enough to silence them. It distracted Marlowe not at all. He kept the LMG shooting downslope, and turned only long enough to yell to Pfaff, "Go to the next bunker; they need help."

At the door of the next bunker stood Pfc. Rivera W. Rodriguez, a Puerto Rican, firing down the trench toward the chogi trail with his M1. Within the bunker were five engineer privates who had come to the hill in early evening to work on fortifications. As the fight started, a satchel charge put through the embrasure had mangled all five men; three were unconscious. Rodriguez, with a bullet through one arm, was trying to guard them. Pfaff dressed Rodriguez's wound crudely and then said, "Cover them a little longer; I'll get more bandages at the CP."

He could barely force his way into the ruin. The air was heavy with dust and powder fumes. A thin voice called to him, "Help GI, help GI, help GI." He knew it was Bressler. He crawled along the floor. A second voice, still closer to him, kept whispering, "Help . . . help . . . help." He could barely hear it but he crawled toward it. In the darkness, he felt over the body of Sgt. Chapman T. Spencer. He was legless from the hips down.

Bressler called to him again, "Come to me! Come to me!" Weak, the note was still insistent. He left Spencer and crawled toward Bressler. From the ruined doorway a Chinese opened fire with a tommy gun. The bullets splashed among the fallen timbers as he crawled. He got to Bressler. The lieutenant's legs were pinned by two of the fallen beams. Pfaff strained and sweated to free him. The effort was useless. Sandbags from the ruined roof pinned down the beams.

He tugged on. Three grenades came through the door and exploded in arm's reach of him. The same beams which kept Bressler pinned insulated the explosion and saved his life.

Bressler said, "Quit it now; you can't help me."

Pfaff said, "Then I'll stay with you."

Bressler said, "No, your job is to go get help. That's our only chance. Tell Patteson I said to put artillery fire on the hill and keep it there."

Pfaff wondered at that: couldn't Bressler hear the artillery already pounding the hill?

He said, "I'd better stay."

Bressler said, "You are to go. It's an order."

There was a small exit on the far side. Pfaff crawled toward it. As he made the opening, a wounded Chinese, moving on all fours along the outside wall, tried to raise his tommy gun. Pfaff was carrying an unpinned grenade. He rolled it and the explosion blew the man apart.

Within the wrecked bunker there had been a third dying American. Sgt. Fred Jackson had had his chest crushed by the roof timbers. But he was unconscious and Pfaff missed him in the darkness. Due to Bressler's self-possession the scene had been carried off without emotion. Once more in the open, Pfaff was intent only on carrying out the order, and in his agitation clean forgot his promise to return to Rodriguez. He ran for the chogi trench. Hardly had he entered it when a squad of Chinese blocked his path. He threw a grenade, and without waiting for the explosion, jumped from the trench and went down the slope in a diving roll. By sheer luck he landed in a shallow gully which ran under the concertina entanglement. Then he started for the company position on the big hill. His feet were like lead and he could hardly summon the energy to move them.

By now the fight had been going just a little less than one hour. Mott had walled-in his bunker. The two Smiths and Serpa were playing dead under the lights. Of Second Platoon, only Reasor and his men still stood their ground. But they were no longer fighting. For about thirty minutes, they had maintained steady fire around their circle with M1 and carbine. The concentration kept the Chinese either under cover or at a respectful distance. But at the end of the half-hour all weapons were out of ammunition.

Their predicament was eased only because by then the Chinese in the vicinity were in the same plight. Reasor saw them wandering back and forth across the knob obviously searching for something to fire. They were in such numbers that they could have crushed his group by sheer physical weight had they grouped and rushed the trench. But they moved like sheep, seeming too dazed even to seek defilade against the VT fire. It was agonizing to the Americans to see these targets moving freely within less than 20 yards of where they stood, helpless to cut them down.

Reasor had been annoyed for some time by the periodic firing of an LMG which sounded very close. Finally, he said to one of his riflemen, "Where in hell is that gun?" The boy said, "Just look up: it's on the bunker roof directly above your head." There being no way to shoot him down,

Reasor jumped on the sandbag revetment, grabbed the gunner around the knees and spun him and his weapon down into the valley.

That made the situation scarcely less awkward. The nine men were wholly surrounded. The trench was blocked in both directions. There was nothing to fire and no one paid them the slightest heed. Flares brightened the ground all around. Shellfire continued to rock the hill. They simply sucked in their guts and hugged the shadow of the trench wall. For at least two hours they stayed that way, silent and motionless.

As midnight came, Lieutenant Patteson, at his position in the OP, still could not tell for certain how things were going on Dale. No word had gotten back to him since Bressler's two telephone calls. As he listened, the small-arms fire on Dale seemed greatly diminished, but he could only guess at the reasons for it. After coordinating with Battalion, he called his Second Platoon and told Lieut. George L. Hermman to get his men forward and support Bressler as soon as he was relieved on his own ground by a platoon from Item Company. That necessitated requesting that his own artillery cease fire to let Hermman get to the hill.

Hermman didn't wait. Leaving the rest of his men in place, he started forward with one squad under Cpl. Edward Shuman. By the time this small band reached the chogi trail, another Chinese wave was moving up the saddle from both sides.

At ten minutes past midnight, Pfaff, breathless and shaking from his exertions, got back to Patteson. For several minutes he stood there panting, unable to speak. Patteson, a coldly precise youngster who maintained markedly formal relations with ranks, waited for the storm to subside. When at last Pfaff gasped, "I'm from Third Platoon," Patteson realized for the first time that this was one of his own men. He asked, "What's the situation?"

Regaining his wind and poise in those few seconds by an extreme effort, Pfaff made his report as methodically as an old soldier, "Bressler and Spencer are both badly wounded and pinned by logs in the CP bunker. The CP is in ruins. I tried to move Bressler but couldn't. He said for me to come tell you that the platoon needs help. He said you must keep artillery firing on the hill. The Chinese are all over the trenches and bunkers."

Pfaff said nothing else about his own actions and Patteson asked him no questions. Then the kid's legs buckled under him and he sprawled on the bunker floor. Patteson helped him to his own bed, then called Battalion and reported what he had heard. Bressler's words about artillery were not relayed; because Hermman's platoon was going forward, the fires had already been suspended.

But the Pfaff report, relayed from Battalion to Regiment, convinced Colonel Kern that the outpost was already lost, and that if it was to be regained before morning, he'd have to put at least another company through Patteson's position. He called Lieut. Col. George L. Maliszewski, commander of Third Battalion, and told him to get ready.

Lieutenant Hermman's force, losing almost an hour in traversing the rough ground, got to the chogi trail in a strength of twenty-four men, two squads having overtaken him during the march from the main line. Up to that point, they had moved without incident. Then without warning they found themselves attacked from three sides by the Chinese who were climbing toward the chogi trench on both slopes while a third group blocked the entrance to Dale Outpost.

Pvt. John H. Dawson yelled, "The Chinks are on our right!" and Pvt. Esequiel Leos answered, "They're on our left!" Corporal Shuman, opening fire with his BAR, aimed straight along the trench, dissolving the enemy group in the foreground. With rifles and grenades the men to his rear opened fire down the slope. The Chinese weren't routed. But after a few men died, the others sought protection behind the rocks. Four of Hermman's men were hit by the countergrenading. For the moment the passage became quiet and the platoon surged forward.

Hermman got up to Mott's bunker. Mott heard him yell, cleared the sandbags away from the door and joined the party. Shuman, Dawson, Leos and two others had meantime started down the trench on the other side of the outpost, still thinking that after mopping up a few Chinese, they would become solid with Third Platoon.

Of the group continuing with Hermman, thirteen were new Korean replacements. Mortar shells were now ranging in on the trench line, coming in four-round salvos. Hermman told the Koreans to continue down the trench and clean out the bunkers. They shook their heads and refused to move.

By sheer coincidence Sergeant Reasor was deciding in these moments that if his group was ever to get out, he would have to make a break for it. He had not heard either Hermman's yelling or Shuman's movement, and he was still unaware that a support party had arrived on the hill. Reasor said, "Follow me!" and they went. Corporal Droney had found a last clip of carbine ammunition within the bunker and, being the only armed man, brought up the rear.

It was about 0200 when Reasor's party stumbled into Hermman hard by the CP bunker. Spencer and Bressler may still have been alive at the time. But if there was any thought of them it was diverted by the action of the next few seconds.

Hermman, arguing with his Koreans, was yelling, "Get the hell on!" Some of his GIs were kicking the ROKs in a vain attempt to get them started. They simply looked blank. Reasor heard a noise right behind him.

Glancing upslope he saw two Chinese setting up an HMG not more than 20 feet away. So he grabbed a grenade from a Korean and threw; it exploded at head level, killing both men.

As the sound died, four mortar shells came in dead on the group. Three exploded along the embankments. One landed in the trench. One shard pierced Hermman's leg and went up to his intestines. Three of Reasor's men were also wounded. Another round, exploding through the embankment, had sprayed fragments among the recalcitrant ROKs, wounding four and killing two.

There followed several minutes of confusion. By radio Hermman got word that Shuman and his men on the other side of the outpost had been checked by tommy-gun fire and were starting back toward the chogi trench. He called Patteson and said, "I'm hit and I've lost ten men out of twenty-four." He didn't say he had to withdraw but Patteson drew that conclusion, telling him, "Fall back on Check Point One," which was an outguard position between Dale and the main line.

So Hermman called out to his men, "Fall back on Jackson!" that being the code name for Check Point No. 1. No one had ever told Reasor about that code name. But one soldier in his group was a Private Jackson and this character was already running for the chogi trench. Misunderstanding Hermman, Reasor took out after Pvt. Jackson and two of his men followed. Split from Hermman, they collided with a Chinese party at the mouth of the chogi trench and recoiled, once more taking refuge in a bunker on the other side of Dale.

At this stage of the fight, had the Americans moved quickly, the hill might have been saved by re-enforcing Hermman. His party and Reasor's men (except for the last minor incident) had not been hard pushed at close range for at least forty minutes. They had lost men to grenade and mortar fire. A few Chinese, fighting singly, had harassed them, but no large organized group had come against them. From these signs, it is apparent that the prolonged VT fire had almost liquidated the enemy on Dale, either killing or driving to cover all but a handful of the hardiest.

But the Americans on the ground were too distracted by their own losses to feel the temporary drop in in-fighting pressure, just as the people at the higher levels were physically too remote to sense it. Patteson suspected that the Chinese had lost their grip. But with Hermman hit and half his force gone, he saw no way to exploit the suspected opening. And there was another thing. By suspending all artillery fires so that Hermman could go forward, the Americans had supplied the enemy a helpful interlude. If the Communists were prepared to reenforce, they would come on now, and Hermman would be caught by the counterattack. Reluctantly, Patteson had given the withdrawal order.

Still, it was easier said than done. Private Mott tried to lead the way, and others among the few able-bodied joined him in trying to rally and support the wounded men. But another grenade exploded among them and two more men were wounded. They were now eighteen casualties and nine unhurt men. As this crippled column formed and started toward the chogi trench, the saddle came under full bombardment by the enemy mortars. Before Hermman could complete the passage, the party sank back to earth, shocked into immobility by its wounds, fear and sweat.

Pltn. Sgt. Burton Ham alone got through to Patteson and told him what had happened. 2nd Lieut. Benjamin L. Collins, who had joined the company just that afternoon, was told to round up a rescue group to go to Hermman. Because Collins didn't know the way, Ham volunteered to return with him. There were twelve others. They found Hermman and his party strung out over 250 yards of trail and hill. Some of the nonwounded were so exhausted that they could not rise unaided. Collins wanted to take Hermman out first because he was bleeding badly; Hermman refused to move until the last of his party was evacuated past him. Eighteen men were brought out. Seven were wholly down and made the return journey either on stretchers or other men's backs. By the end of twenty-five minutes, Collins had done all possible; he returned half-carrying Hermman, who had insisted on coming out last. First aid had been applied on the spot while the bandages lasted. It took the tail of the column another forty-five minutes to cover the 400 yards of trail between Dale and the Company CP. By then, all hands, including Collins' men, were exhausted.

In the interval, Patteson, watching from the CP, saw another Chinese company charge up Moore's Finger. One of his own .50 machine guns was mounted in the CP. He told the gunner to fire on the ridge finger. As the gun got the range and line, Patteson saw a few of the enemy fall and others waver, but the great number disappeared into the main trench.

Again he called for VT fire against the outpost. This time there was reluctance to give it. At Regiment there was insistence that only a strong counterattack could clear the hill and prolonged VT fire would interfere with the mounting of it. Patteson was obdurate and kept saying, "I want it." After fifteen minutes they gave it to him and it came in right on the nose and perfectly timed to disintegrate a column of enemy bearers trooping down Moore's Finger with their own wounded.

For the next few minutes, and until the counterattack was ready, Patteson saw no reason to withhold anything. Not knowing that the two Smiths and Serpa were playing dead on the forward slope, he figured the hill was clear of living Americans. By doubling the fire curtain, the artillery still might exact payment for all that had been lost. So the flares played without intermission and hot steel swept the hill all along its length.

To the two Smiths that made little difference until at last one VT frag got Serpa through the back. He groaned loudly and half-arose. Big Smith pulled his feet from under him and, falling flat, Serpa lay perfectly still. As they glanced his way and saw his face buried in the dirt, the Smiths wondered if he was dead. But he was conscious and biting his lip to stifle his involuntary reaction to the pain.

Another Chinese company came forward at the run, charging up Angel Finger. One squad ran directly toward the three Americans. The lead man stumbled across Big Smith, and as he fell, the others who followed him piled up on Little Smith and Serpa.

This was the climax of the ordeal. Their inert bodies rolled with the blow. The enemy squad jumped up and ran straight on. This time Big Smith whispered, "We made it," and when Serpa whispered, "And how!" they knew they were three again.

Not another word was said during the night. Big Smith looked occasionally toward Serpa wondering how badly he was bleeding. He had made up his mind that if help did not come before first light, he would try to carry Serpa out on his back.

Attack and Repulse

At 0300 the artillery fires ordered by Lieutenant Patteson against Dale Outpost were again lifted.

There had not been enough of it to neutralize the hill. But Lieutenant Colonel Maliszewski had reached the big hill with two platoons from Item Company. Maliszewski was ready to counterattack as promptly as he knew the measure of the job.

As well as he could, Patteson described the situation, forgetting, however, to tell Maliszewski that Bressler and Spencer were trapped in the CP and there was reason to think they might still be alive. It was a significant oversight, since Maliszewski presupposed that all installations were solidly in enemy hands and his men should be prepared to blast out every bunker.

After weighing what was told him, Maliszewski decided to attack with two platoons in line, using both of them on the right side of the ridge, which would put the sweep up and over Moore's Finger.

It was a simple plan and he wanted half an hour to mount it, so that his troops could get to the low ground and ready to spring, and to allow time for additional artillery preparation. The artillery was to stonk the outpost with VT and lights again beginning at 0315. At 0330, he would put up a red flare signaling that the fires should lift.

With some nudging from Maliszewski, Patteson built up on that idea. While the two Item platoons were readying on the right side, he would move his own First Platoon from the big hill to the valley. Then, as the artillery fires lifted, First Platoon would attack up Angel Finger on the left side of the hill.

It sounded good to Maliszewski. As seen by the two men from the high ground, the problem seemed susceptible to this two-winged approach and double envelopment. Neither fully appreciated that the outpost was just high enough to separate the two actions, deprive both bodies of any feeling of close support and make co-ordination impossible.

Maliszewski walked down to where Lieutenant Collins stood in the bunker at Check Point No. 1. Seven of Collins' men had sufficiently recovered from their labor of rescuing Hermman to help him man the outguard. Maliszewski told Collins that he would welcome his group as a re-enforcement during the attack. Having his first taste of battle, Collins was perfectly agreeable.

On the other side of the hill, the pincher was in charge of 2nd Lieut. Glenn R. Yokum, also untried in a fire fight, looking almost too small for a soldier suit and too shy to command. Yokum wore thick-lensed glasses and at first glance reminded one of Mr. Peepers. But as the saying goes, the good ones come in all shapes and sizes. Unspectacular, Yokum had something essential in a commander: he was steady.

Yokum marched his men right along. They were at the bottom of the valley and ready to start up Angel Finger when the moment came that Maliszewski's red flare went up and the artillery fires lifted. That far it had been a breeze. The enemy was pitching nothing into the valley and the American shelling was hitting the bull's-eye atop Dale.

Attacking the slope, the men had first to work their way through a double apron wire. They made it without hurt, but some became snagged momentarily during the passage, and so the platoon became scattered. That cut down momentum. Beyond the wire, Yokum lost five minutes getting them collected again within range of his voice.

In that interval, they could hear the mounting rattle of automatic fire from the far side of the hill. And from the crest, several machine guns spoke, though not in their direction. They started again, but the advance went more slowly.

As they got to within 50 yards of Dale's big trench, from upslope one grenade landed among them. It wounded three men. There were some seconds of hesitation. Yokum yelled, "Move on! Move on!", and responding, they came to the solid band of concertina wire. Some tried to force their way through it; others tried to crawl under. As they struggled, grenades exploded among them and from a few yards uphill, a tommy gunner opened fire.

That was enough resistance to turn them, but within seconds a Chinese machine gun, from farther up the slope, was pouring fire on the same line. Then they recoiled about 20 yards and went flat among the rocks. One man didn't make it: Pfc. Antonio Rivera had got some part of his equipment snagged by the wire and couldn't break loose.

Pfc. Robert McKinley, who had fallen back with the others, saw Rivera's plight. On sudden impulse, this 19-year-old bounded forward and hit Rivera with a body block, aimed hip high. The blow bounced Rivera up and over the wire so that he fell on the enemy side.

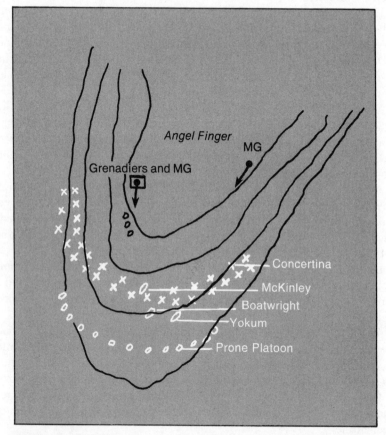

Distribution of Yokum's Platoon when it became held at the wire barricade.

That move, which fully committed Rivera beyond reach by the flattened platoon, undoubtedly led on to the next step. McKinley crawled back the 20 yards to M/S George Boatwright. For some seconds he lay there thinking his idea over. Boatwright was firing his M1 in the direction of the tommy gunner. Briefly, McKinley joined in with his carbine.

Then he said to Boatwright, "Watch me!" Again, he jumped toward the concertina. This time as he hit it straight on, in a diving motion, his arms were up to protect his face. The wire barrier went flat under his weight. Then he yelled back to Boatwright in a voice which rang clarion-clear above the sounds of fire, "Send the men over me!"

Boatwright rushed to within five yards of him and there went flat. He yelled, "Come on! Move up! Go across!" His arms moved like flails as he waved the men toward McKinley's back. But there was no quick response. One other thought made the men more hesitant than their fear of fire. As they later explained, they thought McKinley would be killed immediately, and they couldn't stand the idea of walking on a corpse. So there were perhaps three minutes of agonizing delay while McKinley played bridge, waiting for the traffic that didn't come.

Yokum's main thought during this interval was that if his men didn't stay flat they would all be killed. The concertina looked impenetrable. From just beyond it, the enemy grenadiers and tommy gunner were getting the range. Six more grenades had landed among the men and three more soldiers were crying for first aid. The Chinese machine gun was doing no damage; the fire was much too high. But now there was a fresh worry. A light mortar had opened fire and Yokum counted five rounds as they exploded within less than 30 yards of where he lay.

Yokum's head was averted when McKinley plunged to the wire and so he missed the play. He was yelling, "Crawl forward—one at a time—go under the wire." Then he heard a voice, louder and shriller than his own, "Come up here, come up here, you bastards!" It was McKinley, using his own lungs to give Boatwright an assist. And probably it was the GI language that got them started. Ordinarily, McKinley didn't use it. Later in front of the company, he was to acknowledge that while he lay stretched on the wire, he kept remembering what his dad, a cook in Roswell, N. M., kept writing him: "Keep your head and pray to your God."

Cpl. Virgil Jones was the first man to try the passage. Landing in the small of McKinley's back in the darkness, he lost his balance, banged McKinley in the back of his head with the base plate of his machine gun, and jumped back to the nigh side of the wire, yelling, "Are you hurt?" McKinley shouted, "Jump again and keep going!"

Jones made it this time and Privates Jeeter and Hughes followed directly after. As each man landed on his back, McKinley gave him a shout of encouragement, "Keep going; look for the burp gunner directly ahead!" There had come no slackening of the fire; rather, the few Chinese among the rocks above them were now concentrating both their grenades and the automatic fire toward McKinley. The gunner now kept a stream going, instead of firing in short bursts.

Private Godfrey, a Negro, was the fourth man. As he landed on McKinley's back, a bullet got him through the shoulder. Instead of yelling, he completed his spring, and slumped onto the bank beyond McKinley. The others did not know that he'd been hit. But McKinley had felt it and he pitched his voice toward Godfrey, saying, "If you got it bad, stay where you are."

Privates Naparez and Cox and Sergeant Boatwright went on over. Then Cpl. Harold E. Wright took a grenade fragment through the hip, and in his tumble from McKinley's back, kicked him in the head. He lay down beside Godfrey and waited for the others to clear.

Naparez, who was serving as the platoon's aid man, had seen Wright crumple. Instead of continuing upslope, he dropped beside him and felt for the wound. Wright was already losing blood at an alarming rate.

Nine others, under the spurring of Yokum, who was now standing in the clear and urging them on, made the passage safely. Counting Rivera, that made eighteen whom McKinley had put over the wire. The move had taken approximately six minutes after the initial delay. What had slowed the advance chiefly was that the Chinese grenadiers were throwing in salvos, and each man had waited a few seconds, timing his rush to the break in the grenade fire. Yokum went last.

Downslope, short of the wire, Sgt. William Welcher was having a different kind of trial. The six Koreans in Yokum's platoon were all collected within Welcher's squad. They refused to budge. Welcher booted them until at last one man got up and bounded across McKinley. The others still hugged the dirt. Frustrated and wondering what to do, Welcher simply stayed there, kicking and reviling them, forgetting the platoon's problem.

Sgt. Francis D. Bushman, a go-it-alone kind of soldier, had been on the extreme left of the line, virtually detached from the main body by a rock outcropping. He had not witnessed McKinley's action or heard him. In those minutes he was helping Pfc. Buddy W. Vandvier who had been hard hit by several grenade shards. After giving him first aid and starting him rearward, Bushman crawled forward. By pulling at some loose rock, he was able to wiggle under the concertina.

His line of advance put him on the left side of Angel Finger at the same time that the men who had crossed via McKinley were trying, singly rather than as a collected group, to charge up the right-hand side. It was a better spot for seeing than for fighting. The shelling had set one of the bunkers afire atop Dale Outpost and the glare in the background silhouetted the crest of the finger. Bushman could see two Chinese firing down on the platoon with automatic weapons. Still higher up the finger, though not more than 35 yards above his head, four grenadiers bobbed up in alternate pairs to lob potato-masher grenades down on his friends. From the heights, an occasional grenade exploded on his own side of the finger, but he could not see who threw them nor could he counter the fire ripping into the platoon. Already his carbine was empty. He had grenades and he tried to clear the ground with them. But the height plus the distance mocked his effort and the grenades only rebounded toward him. The slope confronting him was almost sheer and wholly barren, with no shrubs or rock ledges to offer a handhold. He could neither move upright nor crawl. The best he could do was drag himself upward a few inches at a time.

The strain on McKinley had not been eased by the advance of the platoon except that the fire was no longer wholly concentrated in his direction. He still lay stretched across the wire, for there remained the task of evacuating the two wounded men, Wright and Godfrey, the same way they had come. There was no one to help him, since Naparez, after examining Wright, had continued with the platoon. McKinley's way of handling it was to grab them around the knees and pull them back across his own body. That took another five minutes, by his estimate and theirs. After this exertion, Wright could not arise. McKinley heard him say, "Dear God, I'm terribly weak and losing blood." So McKinley pulled back to the nigh side of the wire, intending to carry Wright downhill in his arms. He was surprised to find that his own strength was spent. The best he could do was brace Wright with an arm under his shoulder.

By then the platoon was also reeling. What no one had foreseen was that the act which was intended to save it would perforce give it a fatal diffusion. McKinley's back was in effect a defile. Each man had entered it under fire and, deploying beyond it, was still under fire. In consequence, each man advanced separately to whatever dark object in the immediate foreground seemed to promise the best cover. So all chance for unity was lost immediately.

Pfc. Thomas Nezbella, after crossing McKinley's back, bounded about 10 yards up the ridge, and slid into position behind a rock ledge. He could hear two automatic weapons firing directly above his head; by the sound, they were not more than 30 yards away. He moved five yards closer. Then five times he grenaded toward the sound. Each of his grenades rebounded, exploding closer to him than to the enemy.

Then off to his right a few yards, he heard a shout. It was Private Thacher calling to Private Jeeter, "Come on up with your BAR and help me get 'em." He saw the two men converge and maneuver a short way upslope. Then they joined fire, Thacher using an M1. Within a minute or two thereafter, one of the Chinese guns ceased fire, and Nezbella reckoned that Thacher and Jeeter together had put the gunner out of action. But they, too, had quit fighting, and for the moment, this puzzled Nezbella.

Yokum had tried calling to his men but could get no response. There was too much noise on the hill for his voice to carry, and in the dark (he is near-sighted) he could see no one else. So he went to work as a rifleman. His carbine fire, directed toward the spot where the tommy gunner was operating, endured just four rounds. The piece was so fouled by dust that it wouldn't fire automatic, and after he had spent four rounds manually, it quit altogether. Thus disarmed, Yokum decided to start looking for his men.

Privates Rivera and Rodriguez had moved leftward, which line took them around the curve of the finger, and toward Sergeant Bushman. As they neared him, either a grenade or a light mortar round landed between them. The explosion shattered Rodriguez's arm and wounded Rivera in a dozen places, one frag penetrating his stomach. They started back the way they had come, Rodriguez half-carrying Rivera. Bushman recovered the M1 dropped by Rodriguez. He at last had a weapon and the second Chinese gunner (armed with a Bren) was still in clear profile. Bushman fired perhaps a dozen rounds; it was probably his fire that killed the second gun.

Cpl. Virgil Jones had tried to find a spot along the upslope where he could prop his LMG for a clear sweep against the group of Chinese grenadiers. At last he found it, a rock ledge, flat-surfaced. Before he could open fire, a grenade bounced onto the ledge and, exploding under the gun, wrecked it. One fragment smashed the bridge of Jones' nose. The effect was like a hard blow from a hammer. Jones was stunned beyond knowing what had happened. But he picked up the ruined gun and started downslope. Cpl. Troy Goodman was lying just a few yards below him with a bullet through his leg. He saw that Jones was hit and reeling, so he put an arm around him, and together they continued the journey.

Private Naparez had climbed only a few feet before coming to Private Cox, who was down with a grenade fragment through his knee. He put a bandage on him, and then, supporting Cox, started downslope.

Privates Thacher and Jeeter, whose team play Nezbella had seen knock out the Chinese gunner, were returning even more blindly. Just how it happened, no one ever knew. But both men had been struck in the head by bullet fire, and though neither died instantly, both were in their last moments as they sought the road to the rear.

Of the detail of these blows to his men, young Yokum still knew little or nothing. Until his carbine failed, he had seen none of them and heard no one cry out. It had been as if he were fighting alone on the hill; the rocks and the tumult atop the outpost killed the sounds of his own men giving battle. He reckoned that some of them must have recoiled to the concertina, and if he went that way, he could re-collect them.

The barrier now gaped wide, a mortar round having snapped it just a few yards from where McKinley had lain. As Yokum neared the opening, it was already semiblocked by a cluster of his own wounded and dead. Rivera, Thacher and Jeeter had made it just that far and there died within a few feet of each other. Goodman, Jones and the other wounded were standing by, wordless and motionless, as if shocked by the discovery.

It reacted on Yokum the same way. Counting score, he realized that at most, not more than six of his men could still be whole-bodied and moving up the slope. It was no longer a platoon, not even a squad. That thought made him oblivious to all else. That above him the slope had gone silent, that this could only mean that his men, though falling, had not failed and had won their side of the hill, were facts which simply could not get through to his consciousness.

He yelled, "Come on back!" and this time, because of the stillness, Boatwright, Private First Class Bennett and Private Hughes, who were still trying to move upslope, heard him and withdrew to the concertina.

That left Sergeant Bushman all alone on the finger. He had not heard Yokum's order. But all of his earlier anxieties were now done and he lay flat on the rocks feeling quite content. There was no longer any sign of the enemy and the sounds of fire from on top the hill had diminished to an occasional rifle crack.

When Yokum with the survivors reached the bottom of the valley, he reported by radio to Lieutenant Patteson, telling him what had happened. Patteson told him, "Wait there!"

Aid man Naparez had nipped back up the hill to search for other missing and wounded. He met McKinley coming down. His journey to the rear with Wright had been slowed because two other wounded had joined them, and McKinley was trying to handle all three of them shuttle fashion, moving a few yards at a time.

From beginning to end, the fight had lasted hardly more than thirty minutes.

Yokum's waiting ended when Patteson told him that Item Company had secured the main entrenchments on top of Dale. Patteson said, "Take any able-bodied men you have, move up Angel Finger and join them."

There were seven in all, counting Yokum. They turned back to the hill and climbed it without a shot being fired against them by their enemies.

But it gave them no feeling of victory, for Item stood on the height while they still toiled up the rocky slope.

As dawn came, so did a bearer detail, bringing coffee. They drank and felt a little better.

Stumble to Victory

ITEM COMPANY HAD BEEN IN A BLOCKING POSITION BEHIND FIRST Battalion on the southern side of the Tong Valley when the midnight call came to Lieutenant Hemphill directing him to send a platoon to re-enforce Baker Company on the main line.

Artillery was already falling on Item's bivouac and one man had been killed. Not more than ten minutes after Third Platoon had hit the trail bound for the front, Colonel Kern again called Hemphill telling him that Dale Outpost had been overrun and the rest of Item Company would move immediately to retake it. There was a bad break: the only Item men who knew the ground at Dale Outpost were in Third Platoon.

No one in the company had slept. Hemphill was new to his command, not yet acquainted with his men and without knowledge of the country-side. He assembled his two platoons in the mess tent, told them the mission and then led the column forth. There were 69 men in it. The riflemen all carried basic loads and five grenades apiece. There were 1,000 rounds each for the two light machine guns. Hemphill was about to leave his rocket launchers behind, then thought better of it.

They started at 0130. Their approach march to Lieutenant Patteson's CP was exactly one-half mile, as Cpl. Billy R. Crum knew by reeling off an even doughnut of wire along the trail. But there was much stumbling and checking as more artillery found the mark during the march-up, wounding two men. They were 47 minutes in getting there.

During this time, Maliszewski had been champing at the bit. Having been perfunctorily briefed by Patteson, he in turn gave the picture to Hemphill. Nothing was said about the men still missing and possibly alive on Dale.

Together Maliszewski and Hemphill scanned the outpost from the distance. Save for the precisely delivered VT shower, it looked deceptively peaceful. Nothing could be seen stirring on its surface under the in-

candescent glare of the light shells. To both men the sights and sounds
indicated that Dale had been deserted.

Because of the intense glare above Dale, the valley on both sides of it
was impenetrably shaded. The Chinese would be certain to cover their
back door. The most promising approach was via Moore's Finger on the
right flank. But how the finger was shaped and how its mass intervened
between the valley and the rampart were indiscernible. For that reason and
because Hemphill was new to the scene, the battalion commander dictated
the plan for the company attack.

All of Item would deploy rightward of the chogi trench, with the left
tying in to the outguard position which Lieutenant Collins was holding
with ten men. That group would join the attack. Item's Second Platoon
would be on the right flank, directly facing Moore's Finger. The machine
guns were grouped at the extreme right with the mission of moving up the
finger until they were on line-of-sight to Dale's crest and from there deliv-
ering a covering fire while the rifle line advanced.

Patteson had grown restive over the denuding of his part of the main line
through the commitment of Yokum's platoon. He asked Maliszewski,
"What do I do if the Chinese hit me?"

Said Maliszewski: "Use your cooks and clerks."

Hemphill wanted to know, "Who will I use for a guide?"

Said Maliszewski, "You have one; I'm it."

Hemphill got back to the company, called his leaders together and gave
them orders. The attack was to go at 0330, which, by the time Hemphill
was through talking, left them just 27 minutes to move and get squared
away at the line of departure. It sounded simple enough as Hemphill described it.

But time was pressing. Maliszewski and Hemphill struck off together
leading the column along the commo trench toward the finger. In their
eagerness, they moved too fast. The more heavily weighted riflemen
couldn't keep the pace. So when the lead files reached the dip where they
were to debouch from the trench and form a line on the lower ground to
rightward of it, there was no longer a guide in sight and none to direct the
alignment.

Lieut. Joseph W. Faris led First Platoon. Tight behind him came No. 1
squad leader, Sergeant José Lugo, his BAR man, Private Anthony P. Sanchez, and the assistant gunner, Private Francisco Bermudez-Cruz. And
when they formed, that was all of the platoon. Private Johnson, who had
been behind Bermudez-Cruz, had missed a turn at a gap in the wire and
had led the rest of the platoon off in the opposite direction. With only four
minutes to go, Faris had to radio for a delay in the attack while he hunted
his lost men.

But he was not alone in his embarrassment. Hemphill had already heard from Second Platoon that part of its line was lost or at least missing. Cpl. Donald E. Mullins radioed to keep the artillery going while the slopes were searched for the strayed infantry. Maliszewski, biting his nails, ordered a ten-minute postponement.

Inadvertently, he had helped make this untimely confusion. For in leading off, he had talked it up, yelling, "Let's go! Get the sons-of-bitches!" And the men had followed his lead. The deployment was bedlamized before it had established order. Many of the men were yelling at top voice. Squads already on line were prematurely shouting, "Move out! Move out! Let's go!" All of it would have been great stuff if Item had been set. As things were, the exhorting drowned out the voices of Faris and others who were calling for the lost men.

After hard sweat, Faris found his missing line. Still panting, the platoon was brought abreast the LD. And just then the red flare went off, signaling the starting of the attack. Though most of the squads by that moment were headed in approximately the right direction, they were still scrambled. Several were still far behind and others had come into line in the wrong sector.

Only one group moved directly and steadily to its assigned mission. On the far right flank, the machine guns under M/S Robert J. Jones, with Lugo, Sanchez and Bermudez-Cruz providing the BAR support, moved straight up Moore's Finger to the first knob. From there, they had a straight line to the fire bunkers atop Dale, 75 yards away. Of that, there was no doubt. Automatic fire from the redoubt was already buzzing the knob as they settled among the rocks and began working their weapons. Behind them, the assault line was still trying to collect itself.

On the far right of Second Platoon, two squads had found a conveniently located trench in the valley bottom and were standing fast. Hemphill ran that way yelling, "Move out!" The men echoed the cry but didn't budge. Corporal Crum and Sgt. Joe J. Schindel jumped into the trench and, in Crum's phrase, "did a lot of ass-kicking." That helped to restore motion. But there was no vigor in it. Every four or five yards the men would stop, though they were drawing no fire. The repriming had to be done over and over. Yet they continued to shout, "Move out! Get going! Kill the sons-of-bitches!" as if in the grip of hysteria.

Second Platoon's two squads on the left were advancing upslope, firing as they moved. There were no targets in sight. The brow of Moore's Finger, directly ahead of them, masked the rampart of Dale Outpost, and all of the bullets were being wasted on this dead space. Cpl. Othelius Johnson shouted, "Why are you firing?" Someone yelled back, "Because First Platoon is firing." Helped by Sgt. Edward Gabriel, Johnson moved along the line trying to stop the shooting. Several of the carbines had gone dry before the line could see the Chinese position.

The base of Moore's Finger divides into three subfingers. In the darkness, these divisions could not be seen by the men. The left-hand approach which was taken by Faris' First Platoon is steep-fronted and camel-backed. From the floor of the valley, its last high knob hides to view both the mass of the main finger and the summit of Dale. Not being oriented, Faris' men mistook this cap, not more than 50 yards above their heads, for the silhouette of the outpost. When the red flare went up and their climb started, they cut loose with all weapons. No one had ordered it; nerve tension, mounting high during the approach, found release in the trigger finger. Once started, it was almost impossible to stop because of the furious shouting. But M/S Charles G. Heeg and Sgt. Woodrow L. Schlehofer tried. Obviously firepower was wasting at a rate that would empty every magazine before Item could draw on the Chinese. The two NCOs yelled, "Cease fire! Cease fire!" Their voices were lost in the din. The platoon moved on up the slope, pouring its bullets into vacant rock two heights short of the enemy.

"Getting onto ground we knew nothing of," said Faris, "we were not given time for reconnaissance. And the only effect of our fire was to warn the enemy and give him time to organize against us."

Lieutenant Collins, who had the Baker detachment which was supposed to move with Item, became willy-nilly part of this scramble up the secondary finger. Before he had moved more than 30 yards from the line of departure, he had lost his own ten men in the darkness; knowing none of them by sight or voice, he could not regather them. So he tried to command whatever men were nearest him. It would not work. They lurched forward a few yards at a time, then stopped to fire a few rounds at nothing in particular. He moved among them shouting, "God damn it, keep moving! God damn it, quit firing!" Getting little or no results that way, he started booting them in the tail. And that worked.

When at last they moved off the secondary finger onto the arched back of Moore's Finger, conditions changed swiftly. It was now a straight shoot up the slope into the fighting bunkers of Dale Outpost, not more than 80 yards away. Against the glare of the illumination and the mortar shelling hitting into the rampart, they could see the trench line and see dark figures darting about on the bunker roofs. One Chinese machine gun was firing straight down Moore's Finger, grazing the ground which they had to travel. Now was the time to pour it on! And it was at this moment exactly that the cry, "Cease fire! Cease fire!" which had started in the bottoms not more than fifteen minutes before began to paralyze the Americans.

Barring their path 25 yards upslope was the broad band of concertina wire. Several enemy submachine gunners and a few grenadiers, nesting right behind the wire, were peppering the foreground. A second machine gun, lodged on a bunker roof well over to the right, was firing flankward toward the finger. There was more sound than fury in this automatic outburst; most of it was going high. But with the way wide open for effective return, Item rode the crisis in a confusion of thought and action which directly reflected its early disorganization. Its fire slacked off to a whisper. The will was lacking and so were the weapons. At least half of them had been fouled beyond use during the up-climb because the men had hit the dirt too often while still not under fire.

Pvt. Augustus T. Young's BAR wouldn't work; he didn't know why. Cpl. Terrell G. Parker's BAR wouldn't fire; the magazine was dirty. Pvt. Richard L. Crookston's BAR wouldn't fire; he thought it was because the ammunition was too dirty. Pvt. Julio Lopez' M1 wouldn't operate, though when he yielded it to Parker, it did quite well. Pvt. Earl Johnson's M1 wouldn't shoot; he thought it was because the clips were too begrimed. Cpl. James L. Rector's M1 would fire sometimes if he operated the bolt; he blamed it on the dirtiness of the weapon that in one hour he fired only one clip. And so it went, along a great part of the line.

At his machine-gun position farther downslope, Sergeant Jones decided to explore forward and see what was holding up the company. Private First Class Manning, who had the platoon radio, went with him. From their position on the right-hand secondary finger, they moved on an ascending diagonal toward Dale Outpost's rear. Jones could see clearly the positions from which the two enemy machine guns were firing. The farthest was not more than 120 yards from him. He had kept up a continuous fire with the LMGs on these rather obvious targets and it surprised him that they had not been killed.

As he came onto Moore's Finger, he saw "at least thirty men just milling about." No one seemed to be in charge of them, and instead of resting, they were turning in circles like corralled cattle. Approaching the concertina, he saw Corporal Johnson lying there with the 3.5 rocket launcher.

Pointing to the machine gun 40 yards beyond the wire, Jones asked him, "Why aren't you firing?"

Johnson was in tears as he replied, "Hell, they won't let me."

Sergeant Heeg had given the order. The slope behind Johnson was thick with men still not under control and Heeg was afraid of the backblast. Restoring command unity was the main problem; effective response had been made impossible by the intermingling of the squads. And until the rest of the men could be formed in line and pushed up to the wire, the launcher could not be used.

Hemphill, Faris, Heeg, Jones and the other leaders worked at it. Man by

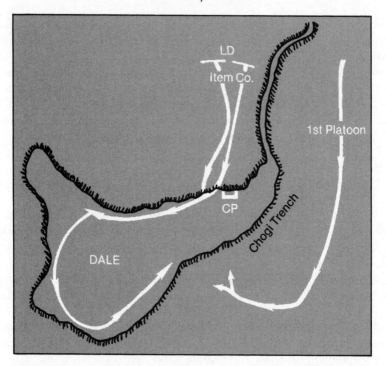

The counterattack against Dale Outpost. Item Company's platoons had
become intermingled before they gained the summit.

man the lower slope was cleared and the line crawled forward. The hardiest
characters tried to push on through the concertina. Pvt. Deforest Small got
hung up in it, and could neither break free nor lie down. He was suspended
there for six minutes. So were four of the company's Koreans. From the
nigh side of the wire, Corporal Beckham stood up yelling, "Get moving!
Crawl through! Crawl under!" It was his last try; a bullet got him through
the brain.

Lieutenant Hemphill bounded for the concertina, trying to break
through. A heavy potato masher exploded next him in midair, and the
fragments ripped his legs and head. The blow stunned him and he sagged.
For a few minutes the men thought he was dead.

That was when Jones decided to return to his machine guns. The slope
was becoming too hot. From behind the wire the Chinese grenadiers and
burp gunners were getting in their heaviest licks. And the machine-gun fire
was now cutting the grass. While Jones walked back to his guns, he was
overtaken by Sgt. Ferdinand Schulz, his own assistant. A grenade had
wounded Schulz in the head while he lay next the wire.

Small broke loose from the wire, as by a miracle, when a Chinese white phosphorus grenade landed under his feet. Said Small, "I got strong quickly." One great heave and he was free, falling back toward the company just before the missile exploded. But two of the Koreans who became trapped in the same way were killed by burp-gun fire.

Of these slight wounds the line again bogged down. A minority quit the hill. The greater number during the next few minutes remained inert next the wire. Even so, that should have ended Corporal Johnson's frustrations. But his bad luck was still running. Someone had landed hard on the 3.5 launcher and bent it, and he could no longer force a round into it.

SFC Burton Ham, who had been with Lieutenant Collins at the beginning, and at the time of their separation had continued on with Pfc. John R. Pennington, was sprawled next to Johnson very close to the concertina. To both Pennington and Ham, it appeared that the in-fighting along the barricade was being carried by not more than six or seven Chinese. Yet they were holding at least forty men motionless, pinning them down and silencing their weapons.

Collins, though he had lost Ham and the others, must have been within a few yards of Johnson, watching the same phenomenon. The line had become transfixed by the strong play of the one Chinese machine gun which fired straight down the finger. Collins heard men yelling, "We ought to get that machine gun!" Others cried, "Why doesn't somebody use the 3.5?" But no one fitted action to words. Collins' impression was that the enemy grenadiers along the wire were using white phosphorus bombs mainly and that most of the stuff was bad and fizzed out weakly.

It is easier to blame inept leadership for this stagnation than to understand that the circumstances of the night attack had stripped it of salient authority. Unity had been lost in the scrambling of the squads. Men command by voice, look and gesture, but the chain of force thus generated is dependent on recognition. Darkness, din and diffusion had militated against recognition on that night to an extraordinary degree. Later when the story of the operation was reconstructed, it was noteworthy that each man told his part as if he had walked almost alone. Not one of them, during the prolonged struggle uphill, identified his own experience as related to the action of more than two or three persons whom he knew. They were a group only in the sense that they had numbers.

Colonel Maliszewski was hardly less susceptible to this lost feeling than the replacements who were having their first time in combat, though because the command was Hemphill's, he did not attempt an intervention which in any case would have been vain. After leading the column to the LD, he continued with the attack, moving first with Faris' flank, then swinging over to Second Platoon, which he calculated would arrive first at the rampart. To a degree, in his detached position, he was deceived by the early shouting and tumult which he believed reflected a splendid verve in the assault.

Shortly thereafter, he began to pay more attention to the enemy guns than to the spell which they put upon Item Company. His interest drawn in that direction, he did not sense the state of disorganization within the American attack. Beating on his mind was the thought that unless the two enemy machine guns could be knocked out, Item would take fearful losses at the wire.

Crossing a draw as he traversed the front, he found a small hole in the concertina and wiggled through. He stood there alone within 50 yards of the fire bunkers atop Dale. He was carrying a carbine and four grenades. Misquoting Confucius, he said out loud, with no one to listen: "The strong example is worth one thousand words." He moved on up the gully scrambling over the rocks to a knob which he reckoned was just within grenade range of the main trench. He had marked the two main enemy positions. It was his intention to attack both of them, working first against the gun on the Chinese left flank by coming up under the blind corner of the bunker.

Hemphill was thinking along the same lines. He was still bleeding badly from his face wounds, and clutching at his hurt leg, though his head had cleared. He moved over to Faris' flank yelling, "Anybody got a 3.5 launcher? Bring it to me!" Pfc. Clarence L. Sparks, the assistant gunner in First Platoon, heard him. The gunner, Cpl. Warren T. Adams, had been working with the wounded and at that moment was loading Private First Class Jessup on a litter.

Sparks ran to Hemphill, carrying the tube and a case of ammunition. Hemphill asked, "Do you know how to load this thing? I don't." Sparks got a round out of the case, but its contact wire had tangled with the spring. Sparks grabbed another round and loaded.

Hemphill wiggled under the wire and ran forward, yelling back to his men, "Watch out for backblast!" It was a needless warning; no one was following him. Sparks stood by the barricade watching him go.

Thirty yards from Dale's main trench, Hemphill halted and fired, aiming at the bunker roof from where the enemy machine gun was firing straight down the finger. Another grenade sailed in on him as he loosed the round and more steel cut into him. Collins, watching the bunker, saw a "great flash envelop the roof." The machine gun went silent, ending the fire from that direction. The one round had hit home.

It was like a dam breaking. Almost instantly, the line of men who had been prone and silent below the wire arose and surged forward. And this time the barbed entanglement detained them not at all. Also, there was an upsurge of the chorus, "Get the sons-of-bitches!" but as Faris later said, this time they knew not only the words but also the right tune.

As to what killed the second gun, the proofs are less concrete. Maliszewski attacked it within a few minutes, either way, of Hemphill's charge against the No. 1 gun with the big bazooka. Jones' machine-gun battery had been plastering that same target for more than thirty minutes, and the gun had operated intermittently, with long pauses, as if the fire was hitting into crew without destroying the weapon. It still fired in weak bursts as Maliszewski approached it. Or at least he believed it was the bunker housing one of the heavies, though it may have been one of the several Brens which the Chinese had brought to Dale. His first grenade toss sailed clean through the opening. There was an explosion and the gun went silent.

Maliszewski then moved toward the several bunkers directly overlooking Moore's Finger. The folding of the earth had hid to his view the dramatic effect of Hemphill's personal maneuver. But as he drew nigh the bunker which he thought was still holding back Item by its fire, a BAR man settled down on the parapet beside him and offered him his grenades. Maliszewski didn't have time to get his name. He unpinned the grenades and threw. Together the two men ducked back into a small ravine just below the parapet. From the main trench several grenades showered down on them. Hemphill's assault force was just then crowding to the trenches, moving upslope on both sides of Maliszewski. Lieut. Claude T. Ford heard a yell out of the darkness, "Come on! Get the sons-of-bitches!" and knew it for the battalion commander's voice.

One big stick grenade found the mark. It exploded under Maliszewski as he went flat. From the ravine came his cry, "Come get me, my right leg is blown off!" followed by silence. Luckily, he had only lost a foot. Maliszewski tumbled back down the slope, then blacked out. Regaining consciousness, he crawled a little way uphill. It seemed to him that an hour passed before any help came. But that was an illusion born of shock. Sergeant Ham had heard his cry and got to him immediately. The medics were working over him within a few minutes and he was carried off the hill while the line was still carrying on a confused fight to subdue the Chinese resistance.

Hemphill's lone-handed sortie had introduced a new if fleeting note of steadiness in the situation. Besides knocking out the gun and jarring loose his troops, Hemphill had given his men that fresh confidence which makes control possible. Once they had broken through the concertina, Faris, Ford, Heeg, Schlehofer and the other junior leaders were able to get them in hand. They obeyed orders and formed as a line of skirmishers just beyond the barrier. There were at least two exceptions. Cpls. George A. Mata and Sisto M. Valeho had been in the forefront of the movement, and they kept

Dale Outpost lay 500 yards beyond the main line and was connected with it by a chogi trench cut along the ridge crest.

right on going, heading for that part of the escarpment where Maliszewski had started his attack.

Mata had an M1, Valeho a BAR. From First Platoon's sector, they cut diagonally rightward across and upslope, firing as they went. Mata's rifle was already sticking. Fifty yards along, they came to another band of wire. They were both in it and Valeho was wedged tight when grenades began to fall on them from out the trench just above their heads. Mata wrenched free. Then just over to his right about 30 yards he heard a call, "Hey over there, come help us!" He ran that way, and hit another small patch of wire. Four members of Second Platoon—one American and three Koreans— were hung up in it, and though Mata strained, he could not pull them loose. Two potato mashers had exploded among the men and all four had been hit by numerous fragments. Mata said, "Give me your grenades!" He got three from them, ran back to Valeho and got two more, and then took Valeho's BAR.

Leaving the four men impaled, he headed straight for the parapet, jumped into the trench and rushed the bunker from which the grenades had been coming. As he bombed into the open bunker door, getting away his five grenades as fast as he could pull the pin and throw, two more potato mashers exploded right at his heels. Hardly pausing, he opened fire with the BAR, dusting the trench in both directions. He stopped only when his weapon ran dry.

Right after that, Corporal Mullins, the radio man, ran past him. With Pvt. James R. Streit, Mullins had observed Mata's whole action from a little way downslope. He had seen the Chinese grenading from the bunker and that had given him pause. Then as Mata's grenades hit among their soft targets, Mullins witnessed the kill and heard the scream of the victims— evidence which Mata had missed in his excitement. Said Mullins, "That was what brought us forward; we knew Mata had done it." Streit had fired his M1 as they advanced; he continued on to grenade the next bunker past Mata, after first singing out, "Hey, any American in there?" Mullins prowled the bunker which Mata had bombed. There were seven dead Chinese inside—the score of a man named Mata.

On its last leg of the uphill sweep, the line started smoothly. There was still fire from the hill. A few burp guns were popping away and the remaining Chinese grenadiers hung on tenaciously. But the machine-gun fire which had raked Moore's Finger was ended. Whether killed by Maliszewski's attack, or by the thirty-minute fire from Sergeant Jones' battery, or maybe the two together, the second gun did not speak again after the line had re-formed.

Not enemy resistance, but the temptation of ground protection, brought about the next unhinging of the line. To men moving in an attack, the sight of solid works draws like a magnet. This is true even in dark and when the works are enemy-held. To take one's chances within solid earth walls seems much safer and more sensible than a slow climb in the open. The Koreans in Item felt this pull far more strongly than did the Americans, and the line rippled back and forth as they tried to break for the hillcrest, only to be restrained.

Renewed confusion came of a peculiarity in the Dale trench line. Where the works of Dale wrap around its command post, the trench for a distance drops down toward the Sidamak Valley, then climbs upslope again. As Item's line advanced, the center where the two platoons hinged was opposite this low point. Because of the dip, the trench ran diagonally toward both platoons. Each could see the opening oblique to its flank but could not see the embankment along its own flank. So the two halves of the line headed for the ditch on opposing angles, and in so doing, the squads again became completely scrambled. Once the line had dissolved in this manner into the works, the restoration of small group unity had to await the end of the fight. Probably by that time it mattered very little. All of the Chinese main weapons had gone out. Group resistance was almost ended. The enemy survivors were little better than fugitives. The fighting problem had become one of smelling out grenadiers and killing them, two or three to a bunker.

On entering the trench Private Small heard smothered calls coming from several of the wrecked bunkers, "Help GI! Help GI!" It troubled him because he had never heard Chinese cry out like that, and he wondered about it as the noise persisted for an hour or more. Having no grenades, he didn't go after the bunkers. He watched others rush the door and throw the bomb home. Unlike Private Streit, not all of them took the precaution to yell, "Hey, any American in there?" Many were having their first night of battle, and of the very special problems in counterattack, they knew only what they had been told.

Whether they in fact unwittingly bombed any of Baker Company's wounded who might otherwise have survived is not known. None remembered having grenaded the CP bunker, toward which both platoons converged. If they ignored its existence, that would be even stranger. Death must have overtaken Baker's commander, Bressler, and his two NCOs before Item reached the trenches. It is simply an oddity in the record that by next morning, Item's recollection of how it had handled the CP was as blank as its consciousness that stricken friends were under the timbers there.

One unwounded soldier, Private Epps, who had lain doggo next a bunker wall, did not wait to be succored. As Item topped the ridge, this Baker man came out of the darkness beyond and ran downhill to Sergeant Jones' machine-gun position on Moore's Finger. He said to Jones, "I'm O.K. as hell; you got anything for me to do?" His arrival tipped off Jones to the possibility that there might be other friends on the hill. His guns had already ceased fire, having burned up all ammunition. Re-entering the skirmishing force, Jones worked forward along the trench. One bunker was being defended from both ends by rifles. It sounded like American fire. So Jones restrained the men around him, thereby saving Sergeant Reasor and three other Baker fighters. These four were the only element on Dale to stay the fight from first to last. They should have felt some satisfaction in it. But Reasor was extraordinarily depressed.

First light was just beginning to break as the final round started. The coming of day afforded the only relief from the confusions already visited on the attack. At last men could recognize each other over a few yards of distance. Platoon and squad unity had been dissolved by the circumstances of the closing rush. The full-length commitment foreclosed any chance of systematic reorganization. But as each man moved along, he saw and joined force with someone whom he knew. The mop-up continued undirected and without cohesion, except as friendship and daylight enabled these little groupings to form and move together. Till the moment when the outpost was at last rewon, the fight went on as a series of separated and unrelated actions.

At the moment of American entry into the trenches, there could not have been more than 50 live Chinese on Dale, though there were 123 dead Chinese within its works. Half of this force made a clean getaway. Corporal Parker ran to Dale's forward slope along the parapet. As he made the front of the hill, he saw at least three squads of the enemy running downslope not more than 35 yards away. Earlier, he had given up his BAR because it wouldn't fire and had picked up an M1 dropped by one of the wounded. Now he made the belated discovery that the rifle was empty.

Private Johnson, teamed with Lieutenant Faris, was looking things over from a crater inside the parados. They saw six Chinese running down the trench headed for enemy country. Johnson fired eight rounds from his M1 but stopped no one. A grenade landed in the crater next to his leg. He jumped straight up and while he was in air the grenade exploded. Such was the jar to his body that he yelled, "First aid! I'm hit!" Faris looked him over. Not one fragment had touched him.

Faris continued on and ran into Heeg. Two Chinese jumped from a bunker within a few feet of them and ran down the trench. Heeg started to fire. A grenade landed just behind Faris, exploded and wounded him. Faris went down. Heeg saw the grenadier jump to the parapet and streak downhill. Heeg ran behind, grenading the Chinese. His third throw, at 40 yards, hit the man in the back just as it exploded.

Private Sparks had teamed with Pfc. Garbell H. Palmer. They stumbled over a wounded Chinese lying in the trench. He was moaning and crying, "Help me! Help me!" Sparks yanked him to a sitting position.

Sparks asked, "Are you a Chinese Communist soldier?"

The man cried, "No, no, no."

"Are you a Communist?"

"No, no, no."

"Are you a Chinese?"

"No, no, no."

"Are you a soldier?"

"No, no, no."

At that point Sparks gave up. He said to Palmer, "He's nothing but a nothing. Anyway, he's wounded. So I guess we better put him on a litter and get him off the hill," which they did.

Hemphill joined Schlehofer, Sparks, Streit, Valeho and Heeg. The party went forward to prowl that part of the perimeter where Mata and Maliszewski had operated. But they found the bunkers dead and the slopes cooled off. While moving, they were joined by Faris, Johnson, Mullins and about fifteen others. With a solid formation at last in hand, they made a sweep over the front of the hill—finding nothing—then started to sweep its left side.

A white phosphorus shell exploded over its lower slope, momentarily lighting it. By its flash, they saw a number of figures climbing upward toward them through the rocks. Somebody yelled, "My God, Joe is coming back!" So they all fired. Schlehofer spent all of a clip as did Sparks, Small, Streit and several others. One man emptied his BAR. For perhaps two minutes, it was vigorous defense.

Then up from the rocks, during a brief lull, came American voices, "Don't shoot! Don't shoot! Baker Company! GIs!" The target had been the little remnant of Lieutenant Yokum's platoon which had managed to survive the attack up Angel Finger. The men had flattened under Item's fire and no one had been hit.

The moment was bitter only for Schlehofer. It ruined his main chance of the day. He had seen three Chinese running toward Baldy down Dale's forward finger. One carried a mortar tube. So he had put down his M1 and grabbed a BAR from one of Item's Koreans. He was just squeezing trigger when the cry was raised, "My God, Joe is coming back!" So he let the three Chinese escape and swung his BAR around to empty its magazine against the slope up which the Americans were advancing.

During the next half-hour, as Hemphill moved about the hill, collecting his men and getting them set on Dale, prior to being evacuated for hospital care, he impressed his followers immeasurably. His clothing was blood-drenched and the head wounds still flowed freely. But as he made the rounds, he said to them, "Don't worry; we're all right now. I know we're out of ammo but I'll get it up to you before I leave here." And the face wore a wide grin. He said to Heeg, "I already have one Purple Heart. Now they'll have to give me a dozen."

The courage of Hemphill and his irrepressible cheerfulness were the impressions which stayed indelibly in the minds of his men long after he had gone. Because of these salient qualities, they spoke gently of him as a leader well worth following. Yet they were not elated about how the company had behaved in this fight, though it had conquered. Their sober judgment was that their failure to become collected was in large part their own fault. After Item regained Dale Outpost, it was never again threatened. The division thought of it as a splendid effort. Its satisfaction was not shared by the men who had won the hill.

Item's losses in this small fight were four killed and thirty-one wounded, not a great bloodletting, but still, one-half the strength of the company, and spent in less than two hours.

If there was shock among the survivors, it was still not enough to blot out curiosity. They wanted to know about the two main guns the Chinese had used to pin them on Moore's Finger, and they wanted to find out even before they outposted the hill. Sgt. Clark D. Stewart found the gun which had fired frontally until it was killed by Hemphill. Only a wrecked barrel remained. There was no sign of the crew. Why that was so is a mystery, unless in flight the Chinese evacuated some of their dead. Pvts. John R. Sessons and James R. Martin reconnoitered the bunker attacked by Maliszewski. They found the gun, with eight dead Chinese draped around it. Seven had been killed by bullets. The eighth Chinese, who sat with hand on trigger, and the gun itself, had been destroyed by heavy slugs of metal as from a shell or grenade.

For the two Smiths and Serpa of Baker Company, who for six hours had played dead on the forward slope of Dale while the fight went on, the relief came in time. Big Smith watched the Chinese survivors flee the hill. Then, carrying Serpa, the two Smiths moved uphill and joined Item.

Shortly after sunrise, Lieutenant Patteson of Baker Company went via the chogi trench to the Dale CP. The morning was quiet save for the singing of birds.

Three dead Chinese choked the lower part of the bunker door. The caving of the roof had smashed the upper half of the doorframe. Patteson could barely get his head inside. Within he could see three bodies pinned under the crashed timbers. It was dark inside so he could not identify the dead, Bressler, Spencer and Jackson.

But the three bodies lay as, from Pfaff's description, Patteson had expected to find them. He knew then that Pfaff had been telling him the truth about his own ordeal within the bunker, a part which Pfaff himself thought not too creditable, since he had failed to stay and die with his commander. It is a simple fact that such men are almost never convinced of their own heroism.

Later, the wreckage of the bunker had to be lifted piece by piece to permit removal of the bodies. Then the hole was filled in and the site leveled to obliterate a brave but wretched memory.

Overture

FROM THE SUPERIOR HEIGHT OF THE ENEMY-HELD RIDGE NAMED HASAK-kol, the light breeze of early evening brought to Pork Chop Hill the sound of music.

For some minutes it continued, rising, then fading out according to the caprice of the wind. Men were singing in chorus. It was a mournful chant-ing, faint, tremulous and uncanny. And though the voices were high-pitched, there was a muted quality to the music, as if it came out of a deep well. Now it became lost in distance again and the men who had paused to listen resumed their supper of steak, French fries and chocolate ice cream.

A private said, "It sounds like they're gathering in the tunnels."

Another answered, "O.K., as long as they stay there."

Asked the lieutenant, "But what does it mean?"

"They're prayer singing," said the interpreter. "I can't hear the words but I know the music. They're getting ready to die."

Said the lieutenant, "Maybe we ought to be singing, too."

In this manner, Lieut. Thomas V. Harrold got his first pointed warning that his men, Easy Company of the 31st Regiment, and their home of the moment, Pork Chop Hill, had been marked for special attention by the Communist Chinese.

Until then, his concern about this particular night had not been deeply personal. For more than a week, the report had been circulating in the division that the enemy would make an attack in main at 2300 on 16 April. An agent working behind the lines had heard it from a Korean woman who was also good friend to several Communist soldiers. After going to higher commands, the story had been passed back down the line to the command posts of rifle companies.

On hearing it from G2, Harrold had felt no special alarm. The report said the blow would fall farther east along the division front. And in past weeks there had been several other such rumors, which had never materialized.

But the music from Hasakkol was like a gun pointing at Harrold's head. If Pork Chop was to be a main target, its commander of the moment had reason to reflect that his situation, and the circumstances of his company, were not bright with promise.

Pork Chop itself was a contemptible hill, ill-formed for all-around defense and too loosely tied in to the supporting neighborhood. Only 234 meters above sea level at its sharply peaked summit, the outpost was not only dominated by the Chinese-held ridges, but in fact extended into their country, being on the wrong side of the main valley. When one month earlier Old Baldy had been wrested away by the Communists, there was good reason in military logic why Pork Chop should have followed it as a gift. That concession would have been in the interests of line-straightening without sacrifice of a dependable anchor. But national pride, bruised by the enemy's rudeness toward Old Baldy, asserted itself, and Pork Chop was held.

These superior heights held by the enemy concealed from ground observation a still more formidable characteristic in the Red Chinese defensive front. They had organized their high ground in true depth by sweating their soldiery and making the most of their press gang labor. Compared to this monumental work, Eighth Army's "deep front" was a hollow shell.

An airborne observer looking beyond Old Baldy or any other main bastion in the enemy line would have reported, roughly, as follows: To a depth of more than 20,000 yards, the Reds had entrenched and bunkered the ridges. Their defensive works had ten times the depth of any belt of entrenchments in World War I. The lines of the main trench systems were traced by our air photo interpreters; it was hard and repetitious exercise because the enemy was diabolically clever at camouflage. Finally on the acetate the picture looked like a giant spider web with successive main lines joined by communications trenches along the transverse ridges. Shells and bombs could be rained on this system day long with little chance of finding a soft target. A miss by a few inches, and the projectile was wasted. Further, there was no way of knowing, at a particular moment, which part, if any, of the works under observation was manned. Every tactical group on the enemy side had multiple fire positions within the general position; underground tunnels connected one position with the others.

It was suspected that, except for a few warning posts, the Red Chinese garrisoning the forward ridges avoided the surface trenches altogether during normal operations in the continuing static warfare and remained deep underground. An army which has thus conditioned itself to live in catacombs is prepared for modern defense in its most terrible aspect.

No less clear to the eye than the vulnerability of Pork Chop as a defensive position was the untimely weakness of its temporary garrison. Easy

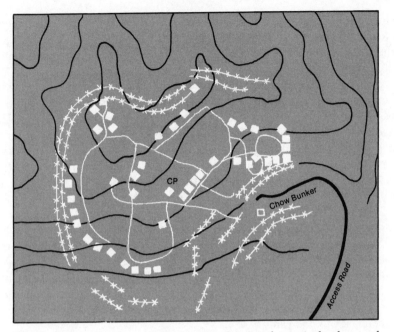

Detail of Pork Chop's entrenched works showing the main bunkers and defensive wire.

Company, normally strong when collected, was only half present on the hill, due to the exigencies of moving day. Harrold's total strength within the perimeter counted 96 men, including artillery, medical and engineer attachments. On Pork Chop, there were but two rifle platoons, the First and Third, and they mustered but 76 men.

Worse yet, not all of them were available to man the main rampart. Twenty had been paired off for duty as outguards. After dark, they would descend to ten listening posts which formed a crescent around the lower forward and flank slopes of the hill. There they would await any approach by the enemy, hoping to sound the alarm and then duck back.

Another group of five men was to form half of a patrol which was to prowl the small valley forward of Pork Chop during the hours around midnight. It did not occur to Harrold that sending a patrol out to brace an expected attack in main could hardly be profitable. The plan had been set several days before. He abided by it.

On one score only the lieutenant felt some extra assurance; the men would be on their toes, and if the attack came, surprise would not attend it. To that end, he had taken special precaution. On hearing from G2 that the Chinese planned to attack on 16 April, he had passed the information along to his chief subordinates, leaving it to them to tell the other men. Now he was happy that the word had been spread around; that meant that the company would be fully alerted and would require no extra tightening during the waiting time.

This confidence steadied Harrold through the early evening. It made him feel better during the fight. While it was a reasonable assumption, based upon what he knew and had tried to do, it was still far wrong. He had given the word but it hadn't trickled down. Finally, only a small remnant of Easy came through the fight. All survivors were asked if they had known an attack was imminent. Three said yes, the others no. Not a man in the outguard or patrol had heard the vital information. They regulated what they did by the accustomed routine. There was no added alertness.

So it was that the patrol departed the company lines not knowing that it might bump a full-scale attack, to be scouted but not engaged.

So it was that the twenty riflemen in the outguard listening posts got no special instructions when at 1937 hours they quit the main trench to take watch positions on the lower slopes. These sightings had been chosen with an eye to viewing as much of the approaches as possible. Thus, because of the uneven ridge fingers, the posts were at varying distance from the perimeter, 125 to 300 yards.

The twenty listeners did not dig in: they used whatever natural rock or bank cover they found. The positions were supposed to be changed from night to night for greater security. But because few rock projections were available, the rule was honored more in the breach than in the observance.

Once settled among the rocks, the outguards went silent and stayed put. This was the order and they obeyed it. Except for the periodic report by telephone to the company, it was a monotonous and stupefying vigil.

Had they talked, it might have been about the weather, for now the Korean spring was at its best. The slopes of their battlement were fragrant from the profusion of wild plums and chindolea blossoms. The air was balmy. A cloudless day was giving way to a starlit night. The pall of smoke, arising from numerous forest fires, and dressing the far horizon, was the only reminder that the season had been excessively dry.

For the next three hours, life was reasonably comfortable, relatively assuring, among the outguards and in the half-company on the bunker line. Despite its incongruity with the other parts of the main defensive line, Pork Chop in itself was a snug position. The little hill had been engineered according to the pattern then conventional with Eighth Army. It was a buffer intended to break up the Chinese attack before it could violate the main line. A solidly revetted rifle trench encircled it at the military crest, providing wall and some roof cover, which served for defense in any direction. Sandbagged and heavily timbered, fire-slotted bunkers were tied into the trench line at approximately 30-yard intervals. They gave troops protection while affording observation and command of the slope. These were stout, unblemished works. They had been but recently overhauled and fire had not yet marred them.

The top of Pork Chop was pushed in, like the dent in the crown of a hat. In consequence, its works could not form an evenly rounded perimeter. The dent was on the rearward side of the hill. This draw, reaching to the crest, in effect produced a divided perimeter. The two platoons were loosely joined in the center. But the odd shape of the hill nonetheless put them in separate compartments.

Some time after 2200, and somewhat before 2300, approximately two full companies of Communist infantry left Hasakkol, and crossing the valley, got almost to the Pork Chop rampart without anyone atop the hill becoming aware.

They had been sighted and engaged by the Easy patrol in the bottom of the small valley. Before they had climbed more than halfway, they were seen by at least ten men in the outguard line. Still, due to the extraordinary mischance of battle, the company got no warning until the assault broke like a flood against First Platoon's sector on the left hand of Pork Chop. Its surge is therefore best followed through the eyes of the sentinels on the lower ridge. There are gaps in the story. Of the twenty men, only seven got back.

On Outguard No. 41, Pvt. Kim Tong Ki was paired with Pvt. Mike Cowles. They were nested behind a large boulder which partly concealed them. Looking downslope, Kim saw three Chinese approaching; in the darkness he could not see how they were armed. He whispered to Cowles who tried to get Harrold on the telephone. The line was dead. By the time that fact registered the Chinese were within 15 yards. Kim threw a grenade. It exploded between the first two men, killing both. The third man ran. Not knowing what to do, Kim and Cowles waited there.

Artillery began to pound the slope, hitting just below them. Kim asked, "We better go top of hill?" Cowles answered, "No, the lieutenant didn't say so." This difference of opinion caused constraint between them and they both relapsed into sullen silence. Kim started to pull out and Cowles held him by the legs. Then an artillery shell exploded just a few yards behind them and part of the blast struck Cowles' head. Kim crawled over and leaned above him but did not touch him. The steel had cut the head badly and the blast had almost covered it with earth and small rock. Cowles' pulse wasn't checked. Kim simply noted that he was motionless.

Stopped by superstition, he was equally afraid to touch Cowles or leave him. He simply lay down beside him and remained the night, shaking all over and unable to sleep. When dawn came, he ran for the company trench and made it. Three other shells had exploded so close to Outguard No. 41 that Cowles' body was already half buried by the dirt spray. Kim reported of him, "I look. No see much. He no talk. No move. Seem dead."

On all outguard posts, it was the company custom to team GIs and Koreans, under the peculiarly limiting instruction that only the American would use the telephone or exert other initiative. At Post No. 41, Pvt. Cho Sung Man was paired with Pvt. José St. Nicholas. They had not been told that an attack was expected. They knew it first when, under the light of a flare, as the artillery opened fire, they saw three Chinese walking, moving upslope straight toward them.

St. Nicholas got through on the phone to his platoon leader, and while he was speaking, Sung tried to fire. But his M1 was dirty and wouldn't work. The lieutenant told St. Nicholas to withdraw at once. They made it to the trench before the artillery had shifted to the upper slope. There they separated, Sung heading immediately for the company chow bunker because he was hungry. He still did not know that the company position had been penetrated. As he entered the chow bunker, four Chinese held him at rifle point. One of them said in clear English, "Put your hands up!" Sung dropped his M1 and reached. Two other company Koreans entered the chow bunker door perhaps twenty minutes later. There was no need to disarm them; they had thrown their weapons away. Without difficulty, the four Chinese made them prisoner.

On Outguard No. 43, Pvt. Koe Kop Chin was teamed with Private Fugett. Neither had been warned that an attack was expected. So when they heard the sounds of distant firing from the direction of the valley, it did not particularly alarm them. After that there was a brief interval of silence. The telephone rang; a voice on the hot loop said, "An attack is coming." Then they saw a Chinese company—upwards of seventy men—marching uphill in three platoon columns, straight toward their position. Fugett tried to call the company, and on finding that the line was dead, he called to Kop, "Follow me, I'm getting out."

As they sprang up and into the open, running for the main trench, the Chinese saw them and raced in pursuit. Fugett was slowed by the weight of his weapon, a light machine gun, and continued to lose ground. As he landed in the trench, the foremost Chinese were already swarming over the parapet. Fugett tried to swing the weapon around but didn't have time. One Chinese tried to wrest the gun from his hands. Another Chinese, standing atop the parapet, fired a tommy gun burst into the two struggling men, killing them both.

Kop had watched this, but was powerless to help Fugett, having thrown his rifle away during the dash uphill. He moved on down the trench, expecting to find help at the chow bunker. He was one of the Koreans who walked into the trap which had already caught Pvt. Cho Sung Man. Their four captors prodded them with rifles and they started marching, beyond the perimeter and downslope toward Hasakkol. A grenade, thrown by an unknown hand, killed one of the guards before they got clear of the main trench. Two hundred yards downslope, an artillery shell landed amid the party. Captors and captives hit the dirt together. The round killed one Chinese and the unidentified Korean. Private Kop jumped for one of the other guards while he was still down, wrested his tommy gun free and shot the two remaining Chinese. Then Kop and Sung ran back to the trench.

Each of these incidents among the outguards was like a play within a play. It ran its own course from beginning to end and did not alter or moderate the sequence of events affecting the company. Harrold did not hear what had befallen any of his outguards until the following day. No message got back to him. The few who escaped the Chinese were caught by separate eddies of the fight as they jumped into the main trench, and no man returned to Harrold.

His view of the way in which the company became beset necessarily differed from theirs. Harrold could be impressed only by what he saw, heard or felt while within the CP bunker. And for the same reason, First and Third Platoons, each fighting an isolated battle, had neither light nor guide, nor any exact knowledge of what was happening to any other element on the hill. Each saw the storm break in a different way and felt it mount to crisis in a different hour. The outguard was finished, its members either dead or in flight, before the others knew.

In First Platoon's sector, SFC Carl Pratt and his men could hear both the yelling of the enemy and the pounding of the artillery fire against Pork Chop's slopes. But while these effects were unnerving during the early stage of the action, there was no great tension among the men.

The enemy was not to be seen and the fire, obviously, was going high. So the platoon stayed in bunkers, or sought cover under those parts of the trench which were roofed with logs and sandbags, lest the flash fires suddenly shift. During the first half-hour of the battle, its men had no feeling that their sector was close-pressed or that the Chinese assault was tightening around the hill.

This illusion of relative safety was in sharp contrast with Lieutenant Harrold's reading of the situation from the far side of the perimeter where sat the Company CP.

His own ground was not yet under attack. As of 2300 hours, he was not yet sure that a general assault was gathering. He had received no messages either from the patrol or the outguard posts which warned him that the Chinese were coming on in large numbers. So he was still playing it by ear, lest by premature and exaggerated warnings, he give higher command the idea that his own nerves were edgy. His trouble was that he had heard or seen no positive sign of a major change in situation and he was loath to guess.

Yet in the end, that was what he did. As the minute hand of his watch passed 2300, a few enemy artillery rounds came in singly. He had seen it happen before, a few teasing shells, followed by a double whammy.

Sure enough, the steel deluge followed in less than a minute. But he had already told Lieuts. Jack Attridge and Harold Wilson to phone the men on outguard duty telling them that they must immediately withdraw. The call to Wilson got through both by radio and telephone; but with two exceptions, Wilson could get no response from the men on the outguard line. When Harrold tried to get an O.K. from Attridge on his message over the single wire, suddenly the line went dead. Via the hot loop, he was still connected with the battalion commander, Major Swazey, and the other companies, but the cutting of his line to First Platoon made him suddenly anxious.

As he listened in that direction, he felt certain that he could hear a strong buildup of submachine-gun fire against First Platoon's sector. He still had seen no Chinese; nor had any enemy movement been reported to him. Still hesitating over his course, he picked up the phone to talk things over with Battalion. That line also had gone dead meantime and its failure, coupled with the intensity of the Chinese bombardment, forced his decision.

He stepped to the CP doorway and fired a red star rocket, signaling, "We are under full attack." Within seconds thereafter, he fired a second rocket, this time a red star cluster, meaning, "Give us Flash Pork Chop." The second flare didn't quite clear the doorway; its backlash set the bunker afire and for several minutes the men in the CP had to bail out of their shelter to fight the blaze.

Even so, the badly directed rocket did its work. At 2305, the lights came on over Pork Chop, and most of the men still in the open trenches ducked for cover, reading aright the signal that a killing proximity fuse fire coupled with high explosive shell would shortly follow. Two minutes later came the VT, not in overpowering volume but fired by a single battery of artillery. Even so, Pfc. Richard Long, of the CP group, having missed the flare signal, was struck down by the fire.

He was probably the only victim of this weak, opening American counter to the enemy barraging, since there is nothing to indicate that the main body of Chinese was yet closed upon the Pork Chop works, and much to suggest that they were delaying their final rush until their own preparation fires subsided.

First Platoon's side of the hill, which had given Harrold the greatest concern in the opening minutes, was still unviolated when the first VT shower came down. The men cleared into the bunkers, still not having seen a live enemy.

For approximately twenty minutes thereafter, the mixed fires, part Chinese, part American, kept them there. At 2325, the hill became absolutely quiet. Attridge called to Pratt, "I think we better walk over to the CP and see about repairing our communications." But when they got into the trench a few minutes later, Pratt suggested that while Attridge was visiting with Harrold, he would talk things over with the platoon's own wire man, Corporal Renfrow.

As Pratt neared Renfrow's bunker, a first aid man, Private Rice, came running from it carrying a carbine, and yelling, "Look! Look!" Pratt followed his point; under a covered section of the trench, not more than 30 feet away, six Chinese walked toward them. Rice was already firing. Pratt joined with his M1. Two Chinese fell. The others ran back along the trench and then jumped on the parados, from where they circled back along the high ground to grenade the ditch with potato mashers. Too late Pratt yelled, "Watch out!" The second grenade exploded between him and Rice, killing Rice instantly and driving Pratt back against the trench wall. He came out of it with a broken shoulder and both hands riddled with grenade frags. But not until two days later could he find time to get first aid.

Corporal Renfrow and Pvt. James O. Harris had sprung from the bunker in the same moment as Rice, and behind them came Private Hayford, another aid man. Facing in the opposite direction within the covered trench, they saw a still larger Chinese party coming toward them. Both Renfrow and Harris opened fire with their carbines, and the Chinese, for the moment, pulled back beyond a turn in the trench wall. So swiftly had the action taken place that neither man realized he was fighting almost back-to-back with the others from the bunker.

Then the grenade shower which felled Rice and Pratt dropped. As the first bomb exploded, Renfrow and Harris ducked back into the bunker. They didn't see the other men fall. But from inside the bunker, Renfrow heard Hayford screaming, "Come help me!" He returned to the trench and taking Hayford by the shoulders, dragged him inside. Then he saw that a grenade had blown off Hayford's left leg at the knee. For the next few minutes, he was busy tourniqueting the leg.

That was the beginning of a dance with death for the two able-bodied men. Renfrow threw sandbags against the door. The Chinese went downslope and grenaded through the bunker embrasure. Harris and Renfrow tried to field and return the grenades. But six exploded within the walls. Two of them blew fragments into Hayford's good leg and the lower part of his body. The grenading was followed by a strafing by two Chinese armed with tommy guns. They also stood at the window. Renfrow and Harris escaped the fire by pressing tight into the corners on either side of the embrasure. There was no escape for Hayford.

By then, Lieutenant Harrold was already calling for VT fire in maximum volume on Pork Chop, sending the message via the radio of his artillery observer, Lieutenant Anderson. When it came in, the Chinese were driven from the embrasure, and the men in the bunker knew an interval of relative peace.

What happened there was typical of the scene elsewhere on the hill for the next hour or more. Both in the assault and defense, there was virtual infantry paralysis because of the intensity and accuracy of the artillery concentrations coming from opposite directions against the crown of the ridge. The Americans had not been permitted time for collected action. The Chinese had not hit hard as tactical groups during the few opportune minutes of relative quiet when they might have wiped out Easy Company fraction by fraction. With the renewal and intensifying of the artillery duel, the open was forbidden to both sides. Their riflemen huddled wherever they could find a protecting wall or roof.

Lieutenant Attridge had gotten back to Harrold's CP just in time to become confined there by the fire and separated from his own platoon by the crowding of the Chinese into the roofed portions of the trench.

The group there survived mainly through the personal fighting power of 1st Sgt. Howard Midgeley and Corporal Riepenhoff, the company clerk.

Midgeley stood at the bunker door guarding the party with a submachine gun. Others tried to relieve him and take their turn at the point of main danger. He shrugged them off silently and pointed to the results of his marksmanship as if asking whether anyone could do any better. He was a methodical man. When he downed a Chinese, he dragged the body next the sandbags so as not to clutter his field of fire. Finally, the bunker had an extra revetment of thirteen dead Chinese.

Riepenhoff, being a clerk, was more deferential. Armed with an M1, he lay on a pile of sandbags at the embrasure, covering the downslope area. When he saw a Chinese, he said to Harrold, "Sir, there's a Chinaman. May I have the lieutenant's permission to shoot him?"

Harrold answered, "Permission granted."

Five times it happened, and each time this solemn ritual was repeated.

Though there were three officers and two other NCOs also present, the salvation of the CP was worked chiefly by these two hands. Their fire made a blockhouse of the bunker, barring the rear door to Pork Chop. The Chinese who had stormed the position and gotten inside the works could not pass it to gain the hill's rear slope and cut the route by which help might come. In the opening thrust, some of the enemy had won to that point and captured the chow bunker. But it was a brief hold only, and once released, was not thereafter recovered.

Otherwise, the defense of the hill was without a linchpin. Such of Third Platoon's 37 men as still lived (six had been killed on outguard duty as the fight started) were pinned to their shelters by the bombardment. Of First Platoon's 39 men, there remained, other than Attridge, not one person who could still move and fire.

First Platoon's only survivors were the half dozen men who have been mentioned here. Its only acts of successful resistance are the few pitiful examples which have been described. The platoon was not only whipped but, in effect, destroyed before it could make a fighting start. The Chinese assault columns had hit the main line at both ends of First Platoon's trench sector and then pinched inward toward each other. Most of Attridge's men were grenaded and machine-gunned while in their bunkers. What toll they took of the Red Chinese in their last minutes is not known. Later it was impossible to determine how they had died, for their bodies were either crushed by falling walls or shredded by the artillery pounding. The difference between Renfrow and Harris and the majority of their comrades is that the two men lived to tell the story.

By the logical process of killing the tenants and then moving into their quarters, the Red Chinese came into possession of half the hill. They had come like phantoms, their swift, silent movement facilitated by their rubber-soled running shoes and lack of heavy burdens in the attack. It was their custom to enter a fight carrying only enough ammunition to create the initial shock; they counted on capturing American stores to continue the fight. That risk usually paid off because of the defender's bad habit of oversupplying the outposts. This time, having staked their claim to half the hill, they squatted on it, holding the bunkers instead of continuing down the trench line. Either they were stopped by exhaustion and fear, or the haul of captured ammunition was not sufficient.

To Harrold's listening ear, the silence from that direction spoke eloquently. The lack of small-arms fire told him that First Platoon was dead and he could only surmise that the Red Chinese were reorganizing at the scene of execution.

To higher command, he had radioed these forebodings, saying that as he viewed it, there was no longer an American garrison on Pork Chop Hill. Battalion relayed the information rearward and Col. William B. Kern took it at face value.

Shortly before 0200, Kern sent word that he was sending one platoon of Fox Company and another from Love Company to attack up the rear slope of Pork Chop with the object of "re-enforcing" Easy Company. That was how Kern ordered it and that was how he supposed that it had been done.

The maneuver is so described, as a two-platoon attack, in the regimental record.

But there had been many a slip. The Fox platoon, becoming lost in the night, never arrived at the fire. The Love platoon, moving with alacrity on its mission, was not told that the Red Chinese already swarmed over Pork Chop, and took literally the guarded statement that its task was the relatively simple one of "re-enforcement." So it marched up the rear slope in a closed column, not expecting a fight.

This was the body that a few minutes after 0200 got to within 20 yards of the chow bunker. There a few machine-gun rounds struck its van, inflicting minor casualties. And there, because of its closed formation and the total surprise, it went into recoil, its members running back to the valley. (See the chapter "Love Alone" for details.) After Love platoon had slipped away, Red Chinese barrage fire swept the valley.

But the realities of this inevitable failure were not known to Harrold. He had been told that two platoons would hit and he took it for granted that they were moving in attack order. To accommodate them, he ordered that the flash fires be lifted from Pork Chop's crown and shifted 250 yards closer to enemy country.

So when he saw the forefront of the succoring force dissolve, its dissolution followed immediately by the Red Chinese barrage fire, he decided that the Red Chinese were manning the rear slope in great strength and were directing their artillery by radio from inside his position.

From the roof of Harrold's own bunker, a Chinese machine gunner was streaming fire in the direction taken by the Love platoon. Harrold had no way of knowing that almost single-handed this enemy fighter had precipitated what Harrold believed to be a two-platoon repulse. A few yards down the trench from the bunker, a Chinese tommy gunner was firing toward wounded Sergeant Pratt who was trying to crawl to the CP. So Sergeant Midgeley, the one-man show, resumed fire and shortly killed the two enemy gunners.

Midgeley had stopped briefly for first aid. The Chinese had pushed a grenade through a crack in the sandbags and he, Harrold and Lieutenant Anderson, the artillery FO, had all been wounded by the fragments.

Both artilleries now resumed their heavy pounding of the hill. The sealing-in effect to the two infantries became ever more complete. Now holding the greater part of Pork Chop in numbers which otherwise should have been sufficient to complete the mop-up, the Chinese didn't venture into the open.

Anderson's radio had at last been killed by the grenade explosion. Harrold's one remaining tie to the outside was a telephone line to his Fourth Platoon, which wasn't on the hill. Via this roundabout relay, at approximately 0400, he got a garbled message from Division warning him that, at the first chance, the Chinese would try to blow up the CP bunker.

He already well knew it. But he answered, "Tell them we will try to hold. Tell them also that any force set to relieve us will need flame throwers and heavy rocket launchers." He was thinking that, with the Chinese solidly lodged in his works, the soundest tactics would be to burn and blast them out.

At that point, Sergeant Hutchins, FO for the 81-mm mortars, counseled an opposite course. He said to Harrold, "I think we ought to make a break for it now; we may still have time."

But Harrold shook him off. He was convinced that the enemy already swarmed over the hill and he was afraid that by withdrawing now, he might desert those few of his men who could still be holding in the other bunkers.

So with the help of the others, he now closed the bunker tight by piling sandbags, the dead radios, the ammo boxes, sleeping bags and everything else movable against the door and embrasure.

Then he called through Fourth Platoon to ask for a continuing illumination of the hill. His idea was that if full light was combined with the VT fire, the Chinese would have even less inclination to move along the trenches for fear of being picked off by snipers.

For the next hour the CP group remained virtually immured. As dawn arrived, the American artillery lifted. That was the first sign to Harrold that a relieving force was knocking at his back door.

Lieutenant Attridge, the only man in the CP not yet a casualty, started down the trench toward the chow bunker, intending to guide the relief onto the hill. He was wounded in the head before he could reach up-coming King Company. So he returned to the bunker, and its door was sealed again while the party waited rescue.

The Easy Patrol

T HOUGH IT IS NOT NORMAL PROCEDURE TO LAUNCH A PATROL against the face of an anticipated attack by the enemy, it was done on that night.

Some days previously 31st Regiment had scheduled a patrol action out of Pork Chop Hill for 16 April. It was to have the routine mission familiar in Korean operations. The patrol would advance to the valley bottom which divided friendly and enemy country. On the low ground it would rig an ambush. Should it encounter Chinese, it would try to capture a prisoner.

This was a sensible object along a quiescent front where the only fighting came of contact between patrols. But it had no orthodox relationship to preparations against full-scale attack. The taking of one or two prisoners out of an already advancing line was not a sure way of getting information and, in fact, could jeopardize only those who made the attempt.

But having been scheduled, the patrol was not called off. Why that measure was not taken is subject to but one explanation or excuse. There was no certainty that the attack rumor would prove true. And when in doubt, as higher commanders usually see it, it is best to keep patrolling or troops will go slack.

So for two days preceding the appointed night, the patrol went through the accustomed rehearsals in the rear area and got the usual briefings. The men were told that they would move out from Pork Chop at approximately 2000, advance to within 100 yards of the shallow stream which wound through the valley bottom, and there lie in wait until they saw some Chinese coming.

Even when the rumors of an attack were totally discounted the circumstances were not auspicious for such an undertaking. Easy Company, having just relieved Item, still stood on Pork Chop in less than half-strength, with only 96 men guarding the hill, including forward observers and medics.

Consequently, to give Easy a fighting chance, it was decided that half of the patrol of ten enlisted men would be drawn from Fox Company, with Easy also supplying five. One group would compose the assault force and the other the support. That the men did not know each other presaged a lack of organizational unity within the patrol from the beginning.

Sgt. Henry W. Pidgeon of Fox Company got back from a brief leave at 1600 on the afternoon before the mission to discover that there is something in a name. Lieut. Robert Grimes met him at the CP with the word that he would lead the assault group and be responsible for the patrol as a whole. The support would be under Sgt. Lovell Poole of Easy Company.

Pidgeon, who is a physically rugged and emotionally mature soldier, was skeptical from the first about the arrangements, though he had not yet heard the attack rumor. But when Grimes asked him, "Are you prepared to lead it?" he answered, "Sure."

The show was jinxed from the beginning. During that evening between 1600 and 1830, 200 enemy mortar rounds fell on Pork Chop. There were no casualties but the shelling drove the men to their shelters. In consequence, the two groups, occupying bunkers on opposite sides of the hill, did not rendezvous until the last moment, and had time for only a hit-and-run final briefing before they got away.

Possibly Pidgeon, in his eagerness to get set, pushed his own group too hard. Poole's men never quite caught up. Both parties had perforce gone single file through the barb wire, which scattered and slowed them. By the time Poole's group had re-collected, Pidgeon's diamond-shape formation had advanced beyond sight. So Poole led his people to the last knob on the ridge finger, about 350 yards beyond the main line. There he set up a horseshoe defense, with Pfc. Joe Miezejewski on the BAR covering the line to the rear. By phone, he reported to Lieutenant Harrold what had happened.

Pidgeon, arriving in the bottoms and there halting his men for the moment, started advancing alone to reconnoiter the spot for the ambush.

Right then, a dozen or more flares from the 81-mm mortars brightened the sky directly behind the patrol, throwing its members sharply into silhouette and casting long shadows down the vale before they could go flat.

Pidgeon called Harrold, "For God's sake stop the flares!" There were three more rounds before the valley again went dark. He then called a second time to report that his men were on position. The hour was then 2115. Harrold said, "Keep a sharp lookout. We are expecting a main attack." That somewhat baffled Pidgeon. By his account, this was his first information that the patrol had been sent forward into an other than routine situation.

But another hour and fifteen minutes passed before he saw the enemy for the first time. During the interval, his men had stayed flattened but alert. The warning of the attack kept them edgy. Yet they didn't quite believe it until looking at the slope of the enemy hill called Hasakkol, they saw about fifty Chinese in line advancing toward them.

Pidgeon sent his point man, Cpl. Robert L. Noel, forward to scout the moving line, telling him, "See all you can and report immediately to me." He had not yet called Harrold.

Noel was back within one minute. He said, "They're all around us. They cover the slope. For Christ's sake, do something."

For the moment, Pidgeon saw nothing to do except re-enforce the point, sneak it out and attempt to get close enough to the Chinese to stop them with grenades. He still was not sure that an attack in main was developing, and being unsure, he did not call Harrold.

So taking along Private Hall, he joined Noel, and they moved forward about 25 yards. One group of four Chinese got to within 20 yards of the rocks which hid them. The Americans grenaded together, throwing twelve bombs. One Chinese ran back. The others disappeared. Though Pidgeon didn't know whether he had scored any hits, he was surprised that he got no reply. And he was quite unaware that he had loosed the first shot in a general battle.

It was then that he tried to call Harrold on the sound power phone. But it was too late. He had forgotten that minutes earlier he had explored the forward ground while carrying the phone, and that its wire had looped around the rocks there and was not later withdrawn. His own grenades in exploding had killed his last line of communication. Quickly he went to Cpl. Henry T. Settle who held the radio on the patrol's left flank and tried to raise the company. But the radio couldn't cut through.

Thereafter for fifteen minutes he waited, then at last gave the order for the patrol to withdraw. It was too late. The group got only 40 yards. Suddenly a curtain of 4.2-mortar fire, ordered by Easy Company to stem the Chinese advance, dropped between Pidgeon and the main hill, missing his men by scant yards. It was steady fire, eight to ten rounds at a time. Nearby was a jutting rock ledge which offered partial cover. Pidgeon and the others crawled under it. Within a few minutes, flash fires from the artillery built up the barrage and extended toward their refuge. One air burst struck Corporal Noel in the face, neck and chest. He said to Pidgeon, "I've had it," and he died within a few minutes. Illuminating rounds now brightened the valley. The rain of steel was unceasing. There was nothing to do but press tighter into the rock.

In the support position, Poole and his men had not heard the grenading and, for all of Pidgeon's skirmishing, remained unaware of the threat mounting in the valley. But at 2245, Poole, on calling Lieutenant Harrold, was told that the assault group was expected to "make contact" shortly, and that he had best advance to assist Pidgeon's party.

He started moving. Harrold, having meanwhile withdrawn the men on outguard duty to the hill, ordered the barrage. If it was to work, it had to be accurate. Harrold wanted a horseshoe-shaped barrage which would drop even with the outguard positions and work back gradually until it enfolded Pork Chop perimeter, thereby eliminating any Chinese who might be climbing the slope.

But that wasn't what he got.

Poole's party, advancing in a wedge shape, moved 50 yards closer toward Pidgeon. Then the barrage caught it dead on, and the formation dissolved as men separately jumped for rock cover. Privates Williams and Miezejewski, who had formed the back of the wedge, were cut down, though the others still didn't know it. Poole tried to get Harrold on the phone, but the line had been cut by the shelling. Sergeant Taylor, the artillery FO, tried to raise him on the radio "Peter 10." But that also failed.

Then Poole attempted to regroup his survivors, intending to return to the main line. But such was the persistence of the fire that he could neither move backward to the hill nor forward to Pidgeon. Now looking toward Hasakkol, the men could count Chinese to the number of several hundred standing against the skyline. Still other enemy groups, though in smaller numbers, stood out prominently on the ridge knobs between the patrol and Pork Chop. These enemy skirmishers were well inside the barrage.

An artillery round exploded just above Poole. He took the fragments in all parts of his body, head, chest, neck and all four limbs. He said to Pfc. Kenneth Weber, "Now, I'll never make it." Weber said to him comfortingly, "Sure you can, I'll help you along." With Sergeant Taylor helping, Weber tried to carry him. But Poole had lapsed into unconsciousness, and before getting 50 yards, both Taylor and Weber were down from exhaustion. Weber felt it was useless to continue the struggle. So they laid Poole in a shell crater, and uncertain what to do, they rested beside him for the next few minutes, paying no heed to the barrage or the enemy.

There Private First Class Rawles caught up with them. He said, "Woll is down there among the rocks; shrapnel got him through the back." Weber listened, still trying to catch his breath. At last he heard the cry of Private Woll borne faintly on the wind, "I'm hit. I'm hit. Please don't go off and leave me."

Alone, Weber went back for Woll, slung him over his shoulder and carried him upslope to the crater, where he was put alongside Poole. Woll seemed terribly weak and kept whispering, "Thank you, thank you, thank you," as Weber struggled uphill. Within less than a minute after he was placed beside Poole, a VT shell exploded almost directly overhead, and a second shard pierced his groin.

Weber was again flat out, clean spent by his exertions. Woll was still conscious. He said to Sergeant Taylor, "Won't you please take me back to the company? I want to live." Taylor replied, "I'll try."

He hoisted Woll and made the start. They were not more than 20 yards along the trail when another shell exploded directly overhead. One fragment went through Woll's skull. A second fragment hit Taylor's left ankle, shattering the bone. Both men had been knocked flat by the violence of the blow. Taylor crawled over to Woll, felt for the wound and knew that he was dead. So he crawled back downtrail to the shell crater.

Now there were but two sound men left, Privates Weber and Rawles. Not only were they tied to the spot by the wounded, but Weber, by physique, nature and spirit the most indomitable man in the group, was temporarily exhausted. For about one-half hour he lay there on his back, saying nothing and seeing only the stars and the artillery display.

Then he said to the others, "If we expect to live, we've got to start digging." There were two entrenching spades at hand. Weber and Rawles set to work. Occasionally, Taylor spelled them. Though he couldn't get on his feet, the dirt around the crater was loose, and he could still work the spade with his hands.

That task occupied them until about 0400. They had to suspend it when Rawles, glancing downslope, saw eight Chinese aid men advancing straight toward them. His own M1 was so fouled with dirt that it wouldn't fire and so was Weber's. Taylor was carrying a .45 Colt pistol. Weber borrowed it, waited until the leading pair of Chinese got within about seven yards of him and shot them both dead. The others scampered away, dropping their stretchers as they ran. Not a word was spoken during the action.

They stayed there, digging fitfully, whenever they could summon the energy. Now when shells came in, they no longer bothered to dodge back into the crater. Their response to the situation had become almost trance-like. They worked automatically as the ebb and flow of strength permitted it, and they guarded in much the same way. But an awareness of danger no longer possessed them. Later, that surprised them: that they had reached a point where death seemed not to matter.

First light came, and they were still working. Coincidentally, there was a great flash just outside the crater. An exploding 4.2-mortar shell lifted a large rock slab and dropped it into the hole on top of Rawles, breaking both of his legs. The concussion, pounding his head against the bank, knocked him senseless.

There was now left only Private Weber in fighting condition. Taylor could still fire but he couldn't walk. As the sky brightened, he crawled over to Weber's foxhole. For perhaps one-quarter-hour they sat there together, saying nothing. Both were too far gone for speech, but each drew spiritual warmth from the other.

Then at last Weber broke the silence, and for some minutes they talked, going over all of the painful facts in their situation.

Finally Weber asked, "Well, what do we do now?"

Taylor answered, "I don't see that we can do anything. If you went alone, you couldn't make it back to the hill. Not until the artillery lifts."

But the artillery wasn't lifting that morning. Within easy sight of home base, they had to stay there, without food, water, first aid or arms, other than the .45 pistol.

Pidgeon and his party had somehow missed them in the darkness. At 0445, Pidgeon had decided to pull away from his shelter under the rock ledge and try to make it to Pork Chop. He figured there was less risk in passing through the barrage than in greeting the dawn still in enemy country. Having no idea that his support had been shattered, he and the three others moved up hill as noiselessly as possible, leaving Private Noel's body.

They mounted as far as the saddle of the ridge which usually cradled Outguard No. 40. By then they had passed through the fires uninjured. As they walked toward the declivity used by the outguard, they saw that it was filled with Chinese—about two squads of them.

But it was the enemy that was surprised. Pidgeon yelled, "Fire!" and they did it together, two M1s and two carbines. The rifles emptied, they didn't stop to reload, or measure the execution. Bullets were already zinging against the rocks under their feet. Pidgeon turned and ran back down to the stream bed, his three men following. They walked eastward along the river bank until they came out at the Fox Company CP.

In the downward flight as in the upward climb, Pidgeon's group must have passed within a few yards of the crater held by Taylor and Weber. But they saw and heard nothing of each other. The exertion either of moving or digging on a battlefield is somewhat preoccupying.

For Weber and Taylor, the day dragged slowly on. They stayed low in their foxholes. The artillery fires continued to interdict the slope. From where they looked, the hill now seemed to be cratered right to the summit. Within the valley, there was no sign of a moving enemy. Still, they gained no impression of how things were going atop Pork Chop. Taken up with their own problems, they did not guess that the fight there might have gone against the company. It was home base and they yearned to return to it.

By midafternoon both men knew that they would either get out together, or not at all, though they did not express this thought to each other. Poole was now motionless and they thought him dead. Rawles was unconscious from the pain and strain and would be dead weight. Throats so parched that speech had become difficult, they looked longingly at the river. But it was forbidden them by the interdicting shellfire from the Chinese. In fact, it was the enemy mortars and artillery, more than their own, which kept them pinned down through most of the day.

At about 1900, they saw a curtain of white phosphorus shells breaking along the river bank and smoking it for several hundred yards.

Weber said to Taylor, "That must be to cover a screening patrol. Maybe they are sending someone out for us."

For at least thirty minutes the smoke thickened and they waited. Weber had been wrong in his surmise. The smoke was not concerned with the patrol. It had been thrown out to cover a counterattack by Fox Company of the 17th Regiment up Pork Chop Hill.

Then suddenly there was a brief lull in the Chinese barraging with only a few shells coming in. Taylor said, "Let's go." They climbed the ridge with Taylor using an M1 as a cane. Weber carried him through the wire. There was still a handful of Americans atop Pork Chop fighting to hold the trenches. Friendly arms were opened to receive them.

All of King's Men

WHEN KING COMPANY DARED THE SLOPE THAT MORNING ITS STRENGTH seemed ample for the task ahead according to the reading of the situation taken by Battalion and all higher levels.

These rearward views were wishful and perforce badly informed. All that was known of the infantry fight on Pork Chop had come from Lieutenant Harrold and Harrold had not been able to leave his own bunker. All the higher commands knew was that there were some Chinese on the hill who could be re-enforced through the valley.

In King Company were 135 men under Lieut. Joseph G. Clemons, Jr. King had spent a quiet night in a reserve position behind Hill 347. All hands had had a late meal and caught a few hours' sleep. At 0330 Clemons was told by phone to move the company into an attack position behind Hill 200, just to the rear of Pork Chop.

The trucks were already on their way. King was ready when the convoy arrived. For each rifle there was a full belt and extra bandolier. Each rifleman carried three or more grenades. There were six BARs in each platoon with twelve magazines per weapon. Five boxes of ammo were carried for each LMG. Because Harrold had so recommended, each platoon took forward a flame thrower and heavy rocket launcher.

When King unloaded behind Hill 200, Lieut. Col. John N. Davis was already waiting in a bunker. He suggested to Clemons that in counterattacking Pork Chop's rear slope, King should hit with two platoons abreast and one in reserve. The mixed situation on the summit was not made clear to Clemons because Davis did not know the facts. Clemons got the impression that the Chinese held the hill solidly and his own men could therefore fire without restraint.

As Davis explained it, while King assaulted the rear, two platoons from Love Company would attack up the ridge finger on Pork Chop's right. This meant risking a crossfire at the very point where the converging forces would have to take hold. But it also made Clemons feel more resigned to the absence of his heavy weapons platoon which hours earlier had been detached for direct support of Westview Outpost.

American VT fire was still raining on top the hill. "Tell me," said Davis, "when you're ready to go and I'll have it lifted." Clemons got his platoon leaders together and said to them, "Hit the hill hard and get to the top as fast as the men can go. Success depends on speed; we must close before daylight."

They were deployed Second Platoon on the right, First on the left and Third in reserve. The assault platoons walked in column 400 yards down the road to the assault line at the foot of Pork Chop. From there, it was only 170 yards to the nearest fighting bunkers. But the way was very steep, the slope was rocky and cratered and this was, literally and spiritually, darkest hour before dawn.

At 0430 Clemons said to Davis, "We're ready now." Relayed to the batteries, the message stopped the fires. King's men sprang forward, some of them, under prodding by their NCOs, starting upslope at the double.

Haste made waste. By the time Second Platoon stalled at the lower side of the five-fold concertina which circled the hill, SFC Walter Kuzmick felt that the too-brisk start had been a mistake. The spring had gone from his legs. His men, panting hard, tugged at rocks and shrubs to assist them. The more heavily burdened ammo, flame-thrower and launcher carriers straggled. Still, he yelled out over the line, "Keep going! Make it fast!" The front runners found gaps in the barricade, gaps cut by the shellfire. They slipped through and followed Kuzmick. In the dark he didn't notice that the freight carriers quit him, dropped their burdens and lay down next the wire. For the next hour, he was much too busy to note that they were missing.

Enemy artillery and mortars had wakened to the attack but were overshooting the mark. The barrage dropped into the valley 100 yards behind the line of departure. So though the barb wire which confronted First Platoon was still solid, its passage was completed uneventfully. Men weighed down the bands with their bodies and other men used their bodies as a bridge.

Though King's men completed the climb without one shot being fired at them, they took 29 minutes to travel the 170 yards from the jumpoff to the height. It was the longest respite from fire given them during the day. The Chinese artillery got the range immediately when they topped the rise. It doused the hill for ten minutes, then lifted for ten minutes, a monotonous but effective pattern thereafter steadily maintained.

First man to enter the Pork Chop works, Cpl. William H. Bridges, saw two Chinese rise from among the rocks beyond the parados and fire di-

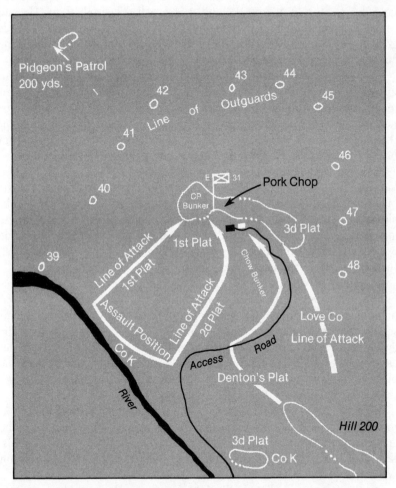

King and Love Companies attacked Pork Chop simultaneously in the morning. Denton's Platoon had already tried in the night and failed.

rectly on First Platoon with submachine guns. He yelled, "Watch out!" and dove for the trench. The burst cut down five men close behind him.

Pvt. Rudolph Gordon made the trench almost at the same moment. Turning leftward, he started for the second bunker down the line. Three grenades came at him from behind its far wall. They fell short. He and Bridges grenaded back. But protected by the bunker mass, the Chinese grenadiers played African dodger, revealing head and shoulder just long enough to heave their potato mashers.

More First Platoonmen piled into the trench. Two squads tried to form up on either side of the first bunker, though in the narrow ditch that merely invited trouble. To protect the assembly, Cpl. Arsenio Correa jumped onto the parados with his LMG and fired two boxes of ammo at the bunker door, 25 yards away. The enemy grenadiers centered fire on him but he was comfortably beyond their range.

Taking advantage of this diversion, SFC Lewis J. Hankey, Cpl. Wilfred Volk and Pvt. Pak Song crawled along the parapet to within five yards of the bunker. From there, they grenaded over the wall, throwing ten bombs altogether. It was even give-and-take. Their sortie silenced the Chinese grenadiers, but in the exchange Pak was wounded in the head by the same explosion that shattered Hankey's leg. Volk treated them where they fell, then left them in the lee of the bunker wall while the fight went on.

Kuzmick's men encountered their first fire as they came to the chow bunker, which was some yards downhill from the main trench. But it was unaimed and going high. On reaching the main trench, Kuzmick kept his squads moving abreast, intending to mop up the ditch while securing the ground both ways from it as he swept toward the Pork Chop CP. It was an elementary precaution taken by him mainly because the hour was 0520, the hill was still dark and he was fearful that if he moved in column through the ditch, the Chinese would close across his rear.

But it was uneven work because of the irregularities in the ground. On this rear rightside of Pork Chop, which was farthest removed from the enemy's point of initial onfall, the trench was still relatively free of debris. Kuzmick's own party was therefore unimpeded as it moved in column down the ditch.

On the outer wing, Sgt. Rollin Johnson's squad became strung out as some men sought rock cover to escape the fire sweeping the downslope. Lieut. Robert S. Cook had joined Johnson to help control the maneuver toward the CP. Walking the rampart, along with Pvt. Edgar P. Bordelon, he got some distance to the fore. At the first fire bunker, Cook was joined by one of Easy Company's Koreans, who had survived the night by hugging the sandbag revetment. The three advanced another 15 yards. From there, Cook could see the CP bunker door. There was no activity. Bordelon fired a few testing rounds at it from his carbine. From within came a voice, "Hold fire! We're GIs." But wishing to see more, Cook did not instantly call warning to the skirmishers behind him.

During these minutes, Sgt. Norbert Huffman's squad had even harder going crossing the infield. The upslope was an obstacle course of rock outcroppings and shell craters. Over this treacherous surface were scattered smoke-blackened tree stumps looking like sitting men in the half-light. The flankers had to move at a crawl. Kuzmick tried to regulate the advance of his center in time with the flankers. But it was impossible.

Huffman got to within 12 yards of the rear of the CP bunker without ever seeing it. There was a prone Chinese on the bunker roof holding a light machine gun. Huffman was still crawling forward when a cluster of five or six heavy grenades, thrown from the far side of the bunker, landed on and around him. One explosion blew away his right hand. Fragments from other grenades pierced his head, neck and chest. As he slumped, the machine gunner fired a quick burst at him.

Cook at that moment had jumped to the rampart, waving his arms toward Kuzmick's men and yelling, "Come on up! Get along! Keep moving and we've got it made!" He still said nothing of the Americans in the CP.

From out the bunker where Cook had liberated the Korean, a Chinese crawled along the rampart. He heaved a grenade. Another heavy grenade came sailing from behind the CP wall. The two grenades exploded simultaneously between Cook and the Korean, shattering one of Cook's legs and hitting the Korean in the stomach and groin.

Before anyone in the platoon could react to fire a shot, five Chinese jumped from behind the bunker wall down into the trench and disappeared from sight into the wreckage forward. Pvt. Thomas M. Dugan stopped to put a tourniquet on Huffman's stump. Then seeing that he was unconscious and bleeding from many wounds, Dugan carried him back to the chow bunker, where he could be given serum albumen to stave off the shock.

The other men did not recoil or hesitate. It was simply that in their state of fatigue they could not change motion quickly enough. For the last several minutes the hill had been quiet of artillery; but while the enemy barrage lasted, they had still pressed on. In a situation for which their training had little prepared them, they had responded as cheerfully as American troops are ever likely to do. No one had told them that in modern war, you may repeatedly get within 20 feet of your enemy, and still not know where his defense is hidden.

Kuzmick dashed toward the bunker door, intending to grenade it. In that tense second, Lieutenant Attridge looked out. His head was bandaged. His arm also was cocked to throw a grenade—an eloquent measure of the confusions of that morning.

The sight of Attridge stopped Kuzmick cold. Right on his heels was Clemons, who was so astonished that he simply gaped. Neither of King's leaders had been told about the party of Easy wounded in the CP. They thought Harrold's company was out of it, and they had no reason to look for any friends on the hill.

This tableau was broken up before anyone could cry out. Three rounds of artillery exploded directly into the scene. Their source was never determined. But because the Communist fire had lifted a few moments before, the men all concluded these were "shorts" from their own support batteries. One round exploded into the bunker door, giving Attridge his second wound in the head. The other two fell about 25 yards behind Kuzmick, wounding three of his Koreans.

To the platoon it was a kick in the groin. Until then, the flank had kept pressing despite the leg weariness of the men. But the impression that they had been fouled by their own guns impacted on them more heavily than the wounding of Cook and Huffman. Shock had stifled elation in the worst possible moment. Kuzmick's men recoiled bewildered and listless and for minutes made no attempt to do anything. The flank as a whole never got going again. In war, one resolute soul can bind the excited minds of many men in a kind of bloody mesmerism; and one small accident can in a twinkling snap that chain of force.

Followed the dull anticlimax. Pvt. Samuel K. Maxwell went on alone to the CP. There were five wounded men inside, one with a leg missing. Attridge was still conscious. Harrold told Maxwell to return to the fight; he would look after his own party.

The sun was edging the horizon; the dark had gone. Pvt. George Atkins, covering Second Platoon as rearguard, brought news to Clemons. From a high knob, he had looked westward and seen "many Chinese" moving on Pork Chop from the direction of Princeton OP.

Clemons called on radio. Would the artillery plaster Princeton Hill and drop a curtain in the valley between Pork Chop and Hasakkol to choke off re-enforcement? The answer was yes, but the requested fires never came in. Three medium tanks, which had been attached to King as support, were still idling around the base of Hill 200, some 500 yards rearward. Clemons switched them to the low ground west of Pork Chop. Their guns diverted the enemy approach from the westward but couldn't dam the flow of Chinese from Hasakkol through the valley.

Some hours later the tankers asked, and received, permission to withdraw, apprehensive that if Clemons was re-enforced, their vehicles would become the target of the Chinese artillery attack. Clemons watched the tanks pull out, reflecting bitterly that because of the withdrawal, his riflemen would get the undivided attention of the enemy guns.

A few of Kuzmick's men picked up and started moving down the trench. Before they could pass the CP bunker, they were stopped by a blast of bullet fire coming from downhill on their right. This time there was no choice about returning it. The fire was from Love Company, attacking up the right-hand finger. King's men tried to signal Love to shut it off, but the fire was too intense to stand against. It died only after Love had been bled into silence.

By these stages, all group initiative became lost to the company. Such energy as remained to King's leaders was channeled for the most part into personal effort. The attack carried on only because a number of the more resolute individuals engaged in widely separated and almost unrelated actions.

Clemons personally was between the devil and the sea. The harder he pressed the fight forward, the greater became his disorganization to rearward, where evacuation of casualties was still proceeding empirically, supply remained unassured, his channels to outside were narrowing and his heavy weapons carriers were shirking the fight. He did not have enough able-bodied men to take the hill by storm; he had too many to plead fatal weakness. The few who remained fighting were dangerously dispersed; to withdraw and regroup them would yield hard-won ground to the enemy snipers. It was time to look things over more carefully and get his house in order—if possible. With his executive, Lieut. Tsugi O'Hashi, he walked back to the chow bunker.

On the right of Pork Chop, Sergeant Johnson, joined by Sgt. Robert E. Hoffman, continued to bore in, moving straight down the trench. They came to a bunker where two men from Easy's third platoon had survived the night by playing possum. At dawn three enemy grenadiers had discovered them and begun to bomb their hiding. Having snatched a few hours' sleep, the two Easy men had freshened. They decided to fight back, though between them, they had but one dirty carbine, which wouldn't fire automatic, and one steel helmet. So they took fifteen-minute turns at the fire post, one man operating as sniper from behind the bunker wall while the other man stayed inside. They had bagged no game but their show of resistance had been enough to keep the three grenadiers from rushing them.

One of the men motioned to Hoffman and Johnson to move on along the trench and try to take the grenadiers in flank while he held their attention from in front. By then, several other of King's men had reached the spot. Before Johnson could start his deployment, seven artillery rounds

(Chinese) exploded along the embankments. One round silenced the Chinese grenadiers. Another landed among the Americans.

Cpl. Robert Rossrilli was arm's length from Johnson as the round came in. The explosion sat him down hard on his buttocks and the shock was so violent that he at first sat there stunned, certain that half of his seat had been shot away. Because the trench was partly covered and half-filled with wreckage, he momentarily lost sight of Johnson.

Then he heard a voice say calmly, "Well, I'll be damned, I am wounded." Johnson got up, not more than six feet away. The shoulder of his jacket was already blood-soaked, one large fragment having cut him to the bone. He called out in a booming voice, "Hoffman, it's time for you to take over." Then he walked rearward along the trench. But for the time being, he didn't get very far. For the next twenty minutes or so, Hoffman could hear him belaboring the stragglers farther down the trench, "Damn you, get up there and help Hoffman." There was a payoff even in the sound of his voice.

Almost coincidentally, the first flame thrower got up to Clemons. Its operator, Pfc. William W. Sykes, was given a squad under Sergeant Asman to run interference for him, as he advanced toward a bunker 50 yards forward on the left side of the hill. Approximately a dozen Chinese grenadiers were nesting there, some inside, and others behind the sandbag revetments, and their combined efforts had kept that alley tight blocked.

Asman and his party moved forward cautiously, spread over both embankments. As their forefront got to within throwing distance of the bunker, a shower of grenades exploded among them, battering Asman around the head and neck and wounding every other member of the squad. The Chinese had quit the bunker, then regrouped on the high ground inside the trench and grenaded the party from the flank as it came abreast.

Not seeing how it had happened, Sykes continued right down the trench with his flame thrower and, getting to the bunker door, flamed the inside for thirty seconds. The door frame caught fire. Then another grenade landed in the trench, exploding its fragments into Sykes' buttocks. He couldn't make his legs move. Pfc. James Freley helped him from the hill, surprised that Sykes had made his run, gotten hit and then retired without uttering a sound. Sykes still carried his flame thrower. It was now empty but no one thought to relieve him of it.

When Asman's party was dissolved, the Chinese grenadiers returned to the trench, beat out the fire set by Sykes and reoccupied the bunker. By then Clemons was ready with a new weapon. Another of his stragglers had at last come forward with a 3.5 rocket launcher. But the boy looked too frightened to do a job with it. Clemons handed the launcher to Sgt. Frank Krohn who crawled along the trench and from a range of 20 yards put four rockets against the bunker. It brought down part of the wall and ended the grenading.

A trio of riflemen who had followed Krohn, keeping flat while he fired, ran on past the bunker. For most of the rest of its length on the west side of the hill the trench had been covered over with beams of pinewood and blinders, heaped with sandbags and, in some places, with several feet of earth. The theory behind the covered trench was that it would prevent enfilade and afford protection against overhead fire; the fault in the theory was that it assumed the garrison would always be able to hold more tenaciously there than elsewhere. Artillery had crushed in the roof at several points. These splintered sections had become successive barricades. A slight rise in the trench floor terraced them one behind the other, making each a concealed fire port. Fire came from them but the firers could not be seen. No hand-carried weapon could batter through these successive layers. The three riflemen took a quick look and then pulled back.

Such was the dispersion that it was impossible to count noses. But Clemons made a rough guess that he had lost at least half of his men. Most of them had been knocked out by grenade fire. The enemy had been prolific, but unskilled in his use of the tommy gun. Apart from the worrisome noise, it had done little damage. What plagued Clemons worst was the fear that his own men were about out of ammunition, though fanned out as they were, he could get no accounting of it. He decided that it was time to call his reserve platoon into the fight.

On the right of the hill, as on the left, progress was made possible by the action of one weapon in the hands of a determined man. Two enemy-occupied bunkers, on opposite sides of the trench and 40 feet apart, had stalled advance there. Burp-gun fire laced the ditch, the gunners operating from the bunker doors, while from behind the bunker walls, grenadiers covered the embankments.

Thirty yards short of this enemy block was an unoccupied bunker partly collapsed by the shellfire. Timing his advance to Krohn's attack with the 3.5 rocket launcher, Sgt. Lovell Jenkins ran for the bunker's nigh wall, carrying a light machine gun. From its shelter, he emptied four cases of ammunition into the two fighting bunkers. The gun was "behaving like a lamb" and as fast as it emptied, Sergeant Kuzmick was getting up to Jenkins with resupply. Quite suddenly, resistance died. Looking to the right, Jenkins saw about fifteen Chinese break into the open just beyond the two bunkers and start downslope. They were close bunched and almost tripping on each other's heels. He turned the gun that way. They seemed to stop "quite suddenly, as if someone had pulled a string on them." Then, almost as one, they pitched face forward down the slope.

Sergeant Hoffman looked at his watch. It said 0745. The company had been on the hill approximately two hours. Its attack under fire had not yet carried more than 200 yards. Not more than one man in five had pushed hard in the forefront of the action. But it was clear to Hoffman that the company already was at the point of physical exhaustion. There was no talk among the men and very little movement. Some of the riflemen were dragging their weapons as if too spent to carry them. Others sat in the trench staring vacantly. When the NCOs tried to direct them, their words blurred.

Kuzmick was astonished at his own physical weakness. For the march-up, he had loaded himself as lightly as possible to conserve strength, carrying only his rifle, canteen and one belt of ammunition. Now he felt as if his legs couldn't take him "to the next bunker" and as he looked over the other survivors of Second Platoon, he could see that they were in no better shape.

But the job was not yet half-done. The Chinese still sat in the bunkers along two-thirds of the trench line and held all of the covered parts of the trench. The battering which the artillery had given the works in order to kill men had but made it easier for the remnants of the two garrisons to stand off each other. The collapsing of a great part of the trench wall made impossible any sighting along it. Bunker doors had broken down under the weight of their own sandbags and no longer served as a portal for grenading. Timbers which had supported the near ends of the covered trench were splintered and fallen, closing the trench to sight and sortie and giving tactical cover to its defenders. From within this jumbled ruin, potato-masher grenades were hurled toward the Americans in large number, and an almost incessant burp-gun fire on both sides of the hill kept them pinned to the defilades churned up by the night's shelling. But the wreckage hid all other animation and they looked vainly for the coign of the firers.

Feeling that King's men had stretched almost to the breaking point, Clemons saw no choice but to mark time while waiting for help. He was no longer in touch with higher commands. The artillery had cut his telephone lines and his five radios had been killed one by one by direct fire. Three of the operators had been hit and evacuated from Pork Chop. From the chow bunker, where the wounded were taken, back to Hill 200, a personnel carrier was now on continuous shuttle taking out the worst cases. One vehicle had been smashed by a mortar shell which killed the driver and rewounded two passengers. It was quickly replaced. From Hill 200 the casualties were moved rearward by litter jeep and chopper.

The Love force which had fought its way up the right-hand finger at last closed on the trench. There remained but twelve beat-up men, as worn as Clemons' own, under command of Lieut. Arthur A. Marshall. Sixty-two had started with Lieut. Forrest J. Crittenden. Wounded, he had given way to Lieut. Homer F. Bechtel who was quickly struck down by a grenade. Before Marshall could fit his twelve men into Clemons' lines, submachine-gun fire cut the number to ten.

They had tried but they had failed. The maneuver had no pinching-out effect. Those who had arranged it did not foresee that with both attacks proceeding on a narrow front, the entrenched enemy, having the advantage of interior lines, could keep the downslope hot without lessening resistance to Clemons. So Love simply withered away under the blast, and its beaten remnant at last joined King's men without having aborted any main portion of the enemy-held works.

Not all of Crittenden's men, however, had been as ready as their leader to make a good Purple Heart try. Early in the maneuver, under cover of dark, some had slipped away, rather than face the fire. Lieut. Virgil W. McCall of Mike Company rounded up two squads of Love stragglers along the slope of Hill 200. He marched them back to help Clemons and, en-route, captured an unexpected prize. The Red Chinese also had their duty dodgers. McCall pinioned one of them he found hiding in a bunker. With the aid of the prisoner, he lured out four other Chinese who had holed up in a covered trench.

Presenting the bag to Clemons, he said, "We might try the same thing here." Clemons was willing. The prisoners, though reluctant, at last agreed to co-operate. McCall pushed his decoys forward to the bunkers nearest the enemy line. Covered by McCall's riflemen, they proceeded to make their surrender appeal. The only visible effect was a sharp increase in the grenading and automatic fire from out the rubble. Clemons said to Pvt. Melvin F. Lucas, "Take the prisoners off the hill before they get hurt."

From the slackening of the fight for the ditch came further dispersion. On both sides, men left the guarding of it to outposts and scattered over the higher slopes inside the parados. Among the Americans, this was not a reaction to orders and the movement was uncollected.

The fighters turned that way individually, partly to escape the death stench befouling the trenches and partly for survival. On the upslope there were defiladed craters among the rocks which might afford more personal protection than the broken battlements which ran head-on to the artillery shelling.

This instinctive shifting brought the two sides closer together than before. But there was no grapple or pickup in the fire engagement. Both sides were touching bottom. In these minutes, either side might have cleared the hill through the collected action of twenty or so men moving and firing together over the high ground in Pork Chop's center, then pressing on to the end of the ridge. But there was not that much unified energy present and the situation all but prohibited organization of it. When men under fire are physically spent, widely dispersed, out of water and short of ammunition, the restoration of group activity is next to impossible. It was a measure only of their common weariness that these rifle lines crawled closer to each other not to court death but to escape it in the rocks and pits of the upgrade.

Such was the situation at 0800. For King's men, the fight had been underway less than four hours, and in that time, they had moved under their own power hardly more than one mile. Canteens had long since been drained in slaking the heavy thirst of the wounded. Weapons had become so begrimed that cleaning required more effort than firing. All of the extraordinary stresses on the hill were of man's making. The morning itself was delightfully cool and fair, a typical day in Korea's loveliest season.

At 0814, re-enforcements began to arrive, at first just a trickle of riflemen, the greater part of two squads. They were from First Platoon, George Company, 17th Infantry. Until then, Clemons had not known that any part of the Buffalo Regiment was within the area. Automatically, he sent the new men along to stiffen his left flank which had been stopped by the covered trench. Then a pleasant voice asked, "Will you please tell me the situation?" Clemons looked up to see his brother-in-law, Lieut. Walter B. Russell, who at the last accounting was still in the United States. Clemons said, "Now what in hell are you doing here?"

Russell was commanding George Company. He explained that the rest of his force was still toiling up the backslope, slowed by the artillery fire. His mission was to "assist Clemons in the mop-up" and then withdraw from the hill as soon as possible. To Clemons' mind, that instruction was a first revelation of the distance separating high command from the realities of his situation. It presupposed that the Chinese were but barely holding and that King remained a mobile and combat-worthy force. One assumption was as wrong as the other. There remained to Clemons about thirty-five tired men from King, the ten survivors from Love and twelve derelicts from Easy who had been freed during the push down the trench line. Harrold had left the hill, and the Easy men, besides being leaderless, were nursing minor wounds. There was no leg push in any of these elements. It was doubtful if they still retained holding power.

Pondering these factors, the kinsmen weighed what should be done. As Clemons saw it, the best course was to withdraw and regroup his people while Russell's men were still approaching, so that the still solid company would have a clear field. Russell, being the green hand, deferred to Clemons, who, though battle experienced, was brain weary. The displacement and flankward shift under fire, always a danger, was begun immediately, and proved to be a mistake. Though Clemons did not know it, a fresh

Chinese company was arriving at the other end of the ridge and closing to contact more swiftly than Russell's men. When Clemons' advanced skirmishers pulled back, thus easing the foreground pressure, the enemy snipers and grenadiers rushed into the vacuum. The momentum which might have been gained by Russell's coming was dissipated before he could get his men into the fight.

Suddenly, the hill was again ablaze. The Chinese artillery and mortars ranged in and where the earth was not shaking from heavy metal, bullet fire was pinging off the rocks and cutting the grasses. Re-enforced and resupplied, the Chinese grenadiers doubled their aggressiveness. These were the conditions in which the maneuver, made to apportion sector responsibility, took place. The new men were down and breathless, their weapons fouled by dew and dust, each seeking to hold a little patch of ground, before any platoon, any squad had a chance to see its situation as a whole. Lieutenant Marshall with the ten Love men and Lieutenant Ess with a platoon from George took over the left sector. Russell with the rest of George moved to the right flank and extended down the finger. Under Lieutenant O'Hashi, King's men regrouped and moved to the center, which put them on the high ground looking to Hasakkol. Man by man and yard by yard, they continued with the shift until the wanted dispositions were complete. Thereafter, nothing came of it. A few men were killed and another score or so wounded. Otherwise, there was no change. George Company settled into the line, and for some hours, helped hold it. But it had already burned up the energy needed to extend the mop-up. The re-enforcement by both sides had only the effect of getting more bodies into the meat grinder without changing the tactical balance. The stagnation of the fight was not less than before. The morning wore on with both Chinese and Americans acting defensively.

Clemons and Russell moved into Harrold's old CP. Using Russell's radio, Clemons messaged Battalion, "I must have water, plasma, more medical assistance, flame throwers, litters, ammunition, several radios." At 1100, a party of Korean bearers got as far as the chow bunker bringing a load of C-rations and water. Distribution of these supplies among the men in the forward foxholes was no longer possible, due to the intensity of the barrage fire on the hill.

At noontime, Lieut. James Blake, the battalion S2, entered the CP. He had a written message from Colonel Davis for Clemons. Any of the survivors of Easy and Fox companies were to be sent to the rear immediately, and George Company as a whole was to withdraw promptly at 1500. Clemons said to Blake, "Take this message back. Tell them I believe that the crisis here is not appreciated either by Battalion or Regiment. I have left but very few men. All are exhausted. Russell has only fifty-five men left.

When they go out, it is not reasonable to expect that we can hold the hill."
One hour later, his message was acknowledged by Battalion, but nothing
was said about amending the order.

By 1200, the flame throwers, ammunition and litters which Clemons had
requested had arrived at the foot of Pork Chop's rear, carried by eight
Korean Service Corps cargadores. But the barrage-swept crest looked too
formidable to these men. So for safety's sake, they marked time on the low
ground during the hours of early afternoon when their cargo might still
have been of some use to the embattled force at the summit. Falling 170
yards short of their target, they failed it altogether.

The last touch of irony was supplied by Lieut. James Barrows, a division
public information officer. Daring the fire which had stopped the Korean
bearers, Barrows entered Clemons' CP at 1445, with two staff photogra-
phers in tow. He had come to take pictures of what he thought was a
successful American action. Clemons said to him, "Forget the pictures. I
want you to carry a message to Battalion." He wrote it out: "We must have
help or we can't hold the hill." Barrows started immediately. Within the
hour Battalion acknowledged the message. But that was all.

Whether it was an oversight by Clemons due to fatigue, or the consequence of a professional training which unduly emphasizes the virtue of
brevity in communications, his messages to the rear had not clearly stated
his own losses, which was the critical point.

Knowing their man, both Battalion and Regiment gave full weight to his
distress calls, accepting it as fact that the force on Pork Chop was "dead
beat," though Colonel Kern was still not informed that both King and
Love had taken excessive losses.

Kern emphasized the physical exhaustion of the force, and not its deple-
tion, when he called up Division to urge that King, if not relieved, must be
re-enforced. Being still more remote from the fire fight, Division was even
more sanguine.

Besides, Division was concerned with a more complex question—
whether Pork Chop was ultimately worth the indicated price in blood. If
the hill were yielded, the Communists would strike next at Hill 347. If it
were fought for, Pork Chop might become another battalion-per-day affair
like Triangle Hill.

The fight was local but the issue was national. So Division asked a
decision of I Corps, which asked it of Eighth Army, which asked it of Far
East Command. The basic question was amazingly simple: "Do you really
want to hold Pork Chop?" But while the big wheels debated the answer,
the task of holding devolved on a picket squad of worn-out men. After
hearing Kern, Division said that, for the time being, King would be given
no help. It was not a hard-boiled refusal. Division simply had to be sure

that the fight was in dead earnest before wasting another company. Maj. Gen. Arthur G. Trudeau and his ADC, Brig. Gen. Derrill M. Daniel, got in a chopper and flew to Davis' CP to get a clearer view of how King was faring. They landed at 1500.

At exactly the same hour, taking advantage of a lull in the cannonading, Lieutenant Russell pulled his George Company survivors out of the Pork Chop works and led them down the hill. He had lost half of his command in less than seven hours. While his column was getting out, the six Korean bearers, heartened by the lull, climbed to the chow bunkers carrying the flame throwers. It was now too late to use them. Some of Kuzmick's men tried to lug the throwers forward. They lacked the strength even to lift them.

There now remained to Clemons but 25 men, including the Love survivors under Lieutenant Marshall. The rest of King's men—18 killed and 71 wounded—had all been lost to the day's fire. It was obviously impossible to continue the tactics of the morning. The remnant could not be stretched across the crown of the hill; to attempt it would mean sure death.

Clemons gathered the men and led them as a tight group to the highest knob on the left side of Pork Chop. After deploying them, he returned to his CP, with his radio man and one runner. So positioned, neither the group nor its commander was linked physically with any support to rearward. What earlier had been a rifle company integrated within a general defense line had become three squads clinging in isolation to a defensive island. Clemons stayed in the bunker to save his radio, his one hold on survival; if help arrived, he would be in the right place to make the contact. The other task of keeping the group alive fell mainly to O'Hashi and Kuzmick.

Within the perimeter which the group formed on the knob were three small, partly collapsed bunkers. Eight or nine of the worst-spent men took shelter under their sandbag walls. The others moved into nearby shell craters. The holes were not deep enough for good cover. Using spoons, knives and bayonets for the work—they lacked the strength to wield the small entrenching tool—they tried to widen and deepen them. The only other activity was an endless cleaning of rifles and carbines, done with toothbrushes, the standby equipment of the soldier when nothing else will free his grimed rifle. Kuzmick set the example. The others followed it, though their response was trancelike. Since early morning they had been without water. Faces caked, tongues thickened by the dust shower which plagued the hill, under lashing by the guns and mortars, they no longer talked to each other. Nor did they move from their places except when shaken loose by an exploding shell. From the foreground, an almost constant bullet fire rained upon the knob. Occasionally, a grenade came sailing in. Yet they saw not a single human target, and therefore made no attempt to return fire. In the end that perhaps mattered very little, since most of them no longer had sufficient strength to raise weapon to shoulder and aim. Than this, there is no more moving entry in the record of King, that young Americans too exhausted to fight may still obey such group discipline as their enfeebled resources permit.

It was to be their portion for four hours. "We lay there and took it," said Corporal Bridges. "There was nothing else to do." To the few who endured it, the earlier trials of the day seemed nothing compared with this final test. Hit and harassed, endlessly cleaning weapons with no valid hope of again using them, they still held ground. The earth and rock banks which they had raised above their small craters were creased and scattered by the bullet storm. The enemy artillery, which had ranged widely over Pork Chop, now concentrated against this one small area of defiance. The embankments caved in. The sandbag walls were flattened. Repeatedly, the men were buried under the dirt shower. Weapons freshly cleaned were refouled. Again the toothbrushes were plied. In this way continued the monotonously deadly round. At the end, fourteen had survived it, sick and shaken but relatively whole-bodied. Seven were Americans, the others ROKs. All had repeatedly cleaned weapons. Seven—and these were Americans—had done some digging. Of the fourteen men, only three had fired so much as one round.

Even had he tried, Clemons could not have returned to them. By the time he re-entered his CP, Chinese snipers and grenadiers had already filtered through to the unguarded slopes around it, and he was invested from both sides of the trench before he could make one move to help the company's situation. Clemons and his three enlisted men, having no choice, picked up their rifles and fought to save themselves from being overrun.

In this way, more than an hour was lost before he could get back to his communications. At about 1640, there was a fleeting respite. He called Colonel Davis on radio and said, "We have here about twenty men who are still unhit. They are completely spent. There is no fight left in this company. If we can't be relieved, we should be withdrawn."

Present with Davis when the message came through was General Trudeau. It was like a five-alarm warning. Until that moment, the picture had remained blurred. The information had been too fragmentary. Trudeau had realized that King was being badly punished, but he did not know that the defense of Pork Chop was at a final strait of desperation. Now, with the day already gone, he was aware that the hill could not be held, unless additional troops moved toward it as rapidly as the night. The question was where to get them and how many should be sent. By this time Pork Chop was nigh a total ruin. Its shattered works could not avail cover to more than a few men, and the Chinese artillery would continue unrelenting so long as its people had a purchase on the hill.

Trudeau flew back to his CP to mull over the problem with the other generals and with Colonel Kern, already enroute to the same destination by chopper.

Love Alone

To UNDERSTAND WHAT HAPPENED TO LOVE COMPANY DURING THE PORK Chop fight, it is necessary to return to the beginning and follow its experience step by step.

What the men atop the hill saw and heard of its effort had not been impressive. While the remnant of Easy Company was awaiting succor, one of Love's platoons had counterattacked and had been knocked back. Then when King Company entered the fight, it was disappointed in the hope that the converging movement by the other two rifle platoons from Love would lighten its work. Finally, only a corporal's guard of Love men got to the top. These things the men attacking the bunker line well knew.

But the view from the top was very limited. The men fighting there could not see how the rest of the attack was faring. Its failures, frustrations and problems were far outside their informed understanding, as were the trials of any comrade who happened to fall unseen among the rocks.

Love's luck had not been running in the hour when the fighting started. The weapons platoon was absent and the three rifle platoons were alerted and trucked forward, at first with the idea of back-stopping Hill 347, just in case the Chinese overran Pork Chop and kept coming. Two of the trucks were wrecked by mortar fire before the company got on location.

That interrupted the ride of Third Platoon. About the time its leader, 2nd Lieut. Earle L. Denton, had his men ready to move again, a staff officer out of Second Battalion (Denton didn't know the man) arrived and told him he was to march the platoon to Hill 200 and thereafter "re-enforce Pork Chop by occupying same." The officer added, "When you get to Hill 200, you will pick up Fox Company and they will go with you."

Denton immediately marched on Hill 200, with M/S Aubrey Norcross bringing up the rear of the column so that the men wouldn't get lost in the trenches. Despite the precaution, the column got split.

Arrived at the CP on Hill 200, he met several artillery officers, but found no one who could tell him anything about the location or movements of Fox Company. Having been given his mission, and having gained the impression that time was of the essence if Pork Chop was to be battened down, he decided to proceed alone. By this chance, and due to Denton's own misunderstanding of the situation, there fell upon one platoon the mission which higher headquarters assumed was being carried out by an adequate force.

From the peak of Hill 200, Denton gazed long and earnestly at Pork Chop. To his untrained eye, the view seemed not alarming. The hill was being shelled but the artillery action was not vigorous. He could hear no small-arms fire and there was no sign of human activity. So he concluded that his platoon was being committed to strengthen a defense which already was doing well enough.

Deciding to move via the road which ran from Hill 200 to Pork Chop, he started immediately. It was an easy, uninterrupted march. The platoon got to within 50 yards of the chow bunker, still in column, without hearing one warning sound.

Then from Pork Chop's height, two machine guns opened fire. Both guns were about 100 yards away. The fire from one came straight at the column, the other ranged in obliquely, firing from a bunker roof. The flank gun was right on target. Six men were cut down, four of them from Sgt. Carlin F. Foot's squad, all of them shot in the legs.

Still thinking Pork Chop was solidly in American hands, Denton concluded that his platoon was being waylaid by a nervous but friendly garrison. Denton yelled, "God damn it, quit shooting!"

Foot and Sgt. Frank Hippler had received the same impression as Denton. So they joined in the cry, "Cease fire! Cease fire!" It had effect: the two machine guns became silent. From somewhere near the gun which was directly above the column, a voice called out, "Come on up!" Foot said to Denton, "Say, Lieutenant, does that sound to you like a GI talking?" The question both startled and annoyed Denton. For another five minutes, he stayed there motionless, looking upslope and wondering what to do. The men stayed flat in the drainage ditch off the road.

Finally Denton sang out, "O.K., let's go!" They were up again and barely starting. Again the two machine guns opened fire. Pvt. Santiago Alieca got a bullet through the shoulder. The other men were already flat and seeking cover. Wondering now how best to withdraw them, making certain they would stay collected, Denton remembered that on the march-up the column had passed a tank-cut in the narrow gap between Hill 200 and Pork Chop. It was the one easily identifiable object that he had noted along the route. So Denton called out to the others, "Let's everybody get back to that tank-cut!"

They complied without further urging. Though it was rapid, it was not a disorderly withdrawal. Some men ran down the backslope; others crawled down the ditch to defilade. But no equipment was left behind and the wounded were all helped from the hill. Yet when six minutes later Denton tried to reform his platoon at the tank-cut, he counted only sixteen men. It was a nerve-wrenching discovery. Somewhere along the road from Hill 200 to Pork Chop, Denton had lost three-quarters of his force without anyone saying boo, and he had not the slightest notion how or why it had happened.

There was a personnel carrier idling in the tank-cut. Alieca and the other casualties were loaded and started rearward. Then the men fell into argument about what should be done next. Denton was undecided. He felt that he was funking his mission, but hunch also told him that the mission was a blunder, though he couldn't say why. In the circumstances, he would have liked to talk over the problem with higher authority. But his one radio had been smashed by the machine gun on top of Pork Chop Hill and he had no telephone. So for a few minutes Denton listened to the argument.

Hippler said, "We should either go forward or march back quickly. To stay here is no good. This cut is a magnet for heavy fire. I've seen it come in here."

Cpl. Robert E. Chambliss said, "Let's get back to where we were up on Pork Chop, form a line and open fire. Those are Chink guns. I know them; I can tell by the sound."

Foot said, "If those are Chink guns, then we've got no business there. They wouldn't be on the rear slope unless they have the whole hill, and you can't take it away from them with a couple of squads."

The argument became more shrill, and more of the men joined in to call out, "Let's move! Let's get out of here!" Then Lieut. John Nesbitt got up to Denton and explained to him that the "lost" part of the platoon was still anchored on Hill 200. Thereon he decided to withdraw full length and get his force in hand before making another move.

As the party moved out of the cut, the two machine guns from atop Pork Chop cracked down. The bursts were just a few yards short. The men broke into a trot and then picked up speed. Denton, who is a sprinter, ran forward yelling, "Hold it! Hold it!" thinking they were right on the verge of panic flight. The front runners were just approaching a culvert as he gained the lead and tried to turn them. But it didn't quite work. Momentum carried them past him. All that saved them from final disorganization was a Chinese artillery concentration. Arriving in salvos of ten shells, spaced not more than twenty seconds apart, they exploded into the road, not more than 40 yards ahead of the men. Within the next ten minutes, approximately 150 rounds hit and exploded in their immediate foreground.

They had all stopped and hit the dirt at the first salvo—all except Denton. Off on the right of the road, about 30 yards away, two medium tanks were parked. Denton stood in midroad calling to his men, "Get under the tanks! What do you want to run off for? There's only good men in this platoon. We got nothing but the best." They went, and from that moment forward they loved the guy and would have eaten from his hand.

Denton hammered on the tanks with his carbine and finally got one of them to open up. On the tank radio, he tried to raise Battalion, but the radio wouldn't cut through. He then asked the tank sergeant to load his twelve men aboard the two tanks and make the run to Hill 200. In that way he managed to stay collected while getting the platoon through the artillery fire. Two of his men were hit by shell fragments during the short haul.

When he got to the check point and told the company commander, Lieut. Forrest James Crittenden, what had happened, he was told to stand by for further orders. Crittenden then reported to Lieut. Col. John N. Davis that his Third Platoon had failed in its counterattack, and Davis issued orders for the strengthened effort which was to be made jointly by King and Love's other two rifle platoons at dawn. That brought to Denton his first awareness that his platoon supposedly had been carrying out a counterattack instead of executing a more or less routine re-enforcement. No one had rung the bell and so he had failed to come out of his corner fighting. Crittenden told Denton to stand by with Third Platoon on Hill 200 and be prepared to advance against Pork Chop on order. In the meantime, he would try again with his other two rifle platoons.

After first being routed from their bivouac, the two platoons had spent their hours marching to the sounds of fire, though getting approximately nowhere. Almost coincidental with the ringing of the telephone at 2330, when came the order that Love Company was to take position on the finger of Hill 347, and be ready to block, two artillery rounds had struck their camp and demolished two squad tents. A third round wounded a BAR man, Pvt. Ben Williams. They were glad enough to quit that ground and go forward.

For maybe an hour or more, they tarried at the position on Hill 347. Then they were moved forward to the perimeter of Hill 200, the mission being the "re-enforcement of First Platoon of Fox Company." Since no one had explained the situation to them, that meant very little.

It was after Denton's return from misadventure that the other two platoons were alerted for their predawn advance to Pork Chop. Curiously enough, the one lesson which had come of that brief reconnaissance was wholly lost to the rest of the company. Denton and the twelve men who had been to Pork Chop's rear slope came back convinced beyond doubt that the hill was dominated by the Chinese. Denton passed that word to his superiors. But when First and Second Platoons were told the new mission, they were given no clearer light on the real situation than Denton had received.

Said Sgt. Horace Ford, "We were told to assemble for a move to Pork Chop. We were not told we were to make an attack."

Said Sgt. Edward Newton, "My squad was told by Lieutenant Paris that we would march up and re-enforce Pork Chop. That was all; nothing was said about a fight."

After platoon and squad leaders checked men to make sure that they were carrying a basic load of ammunition, the march started. By then, the hill had been lost for more than four hours, and none but enemy guns was firing from its ramparts. Denton's report, the messages coming from Harrold and the lack of steady infantry fire atop Pork Chop all pointed to this fundamental change in the situation. But if there was due appreciation of it anywhere in the command level, it was still not communicated to the riflemen who were expected to redress the balance. They were not steeled for a toe-to-toe scrimmage with small arms, though there was sufficient reminder of danger in the area. As the column slipped away from Hill 200, thirteen rounds of mortar dropped on and around it, and Lieutenant Bechtel got his first wound of the night.

Still, that was not enough to prompt the degree of caution needed in the approach. Upon deploying, the two platoons did not take care to stay tied in so that if hit, they could react together and help each other. Once again committed to an attack without knowing it, Love got away badly for having been imprudent.

No reconnaissance was attempted. First Platoon started walking up one flange of the finger, advanced to within 40 yards of Pork Chop's top, became confronted by the solidly staked and unbroken wire barricade, came under grenade fire from beyond the wire, hesitated and weaved for about three minutes, then recoiled to the valley.

Later the men said that the grenade shower was "heavy." But Sgt. Horace Ford counted only eleven grenades. Sergeant Newton counted thirteen. Three men were lightly wounded. M/S Edward L. Posey, sensing that the others wavered, gave the order, "Fall back!" He crawled among the flattened men, whispering the order to them, just to keep excitement down.

They re-formed in the valley, then moved rightward to another part of the finger where someone had found a small hole in the concertina. That move widened the gap between First and Second Platoons.

They got to the hole all right, and as the leading files started to crawl through it, grenade and submachine-gun fire hit among them. The gap was commanded by a stout-walled bunker about 35 yards upslope. Several men could be seen moving on its roof. The worst of the fire was coming from out the bunker. A few Love men started firing their rifles. The enemy silhouettes disappeared. Within the first several minutes, three more men were wounded by grenades.

Cpl. Joseph R. Munier was for several reasons an extraordinary American soldier. A native of Montreal, he had come to the United States and enlisted in the Army because a war was on and he wished to see it. On Pork Chop Hill he was armed with a BAR and was lying next to Private Williams, another BAR man, who despite having been wounded by shellfire earlier in the night, had continued in the action.

Sergeant Posey wiggled on his belly to the two men and suggested that they try to crawl up to within 15 yards of the bunker which was giving the line hell and try to kill it with their fire. Munier said, "We'll try but you can't knock down a bunker with BARs."

Finding a small gap in the concertina, they continued upslope. At less than 12 yards' range, Munier sprayed bullets through the embrasure, not stopping until he had spent all five clips. Then a potato masher came sailing out of the opening, exploded five yards behind him and wounded him in the thighs and buttocks. Munier dropped flat and Williams took his place, firing into the bunker until his BAR, too, ran dry. Another grenade exploded and one fragment hit Williams in the neck.

By that time, Posey had seen enough. He crawled forward to the two men and said, "I think you better fall back, and I think it would be better if we all withdrew as far as the base of the hill." A great light had dawned on Posey: he was at last convinced that the Chinese were in charge of Pork Chop.

And astounding though it seems, it was not until this incident occurred that the same light dawned on the others in Love Company. Ford, Newton, Paris, Lavoie and the men with them, having started with the wrong idea, had clung to it tenaciously. Not until the bunker resisted Munier and Williams at close range did they at last realize that they were fully engaged by an active enemy. Yet a third BAR man, Private Patterson, had been hit by a bullet, and three of the company's ROKs had been wounded by grenades, before Munier made his sortie.

Posey and the two BAR men slipped about 30 yards to the leftward, mainly to remove themselves from the bunker's direct line of fire. In so doing, Williams found a large gap in the concertina, and while he and Munier held there, Posey crawled downslope to rally some of the others and lead them to the opening.

In a few minutes, he was back with the greater part of three squads. Several Chinese grenadiers had maneuvered downslope through the rocks and were waiting just above the gap. Having emptied their BARs, Williams and Munier couldn't supply a covering fire. A dozen grenades fell among them as the men surged through the gap. Sgt. Edward Newton was wounded in back and neck. Pvts. Lindbergh House and John Swaguer were hit in the face and shoulders. Four or five men behind them were struck down and left the fight, but these three tried to keep going.

With Cpl. William Locklear, Ford's assistant, leading, the rush continued. Locklear ran for the main bunker which Munier and Williams had attacked and heaved three grenades through the door. The other skirmishers fanned out to grenade the bunkers on either side of it. Six more Americans were hit by grenade frags during this swift and successful mop-up, including Locklear, who drew a badly shattered left arm.

On his way out, Locklear passed Crittenden, who said to him, "Get back to 200 and tell Fox Company that I've either got to have re-enforcements or ammunition; I've got nothing with which to fight." It was hardly an overstatement. The BARs and machine guns were all dry; half of the carbines were empty; all grenades had been spent in getting to the first three bunkers. In the clutch, what saved Love Company for a little while was the discovery of two cases of grenades in one of the bunkers.

Newton was still moving with the others but was bleeding badly. Posey looked Swaguer over and said to Newton, "If you don't get him to first aid quick, he'll never make it." So Newton started for Hill 200, staggering downslope under Swaguer's weight. Private Williams, already twice wounded, stayed in the attack.

The wire, bunkers and trench which Love's First Platoon had overcome was a Pork Chop outwork, three-quarters way up the finger, but still several hundred feet downslope from the entrenched crest, though connected with it by commo trenches. Checking his squad and finding that he had only two sound men left, both of whom were out of ammunition, Ford continued upward with Posey and Cpl. Nathan Featherstone.

From out of a smashed bunker just forward of them, two Chinese suddenly jumped into the trench and heaved potato mashers at them, then darted back into the bunker. The blast drove fragments into Posey's left leg while wounding Ford and Featherstone in the face. Ford was not even stopped, so light were his wounds. He rushed the bunker, only to find that the two Chinese had vanished into a tunnel leading from its floor. Within the bunker he found a light machine gun and several boxes of ammunition. After advancing the gun about 50 yards upslope, he put Pvt. Columbus Jackson on it.

Firing at the crest of Pork Chop, and toward the midsection of its works, Jackson kept the gun going until his ammunition was spent. His and Ford's account of how the gun was placed and aimed indicates that the fire was bearing against the face of the King Company attack at just about the time Clemons' men felt they were making headway against the Chinese. If it was a mistake by Love, it was still pardonable. Besides not knowing that the Chinese held the hill, the men had not been informed that King Company would be attacking the rear slope at the same time and there would be a risk of crossed fires.

Jackson's fire noticeably quieted the racket atop the hill. Misreading that sign, Ford thought it meant that the enemy was being scared off and Love was gaining control. He yelled to Jackson, "Boy, we're getting there."

But just as happened with King atop the hill, the moment of highest hope was dashed by the sudden dropping of the supporting artillery. One salvo exploded around the gun, putting a shard through Ford's arm and another through Jackson's helmet; it broke through the liner without even graving his scalp.

Another salvo landed in the commo trench among fourteen members of Love, getting all of them, including Private Williams; it was his third hit in one night's action. Posey was wounded again. Lieutenant Bechtel was hit for the second time.

Bechtel crawled up to Williams and said, "We got to stop that fire. Go to the rear of the hill. See if King Company has arrived there yet. Tell them we don't have ten able-bodied men left. Tell them to come on and help us. And tell them to raise the artillery." The message is eloquent of the degree of misunderstanding in both flanks of this "co-ordinated" attack, and the failure in either to get any feeling of support from the other.

Williams started on his mission. Partway around the hill, he ran into three parked medium tanks. He asked the sergeant to message that the artillery should lift fire. While he was talking, two more rounds hit among the tanks, but Williams ducked under the steel hull in time. He continued his walk, and on getting to the road which winds down Pork Chop's rear slope, saw some of King's wounded come out of the works and start toward Hill 200. This was Williams' first knowledge that the other company was fighting and he returned to the finger, intending to tell Bechtel.

In Love's sector, meanwhile, there had been no slackening of the artillery storm. Whether the initial barrage had come from American guns (as the men thought) and this mistaken fire had merged quickly into an enemy cannonading of awesome power and purpose, there was no real way of knowing. The men who survived the deluge were conscious only that there had been no break in it. For the better part of one hour it descended on them, breaking eighteen rounds per minute into the small acre where First Platoon's remnant was still clinging to life. The men could do no more: to advance, or even to think of taking any fighting action had become impossible.

Right after the first salvo broke, Corporal Munier, the Canadian, found himself in a ruined bunker with Lieutenants Paris and Summers, the medic, SFC James Cooper, and four other wounded men whom he did not know. Paris had been hit at the wire by grenades, and an artillery slug had gone through his shoulder. Munier was working on Paris and trying to stanch the blood flow with his first-aid pack and handkerchief.

More shells exploded in the trench outside. A voice screamed, "Help me! Help me! I can't move." Munier started to go. Sergeant Cooper waved him off, and disappeared through the door. Munier continued the bandaging. More rounds came in, and then a cry from Cooper, "Please come help me!" Again, Munier started to go. Summers stopped him, saying, "No, your job is to stay here and help Paris." As Summers stepped from the door, a shell exploded behind him and one fragment cut through the base of his spine. Munier went out and pulled all three men into the bunker. Cooper was not too badly hurt; he quickly joined Munier in applying first aid to the others. Summers died in about thirty minutes; later, another shell broke through the bunker and decapitated him.

By these stages was completed the wrecking of First Platoon. Of its forty-five men, only five were in the group of twelve which later that morning, under the leading of Lieutenant Marshall, gained the top of Pork Chop and joined the mop-up effort by King Company. One of them was Munier. He was still fighting at 1030 on the following day when a strange lieutenant approached him and said, "You don't belong here. Love Company has left the hill."

The events leading up to the disintegration of Second Platoon are less well-known because still fewer of its able-bodied men stayed with the fight until Pork Chop's main trench was gained and managed to survive the ordeal of the afternoon.

Second Platoon jumped off on the left side of the finger, supposedly abreast of First Platoon's line, which harassed by its own problems, could not stretch far enough to join hands with Second's flank. The ascent was much steeper and rockier along Second's path, and therefore it did not keep pace. Halfway up the hill, it came onto a broad saddle, and paused there to get the squads reorganized. No fire had yet come against it during the climb.

That was when the platoon ground was swept by the cannonading which had culminated First Platoon's misfortunes. Approximately sixty shells exploded among and around the squads during the next fifty minutes. The men jumped for rock cover, when they could, and, for the most part, stayed there, taking it. The effect was to demoralize and disunify them almost wholly before they had moved to close grips with the Chinese. Not many were hit by the fire; the agreed-upon number is at most six or seven. But other men, hearing no orders and shocked by the experience, drifted

Pork Chop Hill lay just beyond the toe of Hill 200 and the supply road which served both outposts was under direct observation by the enemy.

away from the slope, seeking the rear. When at last the cannonading slackened, the platoon stood at less than half-strength.

By then, SFC Gilbert Dobak, the platoon sergeant, was in command. He
said to Sgt. Joseph Lavoie, "We got to move out of here." They started
upward, and some of the others arose and followed. When they got to the
wire barricade, and started through a gap which had been cut by the artillery fire, grenade and burp-gun fire from behind the barricade met them.
The men went flat, and a few of them, including Dobak and Lavoie, replied with grenades and carbines. Seven more men were hit by the enemy
fire before resistance tapered off. A few others weakened and bugged out.

When the climb was resumed, only eleven men followed Dobak through
the barrier. He was hit by submachine-gun fire before he got to the commo
trench. Sgt. George Linker took charge. He was still present when what was
left of the two platoons entered King Company's lines. From beginning to
end, the attack had lacked any semblance of military organization. That in
the end the efforts of a few willing, unhelped men partially redeemed it
was due only to individual dauntlessness. They stayed on Pork Chop until
midafternoon, but their force had been spent in the uphill fight, and they
did little to help Clemons.

Lieutenant Denton was still on Hill 200, with his own survivors, the
stragglers from the other two rifle platoons and the duty-fit men of weapons platoon. At about the time the Love squad on Pork Chop was prepar-
ing to withdraw, Colonel Davis called on Denton to tell him that he was
now commanding Love Company and was expected to take it forward and
defend Pork Chop as promptly as he could get the company armed.

The "company" was resting on the reverse slope of 200. Denton walked
down and counted noses. Of the 187 men which Love had mustered the
prior midnight, there were now left 56. Denton formed them as a three-
platoon company, making riflemen of his weapons people, and then stood
by while ammunition—this time with double the load of the night before—was issued.

Two hours later they were on the road, and by 1630, the company had
moved up to and reassembled at the chow bunker without losing a man.
But the approach had a touch of genius. To beat the artillery and mortar
fire, Denton had advanced his unit from Hill 200 one man at a time, with a
two-minute interval separating files at the point of departure. That cost
him an hour but he figured it was worth it. He explained his purpose to the
men and he felt gratified that they moved right along despite their extraordinary extension.

Denton pushed on to the CP and found Clemons immediately. Small-
arms fire crackled up and down the trench but for the moment Clemons'
fire was keeping the snipers back from his own vicinity.

Clemons said to Denton, "I've got only sixteen men on this hill. I can't tell you how they're deployed at this moment. I haven't had time to look." The figure was approximately right, though Clemons was guessing at it.

It was agreed that Denton had best try to set up his men in a limited perimeter facing the forward slope of the hill with two of his platoons in line forming the front and the third platoon filling in the shrunken circle by covering the rear. This arrangement would still leave three-fourths of Pork Chop's crown, including the CP area, outside the defensive circle, but in the circumstances there was no more promising alternative.

Before Denton's deployment was more than half-complete, his chosen sector was hit by an artillery concentration and he lost six men to the fire. The others took it without jar; they were now acting heads up and Denton felt confident that they would stay steady against whatever came. He kept his war cry of the prior evening, changing only one word, "Nobody but good men in this company! Nothing but the best!" They heard him say it over and over and they believed him.

Nor did it upset Denton when he discovered that in his rush, he had forgotten his communications. He sent a runner back for some AWPR-6s, and before any further damage was done the company, the man had gone through fire and returned with two of them. The incident was typical of Love's closing round, after its several bad starts. For another six hours, it would continue to travel the road of blood and fire. Before sunup, more of its men would die, and others would be wounded. But at long last, the feeling of success was coming, attended by that special magnetism which flows from an inspired spirit. There was a breeziness about young Denton, a gentleness and a manliness which bound others to him. The kid was proud to be commanding his fellow Americans and he was not afraid to let them know it.

After the harsh greeting by the Chinese artillery when they settled in, Denton's men knew several hours of relative quiet. They kept low because of the thickening sniper fire over their area, but except for an occasional mortar shell, there was no heavy pounding of the hill. The King men under Kuzmick and the detachment at the CP also shared this partial respite. With the darkest hours approaching, it seemed the Chinese were withholding themselves before a last great effort. Yet there was no great safety in this quiet. Any movement on the hill was swiftly punished. The badly wounded could not be evacuated. Lieutenant O'Hashi, leaving his position on the crest to talk to Clemons, was directly hit by a potato masher as he entered the CP door. The blow shattered his right shoulder.

During these same hours, decision was being reached at the higher levels. General Trudeau at Division talked to Maj. Gen. Bruce Cooper Clarke at I Corps, asking and getting assurance that if he spent more men to regain Pork Chop, it would not later be yielded. Once that point was cleared up, the Second Battalion of the 17th Regiment was attached to the 31st Regiment. Since George Company of the 17th had already been chewed up during the afternoon fight, that gave Colonel Kern two rifle companies with which to win his fight. The 17th's First Battalion was also moved to the Pork Chop area but not put under Kern.

Kern immediately called Captain King of Fox Company (the time was 1800) and told him to move on Pork Chop and relieve Clemons' force as promptly as he could make ready. He decided to withhold Easy Company, awaiting proof of need, just as Division had decided that it would keep a string on 17th's First Battalion up to the moment when the course of the fight proved that Kern could not win without using it. Now that everything else along the Division front had cooled, all higher headquarters could concentrate on the one neat problem of getting the maximum result at Pork Chop while risking the minimum loss. The results show how narrow is the dividing line between practical economy and the wastage which comes of sending too few men.

Captain King lost some hours in getting Fox Company on the road. He moved after he was at last satisfied that the men were as well equipped and ready as the circumstances permitted. Still, in the end the delay probably cost Fox Company an excessive price.

Fox's men started arriving on the hill at 2130. One platoon was deployed into the Pork Chop trenches. Several of the officers pushed forward to talk to Denton and Clemons. Captain King, moving with the main body of the company, was still some distance down the rear slope. His radio had been jammed by the enemy as he began the approach, and he could get no idea of how his lead platoon was faring, nor could he talk to the commanders he was supposed to contact.

At the same time, there was a sharp build-up of fire against the Love Company front and Denton could see a body of Chinese crossing the valley from Hasakkol. On radio, he called on the artillery to fire "Flash Pork Chop" which would interdict the forward slope with killing fire. The barrage dropped quickly and it scattered the Chinese attack.

Whether it was cause and effect, the Chinese loosed the heaviest concentration of artillery and mortar fire against Pork Chop that had yet hit the hill. (Denton believed that an enemy radio man hiding in one of the bunkers had called for the TOT.) It dropped mainly on the trenches where Fox's lead squads were deploying and on the rear slope where the two platoons were still toiling upward. Before having any chance to engage, Fox Company lost nineteen men; and as the steel continued to rain down, the entrenched men huddled and the columns broke and scattered. Such was the state of disorganization, that it took Fox another three hours to get the greater part of its force set on the hill, and the platoons never did get satisfactorily tied in to one another.

So once again in the Pork Chop duel, the massing of artillery erased the attempt to gain advantage through infantry numbers. The body blows against Fox sapped its energy, leaving it in no better state than the weary forces it had come to relieve.

For these reasons, as well as because of the confusion at the start, the relief was long protracted, clumsy and hazard-filled. Captain King asked Denton to assist him with platoon guides, though Denton didn't know the hill and Fox wasn't fitting into Love's positions. The Fox men forward were already so tightly bunched that they had to be pried apart physically to execute the deployment. As Denton said of it, "At every point the relief was sticky and it was almost impossible to keep the men from bunching or persuade them that they were safer if they spread out; the conditions of the fight made the argument seem unreasonable." Some of the Fox men were still in shock from the hard opening blow dealt by the enemy artillery and their hysterical shouting and screaming muffled the effort to give them direction.

There was also the acute problem of attending the casualties, giving them first aid and arranging a base for their ultimate evacuation from Pork Chop. There being no letup in the barrage fire, the problem kept growing. At one stage, Denton came upon five wounded Fox men piled up in the trench. One man had lost a leg. Denton carried the five to the CP, then returned to his rounds. By then it was wearing on toward midnight. Both he and Clemons were growing increasingly concerned about getting their own fractions off the hill and passing full responsibility to Captain King.

The question of what to do about lights arose at this point in the relief. Under Clemons and Denton, the defense had been making steady use of illuminating shell over the top of Pork Chop and the forward slopes which served the Chinese approach. They reasoned that since their own men were holding tight to the foxholes and their main danger came of prowlers who were already on the hill, the lighting of the hill was all in their favor. But when came time for the withdrawal, Clemons wanted to turn the lights off so that his men, in moving, would not be silhouetted. Captain King felt it not less important that the lights should be kept on to steady his own garrison. In the end, they compromised, continuing the illuminating of the forward slope while keeping the rest of the hill dark.

As soon as that confusion had been cleared away and Denton had examined the wounded and done what he could for them, he started sending his own men off the hill, bound for Hill 200, once again having them monitored out at two-minute intervals singly to cheat the enemy artillery.

Then he returned to Clemons' CP, running a gauntlet of fire his last 20 yards to get there. Enemy grenadiers had crowded in and were throwing at the door. He and Clemons stood just inside, ready to field and return anything hot that came through. On the bunker roof just above their heads, they could hear two Chinese moving a light machine gun into position. The gun opened fire. Corporal Chambliss of Love Company, who had decided to stay with Denton, had been waiting for that moment. Disregarding the grenadiers, he jumped into the trench and sprayed upward with his BAR, shooting both gunners off the roof.

These things happened right around midnight. Besides Chambliss, Newton, Ford, Lavoie, Munier and a hard-boiled, 19-year-old runt from Brooklyn, Pfc. John L. Baron, had stayed with their commander. Baron was a case; the boy talked a blue streak of profane obscenity and thus far in the fight had done little else. Also in the bunker with Denton were Clemons, Captain King of Fox Company, Clemons' two enlisted helpers, Sgt. Richard Falk and five (unidentified) wounded men. Though the casualties had been stowed in the bunks, it was rather crowded.

Ready to leave, Clemons, Denton and their men had been awaiting a respite in the close siege of the CP. Hence when Chambliss killed the machine gun on the roof, as many of the others as were weaponed jumped through the door into the open and sprayed fire over the embankments and along the trench. That lasted for five minutes and temporarily cooled the area.

Clemons and his men started rearward. Denton and his few retainers were about to follow when Captain King said to him, "I don't know this position at all. Could you stay awhile and help me?" So Denton stuck it and his small "palace guard" stayed with him.

Clemons had been gone one and one-half hours when the fight flared. There were sounds of movement from the roof as of men tearing at the sandbags. Through the top of the CP door sailed three grenades, as if a leaning man had made the toss from above. Two blew off harmlessly. The third grenade exploded metal into one of the American wounded.

Then a Chinese came through the door triggering a submachine gun. Denton was shot through the leg and hand. Other bullets hit Captain King and one of his men, Sergeant Robertson. Shooting from the floor, Baron cut down the gunner with one burst from his carbine, yelling, "Take that, you —— ——son-of-a-bitch!"

Again the Chinese on the roof grenaded through the doorway, and in the same instant, a second burp gunner aimed his weapon through the embrasure. The grenade exploded under the bunk of a wounded man who had already lost a leg. Chambliss, Newton and Ford blasted toward the embrasure and killed the Communist gunner before he could fire. Once more,

Baron jumped into the open trench and, spinning, fired at the roof. The grenadier fell and his feet still dangled above the CP door in the morning.

He would have been dead in three more seconds anyway. As Baron rebounded into the bunker, three 122-mm artillery rounds landed in salvo, two crushing in one corner of the roof, the other exploding into the bunker's sandbag base and caving one side of it. One round cut a yard-wide hole in the ceiling and showered fragments over the bunks holding the American wounded.

Hit again, they screamed and sobbed hysterically.

Denton cried, "Shut up! I don't want any cry babies in here. Nobody but good men in my company!"

That silenced them immediately.

Baron shouted, "Jesus Christ, this is worse than Custer's last stand."

Asked Denton, "Were you there, too?"

"No," yelled the kid, "but I've read about it."

Denton's radio was still working. He had already been in touch with two Quad-50s which had parked halfway down the finger waiting for the moment when they might assist the infantry fight. It flashed over his mind that if the eight .50 machine guns could put a grazing fire over the bunker roof, the Chinese could be kept from grenading through the hole blown by the artillery.

Denton called the Quads, "Can you give it to me now—all the fire that you've got—put it right over the CP roof?"

Came the answer, "Which roof, Lieutenant? From where we sit all of the bunkers look alike." And it was too true, as Denton reflected.

He dropped the instrument, grabbed a grenade and wired a flare to it, then looked for a willing hand. Again it was Baron who volunteered to go into the trench and pitch the improvised light on the roof to mark the target for the Quads. He went, grenade in one hand, carbine in the other. As he made the upward toss, a Chinese burp gunner, ten yards away, opened fire. The burst cut three buttons from Baron's jacket without breaking the skin. Yelling, "You —— —— son-of-a-bitch!" he whirled with his carbine and emptied a magazine into the man.

With the light came the deluge. The Chinese correctly read it as a signal for help in some form. Earlier, their attack upon the bunker was a random effort, the unorganized forays of a few determined individuals. Now, as if on order, they pressed on it in large numbers, coming from all sides, grenadiers throwing and machine gunners firing as they ran screaming toward the central target.

The men inside the bunker knew now that they were beaten. The noise was overpowering. No one moved toward the trench. Denton did not try to form them for the last round.

Baron had walked over to the man with the missing leg. He had seemed to be lapsing into deep sleep. "I watched him," said Baron, "hoping he would make it; it kept my mind off things." Suddenly the man stirred and propped on his elbow, crying, "Save the ammo! For Christ's sakes save the ammo! Don't waste another bullet!"

Sergeant Falk spoke, "Nothing can help us now but prayer. That's what I've always heard about spots like this."

Denton said, "Well, Falk, if you can pray, go ahead."

Falk started, "Our Father—who is in heaven—forgive—forgive us our debtors— Oh hell, Lieutenant, I don't know it, I just don't know it."

During the moments of this fervent supplication, reverent in spirit if not in language, they were all silent. (Later, they quoted Falk's prayer verbatim as if it were etched in the memory.) Then as Falk said the last words, outside the bunker there was silence also, broken only by the crackling of rifle fire at some distance. Gone was the oppressive rattle of the burp guns and the fury of the oncoming grenadiers. The storm ended as suddenly as it had arisen.

Easy Company of the 17th Regiment had arrived on Pork Chop. Under the impact of Easy Company's advance, the Chinese resistance for the moment was diverted and almost stunned to silence. Some of the enemy, who still saw a road of escape down the northern fingers, fled toward the valley. Others, becoming trapped between the advancing skirmish line and the debris, died fighting. The greater number simply crawled back into the woodwork, letting Easy Company have the field temporarily, while saving their shot and storing their strength until the moment when more comrades would reach the hill. This was the typical, well-seasoned reaction. In two years of trench warfare, the Red Chinese soldier had become like Brother Fox. Any part of earth was his covert and he had learned to bide his time.

Colonel Kern had heard about the difficulties of the relief and Fox Company's early ordeal. About one hour before midnight, reckoning that Pork Chop was again slipping from his fingers, he called General Trudeau and said that he was committing Easy Company immediately. Trudeau agreed with the decision, saying, "If we've got to counterattack again, lay it on before first light." To double the insurance, Trudeau at the same time released the 17th's First Battalion to Kern. Within five minutes of its authorization, the attack was underway.

Given a task to do, Easy Company solved it with a new maneuver. The direction of its movement, rather than the power of its small arms, made the decisive difference. Instead of attacking obliquely from Hill 200 via the supply road and up the rear slope of Pork Chop, as the other companies had done, Easy risked a plan which carried it out and around the hot

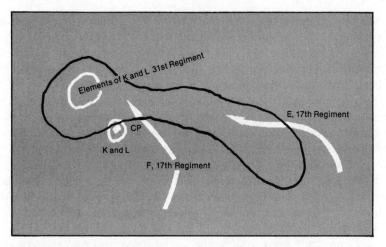

When Easy Company counterattacked Pork Chop from in front, the hill mass was enemy-held except for the two encircled areas.

corner. From the cut between the two hills, Easy marched forward into enemy country and, from a line several hundred yards beyond the American front, attacked directly up the face of Pork Chop, its back turned on enemy-held Pokkae as it jumped off. Had the Red Chinese been trying to re-enforce Pork Chop at that moment, or had they suddenly shifted their artillery concentrations from the rear to the east slope of Pork Chop, Easy might have been killed before it could start. But the boldness which prompted the stroke earned its due reward. The local surprise was complete. No fire interrupted the charge. An approach designed to cheat the artillery also had the effect of boxing in the enemy infantry.

The plan was the inspiration of Easy's young commander, Lieut. Gorman Smith. When his battalion first moved up, Smith noticed that the back slope of Pork Chop and the valley between it and Hill 347 were directly under the eye of the Red OPs on Old Baldy. He said to his commander, Lieutenant Colonel Tully, "If I have to re-enforce that ridge, I want permission to move through the front door." Smith was so certain that this was the right way to do it that he schooled his company on the approach 24 hours before he drew the assignment.

When the order came, no additional instructions had to be given. Every man knew the reason for the unorthodox march; all had been briefed on the route. They started immediately.

While Easy Company worked its way along the front of Hill 200, Smith's forward observer, Lieutenant Clark, laid a covering barrage in the valley east of Pork Chop about 200 yards beyond the assault column. The extra novelty in this protective move was that it risked calling attention to what was being done. The barrage was maintained as Easy's line charged up Pork Chop's east-running finger. Smith's main safeguard against head-on collision with a mobile enemy force, Clark's fires helped Easy reach Pork Chop's crest without losing a man or ducking a hostile round.

But Gorman Smith felt no illusions about his success. He said, "Our route and our plan were proved good only because they worked; had we not made it, had we become trapped, I feel sure I would have been called a three-cornered fool for going that far forward of my own main line to attack Pork Chop."

Be that as it may, of Smith's bold thinking came the extraordinary speed of Easy's assault to the crest. For the embattled group within the Pork Chop CP, the minutes thus saved by one man's intuition and hard work were as decisive as a last-minute reprieve to the condemned.

To Denton and his assistants, the fact of deliverance was at first unbelievable. Once again the irrepressible Private Baron jumped into the trench to see what was happening. His first impressions are given in his own words, "There's a ROK soldier going by me, firing a BAR, going to town. Jeez, can that guy use a weapon! Leave him alone and he'll go clean to China. Hey, and there's a hot shot of a little kid, just a small punk, hasn't even got a man's voice yet, screams like a girl, but he's all over the place, doesn't seem to know how to turn that carbine off. Jeez, what a guy, the little bastard's a one-man army."

Easy's assault was the pivotal event in the battle. While it determined the outcome, it did not immediately end the fighting. Thereafter the Communists challenged again and again but the advantage stayed with the Americans. Their grip was not again loosened until three months later when they gave Pork Chop away feeling that it was no longer worth the price of a squad or a man.

By 0250 Easy Company was deployed fully over the wrecked battlements and Colonel Kern was hearing the report that "Pork Chop is under full control." Smith knew, when he said these words, that they were more comforting than accurate. It was an unprecedented situation and he was at a loss to describe it. The position was "secure" in the sense that for the time being there was no fighting and at all points Smith's men were temporarily in control of the surface. But under the surface nothing was yet secure. Scores of armed and able Red Chinese still infested the ruins and would come fighting from the refuse heaps and smashed bunkers after a breathing spell. Despite the deceptive quiet, custody was still divided.

At 0320, another Chinese counterattack came via the northern finger and promptly the Red snipers on Pork Chop emerged from their holes and resumed fighting. So began the blood bath of Easy Company. At 0429 still another company of Chinese climbed Brinson Finger on Pork Chop's left flank, gained the height and dug in.

On getting that message, Colonel Kern read it as a five-alarm warning. Calling General Trudeau, he said he thought it time to commit the additional battalion of the 17th Regiment. Trudeau replied, "No, we're chewing up one battalion a day. We can't keep it up. Send just one company. Then withdraw the extra company the moment we get the position under control."

So as the second dawn came, Able Company of the 17th went to the fight. As Trudeau had hoped, its weight was sufficient unto the end. The struggle lasted all day, its fury unabated. Fox and Easy were punished hardly less than the early garrisons. Able's strength was still needed to stiffen their depleted ranks when that night, after sunset, the enemy gave over, Pork Chop became tranquil, the smoke blew away and men could see the stars once more.

Denton and his crew of diehards had stayed the fight until midafternoon. Some of them had dozed for a few minutes after Easy gained the hill. A bit refreshed when morning came, they discovered that the Chinese had systematically booby-trapped the CP area during the night. So as a gesture of hospitality to the new tenants, they got the house clean again before they left.

When Pork Chop cooled, the battle ended. For the troops who stood guard along the ridges to rear of Pork Chop, Arsenal and Dale, it had been a mildly unpleasant 48 hours, made so by the persistence of the Chinese artillery. But save for that small pinch of danger in the air, and the molten downpour which cost a few men their lives and many more their sleep, they were hardly more than nonengaged onlookers. The battle of Pork Chop was an artillery duel. The American guns won it. The relatively few riflemen who struggled to hold the outposts, doing it with their flesh when their weapons would no longer work, only validated the guns' claim on victory.

A minor affair as to infantry numbers, it was impressive in weight of metal. Nine artillery battalions were kept operating under the hand of Brig. Gen. Andrew P. O'Meara, due to the presence in 7th Division's neighborhood of 2nd Division's organic artillery.

During the first 24 hours the guns fired 37,655 rounds in defense of Arsenal, Dale and Pork Chop. The proportions were 9,823 rounds fired by the heavies and 27,832 by the light howitzers. On the second day after Arsenal and Dale had been saved and only Pork Chop was in jeopardy, the supporting fire built up to 77,349 rounds total.

Never at Verdun were guns worked at any such rate as this. The battle of Kwajalein, our most intense shoot during World War II, was still a lesser thing when measured in terms of artillery expenditure per hour, weight of metal against yards of earth and the grand output of the guns. For this at least the operation deserves a place in history. It set the all-time mark for artillery effort.

Pork Chop when the fight was over was as clean picked as Old Baldy. And its cratered slopes will not soon bloom again, for they are too well planted with rusty shards and empty tins and bones.

Book 2 ❧ The Patrols

Into the Alligator's Jaws

THEY WENT SINGLE FILE, WITH THE COLUMN OF TWENTY-ONE MEN STRUNG out over approximately 65 yards of trail space. This was their normal way of going when operating conditions, by their standards, seemed reasonably good.

When fog, rain or dark cut the horizon to nothing, with consequent risk that the column might split through some follower taking the wrong path at a trail fork, it was their custom to lock hands from front to rear. Then, in the manner of a daisy chain, they would advance into enemy country. This practice, which western troops would be disposed to scorn as being beneath dignity, they accepted gladly as an extra safeguard against danger. When close to the enemy, they linked themselves with wire to signal what came.

Americans thought the night of 28 April formidably dark. There was no thickening of the atmosphere at ground level, but a heavy cloud wrack had blacked out the stars. Still, as the Ethiopian column began dogtrotting downtrail, 2nd Lieut. Wongele Costa could see as far as the back of the fourth man. That seemed adequate for the mission and he saw no reason to contract the column or restrict its movement.

The ridges which bound the Yokkokchon Valley are exceptionally rugged and deeply eroded. From Second Company's home on the big ridge to the patrol's rendezvous at the extreme end of the forked, low-lying ridge called the Alligator's Jaws the distance was 2,000 yards air line. But the trail cut obliquely across country, dipping into three draws and rising steeply over as many sprangling ridge fingers. The actual walk to the object approximately doubled the air distance.

It is a matter of record that at 2028 hours, Wongele Costa reported by radio that he had arrived at the appointed ground on the tip of the Alligator's Jaws and his men had already set up their weapons and were ready to fight. He also said, "These are the first words said by anyone since the start." The advance had been without incident and is noteworthy only because of its express-like speed. We had witnessed the patrol depart the company lines at exactly 2000. In less than a half-hour, in dark and over formidably rough country, they had progressed as far as average infantry can go in sixty minutes.

They had come to a position which, so far as terrain features were concerned, was almost identical with the ground which brought disaster to a patrol from Charley Company, 17th Regiment, several days later.

Where they had decided to rig their intended deadfall, the upper end of the Alligator's Jaws tapered down to the valley floor. An irrigation ditch looped around this extreme finger-like projection of the ridge. Atop the finger, approximately 125 yards from the ditch, and rising not more than 30 feet above the valley floor, was a last knob, shaped like a camel's hump, with space enough to seat at least half the patrol.

Here were the same simple terrain features which the Charley patrol tried to exploit toward rigging a secure ambush. The knob obviously should be manned since it dominated the trails around the base of the hill along which the Chinese patrols were likely to move after midnight. But a ditch is a dilemma in night operations. Used defensively for cover, it is quite satisfactory, provided one finds the right spot and the enemy does not. Otherwise, the consequence may be a dreadful enfilade. There is no final answer to any of the most acute problems in minor tactics. Time and luck are the chief handmaidens of sound decision. Take the situation of an infantry company defending a strategically important bridge. No rule in the book helps the commander to determine the moment when it is better to destroy the bridge than seek to save it. As for a ditch in night fighting, it may be either a lifesaver or a deathtrap.

In deciding to base on the ditch at the Alligator's Jaws and use its walls to the fullest, Lieut. Wongele Costa took on the same setting that flummoxed the Charley patrol, then organized his ground according to an exactly opposite pattern.

His assault group was put on the high ground. Ten men were put on the knob, nine armed with M1s, one with a carbine. All carried four grenades apiece. Other than arms, they carried one radio, a sound power phone, one red flare to signal for the arranged fires, one green flare to request help from the main line and one amber star cluster to message that they were returning.

Each flare was handled by a different man: he would not fire it except on order from the patrol leader. It was an extra precaution taken by the Ethiopians while on patrol but not observed by our own troops. They considered themselves too weak in radio technicians and therefore put greater reliance on old-fashioned signals.

Cpl. Raffi Degene was left in charge of the assault group. They sought rock cover and did not dig in.

Wongele Costa then led the support party to the ditch, a dirt-banked structure raised a foot or so above the flat confronting it. The ditch turned sharply at the point where he established the force. There were but seven men to be deployed. The weapons available to hold the ditch were three M1s, two BARs, two carbines and forty hand grenades. He split his force in two wings, so that three men faced north on the right of the turn and four men faced west to left of it.

In so doing, his thinking was that the two flanks would be mutually supporting along the ditch, if either got hit. The chance of enfilade had been reduced. The approaches to the hill were covered from two directions.

He did not calculate, however, that the group on the low ground was more likely to figure in an initial interception than the men on the heights. No trail led directly to the ditch position, though several paths skirted it and merged where the ditch rounded the finger end just north of the assault position. Hence as Wongele Costa envisaged the main possibilities of his ambush, the Chinese might start climbing the Alligator's Jaws, become routed by the assault group, and in flight to their own country, be taken by flanking fire from the support. That was why he put both BARs in the ditch. He had been ordered to take prisoners if possible. Because of the low visibility, he saw little chance of doing it unless the enemy virtually stumbled over his men.

One BAR man, Cpl. Tiggu Waldetekle, was left in direct charge of the support. Taking along his runner and the two aid men, the leader then moved upslope to a point halfway between assault and support. He was connected with both groups by phone and with higher levels by phone and radio. His preparations complete, he waited.

Until exactly 0300, the hill was absolute quiet. Wongele Costa had just looked at his watch. His men had been on position six hours and 32 minutes. During that time, the only sounds he had heard were his own voice making the hourly report by radio to the company: "Everything negative." But he knew that the men were awake and watchful. Cpls. Degene and Waldetekle had seen to that. At fifteen-minute intervals, each junior leader made his rounds, crawling from man to man. He pressed the man's hand. The man pressed twice in response. It was their way of assuring an alerted unity.

Both corporals had just crawled to his position and completed their hand check. Wongele Costa had called the company and his two assistants were already back with their men.

As Waldetekle slid back into his position with the support group, he saw the men on the left, pointing vigorously out into the enveloping darkness

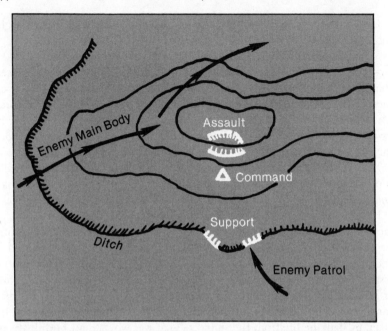

The patrol was split, half of it deploying into a ditch, the other half holding the high ground.

with their rifles. It was the signal that they detected enemy movement. He moved to them. Then he could see a figure in clear silhouette standing not more than 20 yards beyond the ditch.

Waldetekle backtracked along the ditch, then crawled again to Wongele Costa, saying nothing, but pointing with his rifle as his men had done. The lieutenant sent Private Tilahullninguse crawling uphill to give the same signal to Degene and his men. The whole alert had been carried out soundlessly. All weapons were now pointed in the direction where the one Chinese had been seen. Then, for a few seconds, Wongele Costa waited, confident that his own presence and preparations had not been detected.

Waldetekle crawled to him again, gesturing still more vigorously with the rifle. It was the sign that he had seen several other Chinese moving along the same axis.

To Wongele Costa's left, a shallow gully ran unevenly toward the ditch. Using hand signals, he told Tilahullninguse to unpin a grenade, crawl down the gully and bomb into the enemy group. It was done as directed. Wongele Costa was still certain that the Chinese were unalerted and wholly within his field of fire. But he was bent on capturing prisoners and he figured—wrongly, as developments were to prove—that one grenade would hardly more than momentarily upset them and enable the support group to bag them before they could recoil.

Tilahullninguse was 15 yards uphill from the nearest Chinese when he loosed his throw. As the grenade exploded, by its light, Wongele Costa could see about twenty of the enemy. More than that, they were deployed, lying flat and with weapons pointed straight toward his support line, which so far hadn't fired a shot.

As the scene went dark again, the enemy opened fire against the ditch with grenades, rifles and submachine guns. Not more than five seconds elapsed between the explosion and the answering volley. Before Wongele Costa had time to shout an order, the left wing of the support group had joined the fight full blast, three rifles and the BAR.

In this way began a duel almost without parallel in modern war. The opposing lines were just a little less than 15 yards apart. (The distance was tape measured on the following day.) At that range, as the shooting began, the odds were four riflemen against twenty. Only Waldetekle's left wing was free to trade fire with the enemy. His right flank weapons were interdicted from fire by the turn in the ditch. From its position on the knob, the assault group could not bring weapons to bear on the Chinese without risking that the volley would slaughter the four Ethiopians who were fighting. These things, Wongele Costa weighed within the first few seconds while watching the fire flash. He made his decision.

There was just time to call the assault group on the sound power phone and say, "Don't move! Don't fire! Now send a man down to the right flank of the support and give them that same message." Then he turned to Tilahullninguse and his two aid men and said, "Follow me!" On hands and knees, he moved down the gully which cut through Waldetekle's position, stopping every few feet to fire his carbine. The three men behind him did the same.

Their entry into the ditch was timed precisely to save the position, though the re-enforcement did no more than plug the gaps cut into ranks. The ditch, which was running about one foot of water, was deep enough to provide full body cover for the line of riflemen. But to fire, a man had to come head and shoulder above the embankment, and Waldetekle's halfsquad had chosen to face it, though bullets beat like hail against the bank.

A grenade sailed in, bounced off the bank and exploded as it struck just above Waldetekle's elbow. His right arm was blown off clean just below the shoulder socket. He uttered neither cry nor groan. The others didn't know he was hurt until with his left hand he passed the BAR to Private Yukonsi, saying, "Fire, and keep it low." Thereafter, he continued to give orders.

Yukonsi triggered the weapon for only a few seconds. Then a burp-gun burst hit him in the left arm, shredding it from wrist to shoulder. The BAR was still in working order. Yukonsi handed it to Tilahullninguse without a word, then collapsed in the ditch unconscious from loss of blood.

On the extreme left of the line, Pvt. Mano Waldemarian took three bullets through his brain. But in the frenzy of the action, no one saw him fall.

Wongele Costa yelled to the two aid men to take over the grenading. Then he propped against the ditch bank and let go with the carbine, firing full automatic. During the remainder of the duel, he worked as a rifleman, leaving the directing to Waldetekle. The point-blank exchange continued for another fifteen minutes. Wongele Costa—a precise man—timed it with his wrist watch. But once all five weapons were brought to bear in volume, the enemy fire ranged increasingly higher, and there were no more casualties in the ditch.

A messenger from the assault group came crawling down the gully. Word of the action had been sent the battalion commander, Lieut. Col. Wolde Yohanis Shitta. He was asking, "Shall I send help?"

Wongele Costa replied, "Tell him no. Tell him I can hold this field with my own men." The messenger left and the lieutenant resumed fire.

Action was temporarily suspended when at last Waldetekle cried, "There's nothing coming back." Wongele Costa called, "Hold fire!" and then listened. It was true. Either the enemy had been wholly destroyed or its discouraged remnant had been driven off. There was not then time to look. The BAR had gone dry. The carbine was empty and the aid men had thrown their last grenades.

By radio Wongele Costa called for flares over the position, as had been prearranged with the 48th Field Artillery Battalion under Lieut. Col. Joseph S. Kimmitt. Within the next minute he got four rounds. They lighted the hill and the ditch bright as day, and, in so doing, diverted attention from what had transpired in the foreground.

As the lights came on, Wongele Costa glanced toward the hill at his back. Then he saw it: an entire Chinese platoon, deployed in skirmish order, was advancing up the nose of the ridge. The line of approximately fifty men was in that second still upright and marching straight toward the assault group. In the next second, the line had gone flat, thereby foiling the lights. The Chinese were still about 100 yards short of the position on the knob.

"VT fire on White—all you can give me." That was the radio message from Wongele Costa to the artillery. If the proximity fuse shells came in as directed, they would just miss his own men and stonk the enemy in the "white" area. He got his barrage in exactly thirty seconds and it landed right on the button. From his post in the ditch, he could see the rounds exploding into the enemy line and he could hear the outcries of the wounded. In less than one minute the formation was broken. Some of the Chinese ran for the base of the hill. Others ran forward looking for a hole or a rock.

In that interval, Wongele Costa abandoned his position on the left side of the ditch. The casualties were carried to the position on the right flank. But in the darkness, he missed one man, not knowing that Waldemarian was dead. So he called for lights again to assist the search. When the flare came on, he could see Waldemarian in the ditch. He sat there in a natural position, the rifle folded close in his arms. Wongele Costa crawled over to him, found that he was dead and so returned, carrying the body. Thereby he simply followed the tradition of his corps. Fiercely proud of the loyalty of their men, officers of the Imperial Guard are likely to say to a stranger, "Should trouble come, stay with me, I'll be the last man to die." But in battle, it is the officer invariably who takes the extra risk to save one of his own.

There had been no letup in the VT barraging of the nose of the ridge. Costa simply had it shifted forward a short space to choke off escape. Then Corporal Degene called him to say that from the knob, he could hear the Chinese reassembling on the other side of the finger, downslope 70 or 80 yards from his position.

Wongele Costa again called the artillery, "Keep the fires going on White. But give me more VT and put it on Red."

Fifty-five seconds later, the new barrage dropped on the far flank of the hill. Thereafter, for 65 minutes, the fires were continued unrelentingly against the "White" nose of the hill and the "Red" slope.

The patrol merely continued to hold ground. Degene's men neither shifted position nor fired a shot. Unassisted, the artillery broke the back of the Chinese attack.

Wongele Costa and assistants had long since returned to their position between the two groups. The aid men had tourniqueted and quieted the wounded. They would have to last it with the others.

At 0430 Colonel Shitta called the lieutenant to ask how things were going.

Wongele Costa replied, "The only live Chinese in this valley are in our hands."

Said Shitta, "If that's it, you might as well return."

So Wongele Costa got the patrol reassembled and on the trail. To the number of twenty-two, they had counted enemy dead in their foreground. They were confident that with the help of the artillery, they had wounded at least as many more. Two badly shot-up prisoners had been taken.

The wounded and dead were put in the van of the column. Costa helped bear Waldemarian's body. They started uptrail and at last closed on the company lines at 0535. They still looked fresh in the full light of a lovely dawn.

There is but one note needed in summary. Wongele Costa and his twenty men were having their first experience under fire. Theirs was the first patrol sent from the newly arrived Ethiopian battalion which had come to Korea boasting that it would outshine the old Kagnew Battalion, which was a shining outfit.

But these men knew their ground, almost as a man knows the palm of his own hand. Following the method used by the old battalion, four afternoons successively, prior to the pay run, all members of the patrol had marched to the entrenched height on the Alligator's Jaws which overlooked the flat they had chosen to give battle. There they had spent hours studying the distances, the relation of one slope to another and the likely application of weapons, according to the probable contingencies.

The start of their debriefing followed the combat by less than two hours. Wongele Costa said, "Every detail of that ground had become part of a print in my mind. It was like moving in my own house. I could see in the dark."

Double Ambush

At two hours before midnight on 10 may, 1953, a twenty-four-man patrol from Charley Company, 17th Infantry Regiment, started a starlit march toward T-Bone Hill.

They were led by 2nd Lieut. Ronald A. Monier, who had not yet been under fire. As they began the descent from the main-line ridge, moving single file along the trail winding to the valley, there was a normal expectation that within four hours they would return whole and hearty, reporting a negative end to a routine mission.

Their commander, Lieut. Stephen J. Patrick, watched them vanish into the downslope darkness and then went to OP 17 from where he would follow them by radio.

The assigned route took them into no-man's country with its chance of hostile contact. But the Korean night was calm and clear, the men were buoyantly fresh and the mission was too limited to make an open fight seem likely.

Charley Company's trench overlooked two strongly fortified outposts garrisoned by Americans 600 yards forward of the Army main line. The perimeters of these small subridges, Erie and Arsenal, fairly dominated that part of the valley bottom where the patrol would nest.

Monier had been ordered to advance past Arsenal to where its forward fingers tapered to the low ground. There, at a distance approximately 900 yards north of the Arsenal trenches, he was to deploy the patrol defensively and sit tight. The object in all such operations was to ambush an enemy patrol if possible, or capture prisoners, or forestall surprise against the main line. Provided none of these opportunities arose, the patrol would hold ground for four hours and then return to home base.

By Korean war standards, it was a conventional design. The start this time was auspicious. During the march, all things went perfectly. Monier was delighted that his men moved right along and maintained just the right interval. They did their 1,500 yards in complete silence and got to the appointed ground without once breaking their good march order.

Come to the terminus of Arsenal's most forward finger, the patrol split in two. The "support group" of twelve men, led by SFC Julio S. Varela, deployed as a crescent around the last knob of the finger, their backs toward Arsenal, their weapons sighted forward.

Monier and his dozen continued on another 100 yards. That interval put the "assault group" in the bottom of a sandy wash and next the embankment of an irrigation canal which followed a twisting course around the base of Arsenal. The ditch was, in fact, between the two halves of the patrol. Some of the men groused to each other that its high banks gave the enemy a perfect approach to inside the position. But they said nothing to Monier. So the forward group there formed another defensive crescent facing toward the ditch.

There ensued for the twenty-four men under Monier an eventless and prolonged semivigil. At the assault position several old 60-mm mortar holes were convenient to the purpose. Apart from the shallow cover these pits provided, the patrol did not dig in. With the lengthening of the night and the ceasing of all activity, their senses dulled and even the best soldiers among them felt an almost overpowering urge to sleep.

But along the friendly heights to rearward of them, there was a sense of danger not shared by the patrol. This violated the familiar rule in Korean operations. Usually in his movement through disputed country, the Chinese enemy was so furtive that he gave no preliminary warning to the defenders on the heights despite their superior observation. It was a common thing for patrols to get within grenade-throwing distance of an enemy column without any warning being sounded. At such close quarters, getting word back to home base without alerting the Chinese was a main problem.

But on this midnight the closest echelons to rearward knew that the valley was crawling with a live danger though no warning word got forward to the twenty-four men nearest its embrace. It was the fault of no one man in particular. There were small slips at various points. All that the rear knew or suspected was not relayed to Monier by phone or radio, and such little information as Monier received, he did not pass along to others in the patrol. Possibly this reticence came of his lack of experience; most of his men were likewise green and in no mood to prod him. In consequence of several lapses in leadership, the patrol for at least ninety minutes carried out its mission perfunctorily, when all the time the rear was aware of developments which would have kept its members fully awake and watchful.

The communications lag which invoked the penalty is almost exactly measurable. Monier's men continued at a halfway alert right till the moment when they were due to withdraw. By their own account, as 0200 hours approached, they were taking it easy with no sweat. The initial tension had passed completely and most of the men were sprawled and resting. Said Pfc. Eldridge J. Linkous afterward, "Not one word had been said about the enemy; after three hours of waiting, I felt perfectly safe."

But on the big ridge to the rear of Arsenal Outpost, at thirty minutes past midnight, Lieut. Omer L. Coble, Jr., of the battalion staff, had received a message from the men manning Outguard No. 11. That listening post was at the base of Arsenal and covered one of its flanks. Its men had seen a party of twelve Chinese approach to within 50 yards of their ground. Taking a quick reckoning of the terrain and distance, Coble figured that he could put up lights to reassure the outguard and still not endanger the patrol. But he checked with Monier on that point and was told to go ahead. Also, his request for the flares was approved by Maj. Earl C. Acuff, the battalion commander.

The mortar section of Baker Company, which was to fire the flares, was behind Erie Outpost. Because of uncertainty over the target area, possibly compounded by Coble's instructions cautioning against high-lighting the patrol, the shoot was long delayed. Finally, two rounds were gotten off. The outguard reported that the second one had shone directly over the desired spot and had scared away the enemy.

Again at 0145 Coble was called. The reserve platoon on Arsenal had heard an unknown number of enemy moving around on the slope behind the CP. Coble told them, "Grenade your wire and then investigate." This they did, but found nothing. Almost coincidentally a work detail from Charley Company reported "enemy moving" on the forward slope of Erie Outpost. Via the hot loop, Coble passed this information to the companies and again asked permission to fire flares.

By then Lieutenant Patrick's company loop was alive with information. Outguard No. 11, on the slope which faced toward Erie, was again calling. It could see between fifty and sixty Chinese milling around on the ground between Erie and Arsenal. Could the battalion help out by firing some lights over that area? Coble concluded that it was a good idea. He again called the Baker mortar section and ordered the firing of flares between the two outposts. Again, there was the prolonged delay in executing the order.

Adding these reports, then discounting them by half, the indications remained strong that the Chinese in superior numbers held ground between the patrol and home base. Yet what the company and the battalion surmised either did not get through to the patrol, or if Monier heard it, he still did not share the information with his men. They remained sleepily unaware. Pvt. Charles Riddle, who was carrying the phone for Monier, heard Coble request and receive permission to fire the flares. But Riddle was a new soldier and to him the message conveyed nothing. Pltn. Sgt. Jack D. Robbins did not even hear that much and his confidence that the night was clear of danger continued unabated.

At 0200, Monier, checking his watch, said to Robbins, "It's time to call the company." Robbins nodded and walked away a little distance. Riddle handed the phone to Monier, then stepped back a few feet, not noticing that the wire was looped around his leg.

The conversation lasted not more than five seconds.

Monier said, "Negative. Shall we withdraw?"

Patrick replied, "Hold just a few minutes. Someone between us and Baker. We want to check."

As Patrick finished, the sharp rattle of automatic fire and several loud explosions came at him over the phone. Then Monier's voice yelling, "Hell's fire!" At that point SFC Joe Lopez of the support group cut into the loop just long enough to say, "We're hit!" The line went dead and Patrick heard nothing more from Monier.

To say what killed the phone is easier than to explain how the surprise was put upon the patrol. Exactly as Monier called, the Chinese sprang their trap. The triangular-shaped ambush had been drawn up between the two groups so that it covered Monier's crescent full length. Undetected, the enemy had worked to within 20 to 35 yards of the assault party. Apparently timed to some signal—perhaps Monier's call—the Chinese grenadiers and tommy gunners had opened fire together. For a few seconds, Riddle, the phone man, galvanized by shock, stood rooted to the spot. Then he dove for the nearest cover and, diving, with the wire twined about his leg, broke the connection.

Thereby Monier was cut away both from the higher levels and from his twelve men to rearward. All that saved his own party in this first crisis was that the enemy was too eager even as the patrol was too incautious. Except for Monier, Riddle and Robbins, the men were already prone, though not guarding and ready to fire. A flattened, motionless man on a dark night is not a satisfactory target even for point-blank musketry. Had the enemy but marked time for a few minutes, the group might have been caught formed and standing. That opening grenade shower, exploding among the Americans, failed to hit flesh; in fact, most of the bombs fell short. The automatic fire was high. But it was not high enough for Monier's men to feel like raising their heads or turning until they could bring their own weapons to bear. So there was no counteraction. The Americans simply lay there under and amid the whistling steel, helpless but for the moment unharmed. It was a temporary reprieve, made so by the bad shooting and hesitancy of the enemy. Having virtually won the skirmish with the perfectly staged ambush, the Chinese forbore to clinch it with a closing rush.

Robbins, like Riddle, had hit the dirt. That left Monier the only man not prone. He still knelt by the telephone. His first flash reaction, in the seconds when shock passed and his wits returned, was to call Varela for help. But as he fumbled with the instrument, trying to raise the support party, suddenly the sky came bright not more than 120 yards to his rear. Varela's knob stood out boldly under the glare. Monier shouted into the dead phone, "What's happening back there? What's happening?" In his excitement, he didn't realize that the line wasn't working, while Riddle, watching this vain effort detachedly, was too stunned to tell him.

For perhaps one full minute the assault party continued in this weird tableau, the men pinned, Monier trying to raise someone on a dead line, the fire sweeping overhead, the enemy too fearful to close, the front of the patrol full beset and paralyzed, its members counting for survival on help from the rear element.

That faint hope was already dashed, though Monier's party remained unaware. Varela's party, formed in their loose semicircle on ground 30 feet higher than Monier's, should have had the best fighting chance, all other things being equal.

In greater strength than opposed Monier, a second enemy wing stalked Varela. But its skirmishers had not yet fixed the position with a tight ambush. They were still groping and closing when the thing happened.

Belatedly the mortar battery from Baker Company fired its two flares as ordered by Lieutenant Coble. They were intended to illuminate the vale between Arsenal and Erie. But the crew had been listening to too many coordinates that night and the lights missed their target by a country mile.

Flaming on the wrong side of Arsenal ridge, they drifted directly down on Varela's party, transfixing it like a poacher shining deer. Suddenly every man in the crescent was under bright light. Sergeant Lopez got off one last frantic message to Patrick, "The lights are on top of us. For God's sake stop them!" Then Patrick heard the line go dead. It was the final message between patrol and company. But it was too late. The damage was done.

Two lines of Chinese had been converging toward Varela's knob when the lights came on. The physical evidence suggests they could not have been more than 35 or 40 yards away. But the Americans, stone-blinded by the magnesium glare, saw nothing. They knew the Chinese were there in the moment when their spotlighted stage was riven by an intense crossfire from automatic guns.

Pfc. Thomas L. Colvin, the radio man, was hit in the head by a burst which opened his skull and laid his brain bare, though he still lived.

Pvt. Pak Hak Soon, rifleman, took three bullets through his legs and one through his right shoulder.

Sgt. Robert W. Pratt, who was acting as forward observer for the mortars, was hit in the hand, back and chest.

Pvt. Donald B. Bashaw, who had been on the sniperscope, was dead, six bullets in his neck and head.

Sergeant Lopez was also hit six times, both arms, both hands, both legs.

But of these deep and mortal wounds inflicted in the early seconds, the few who survived whole-bodied saw and felt nothing. They were still sightless from the glare's aftereffect. The noise of enemy fire drowned every outcry.

The first flare parachuted down to land not more than five yards from Cpl. James R. Hammond who was third man from Varela. The second parachute hit earth about 35 yards behind the knob. By then the scene was again dark. But while the hapless targets were less naked to the fire, vision did not swiftly return.

Again, had the enemy rushed, every man would have been lost. For at least two or three minutes the Chinese maintained fire from the distance. When at last Varela's sight cleared, a Chinese stood directly over him, arm cocked to throw a grenade. Varela pulled the trigger of his M1 and the man dropped.

Varela unpinned a grenade. Before he could heave it, enemy grenades fell all around him. They came in batches, five or six at a time. He felt that he was surrounded and probably alone on the knob—an inaccurate impression. Instinct made him thresh out with arms and legs as the grenades came in, kicking and pushing them away. His guardian angel must have stood with him. At least a dozen bombs exploded just outside the circle of his reach but not one fragment touched his body.

So unremitting had been the pressure that his own grenade was still in his hand, kept inoperative only by the tight clenching of his fist. There was no time to throw it, though retaining it compounded his danger. If stunned, he would die from his own bomb.

As the bombardment slackened momentarily, Varela rolled off the knob and crawled on his belly toward the irrigation ditch. He still knew nothing of what had happened to his men, his own ordeal having kept him insensible to all else that went on. But he knew that whether any of the others still lived, at least the chance for successful resistance on the group's chosen ground had died with the lights.

Varela crawled deeper into the rice paddy, feeling surprise that no enemy moved to stop him. Halfway along he got his answer. From beyond the canal bank, submachine-gun fire searched the muddy flat. Varela counted at least four weapons firing from behind the bank. With the situation delivered wholly into their hands, the Chinese had "chickened" and sought the cover of the waist-high embankment.

In the muck Varela overtook Pvt. Ronald P. Devries, who was barely dragging along, due to a shattered hip. Beyond Devries were Private Soon, thrice wounded, and Cpl. Robert Fontaine, with a bullet in his right arm. Varela slowed to the pace of the three hit men.

The last to close on this battered group was Pvt. Gonzales Carmela, Puerto Rican, the only man who had used a weapon at the original position, the last fighter to withdraw from the knob.

Carmela is built like a bull, blond, blue-eyed, ruddy-faced, a singular type for a Latin. He speaks no English; so Varela, the boy from the Southwest, had been his channel to the platoon.

While still blinded from the lights, he had fired two clips from his M1, just getting the stuff out as best he could. Then the rifle fouled from a ruptured cartridge. By the time he could see again, there seemed to be no one moving on the knob. Sergeant Pratt, thrice wounded, was still sticking it, and would continue to do so, trying to raise the mortar section on radio so that he could report the plight of the patrol. But this Carmela didn't know.

So he stood up and walked away. When he reached the paddy and the bullet fire came against him, he continued on hands and knees. Until he overtook Varela, he had maintained himself in utter solitude. As he explained, the overpowering sound and fury of the fire fight had excluded all sensation of the near presence of other men. He said, "I could feel me and the fire. I lived. The object of the fire was to kill me. So I fired." Elementary, but still the hardest lesson to drive into an infantryman's head.

Pulling along the others, Varela and Carmela got to within 15 yards of the ditch bank. There Varela called halt. He knew that Soon, Devries and Fontaine were useless because of their arm wounds. So he whispered, "Give me your grenades." With the six which he collected, he had eight. Carmela was carrying three.

Then on Varela's signal, he and Carmela stood together and grenaded into the ditch. As the bombs went off, they could see the water splash. And they could hear the screaming of the Chinese along the embankment. They were certain that their metal had bit into some of the targets and demoralized others. For the moment, the enemy weapons were struck silent.

Feeble as was this action, it was the only piece of timed and collected counterhitting by members of the patrol. And it lasted less than one minute.

With the throwing of the last grenade, Varela and Carmela pulled the other three to their feet, and as best they could, the five men moved

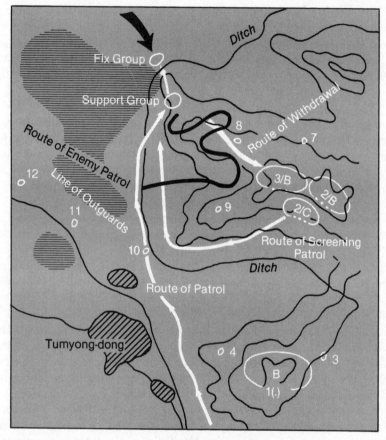

Monier's advance and the Communist penetration.

obliquely across the paddy. Varela wanted to get to Monier; he did not know that the assault group was already close engaged; his own ordeal excluded all impression of things elsewhere.

Devries could no longer walk. Varela carried him piggyback. Carmela put an arm under Soon's shoulder. Their route would take them through the ditch at the point where it cut the line between the patrol's two initial positions. They tried to run because the tommy-gun fire was again nipping at them.

Lopez, Hammond and the few others who had escaped the knob immediately all ran directly toward Monier while Varela and his party were attacking across the paddy. All had been wounded, and none was any longer in condition to fight.

They could not have reached the canal bank at a worse moment either for themselves or for the good of Monier's party. The whole action had not yet lasted five minutes and Monier was still paralyzed by the circumstances. The Chinese who had boxed in his crescent were concentrated between the two halves of the patrol with their center anchored on the canal-bank turn.

Startled by the burning of the flares on their rear, the Chinese skirmishers contracted toward the ditch and, in so doing, disunified and reduced their fire. Thereby for the first time, Monier's men came relatively free to move and to think about using their own weapons.

Pfc. Robert W. Krause swung his BAR into action, aiming at the ditch bank. Sergeant Robbins yelled, "Everybody fire! Everybody fire!" Several riflemen joined Krause.

They barely got started. Then they heard cries out of the target area. "Lieutenant Monier. Lieutenant Monier. Where are you? Don't shoot. We're coming in."

Krause yelled, "Cease fire! That's Lopez." Over the sights of his weapon, he could see five or six men rise up along the canal bank, amid the Chinese, and lurch toward him.

Monier also realized these were his own men. He yelled, "Don't shoot! Don't shoot! That's the support." That stayed all hands just in the nick of time. The position had to go quiet to save Lopez, Hammond and others in the first group of walking wounded. Hobbling toward Monier from the ditch, they masked the enemy position just a few feet to their rear.

This sudden appearance was hardly less confusing to the Chinese than to Monier. They could have won in that moment by redoubling their small-arms fire. Instead, they stopped. Then a few of them arose and, following along behind Lopez' group, used the Americans as a shield while grenading over their heads toward Monier.

By then, Varela and his group were approaching the same canal turn, so

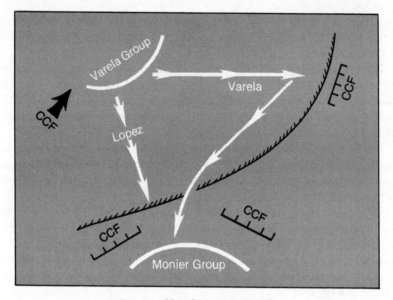

Re-assembly of Monier's Patrol.

that, in effect, the deployment was like a four-layer cake, alternately American and Chinese. Varela still carried Devries. But both he and Devries had been hit by grenade shards during the last stretch.

It was an unbelievable entanglement executed in slow motion. Due to the reeling pace of the walking wounded and the folly of the enemy in not standing as a firm fire block, the agonizingly slow convergence but compounded confusion to both sides. At this stage one eddy of resolute action on either side might have made a stampede.

Varela caught up with Lopez just after crossing the canal. Lopez said, "I'm done. You take over." But there was nothing to take over. Both were aware that they were moving almost cheek-to-jowl amid the Chinese. They could do nothing about it except lurch onward toward Monier.

Sergeant Robbins watched this strange formation approach. Almost spellbound by the spectacle, and feeling his own nerve unravel, he was jarred out of it when a grenade bounced off his helmet and exploded. Suddenly he was at dead center of the enemy grenade shower. As Varela had done earlier, he gave over all else to fend off the missiles landing in his personal circle. While succeeding in this mad scramble, he heard cries from two of his men which told him they had been hit.

Again it was Private Krause, the BAR man, who led by example when all other kind of leading failed. Krause saw one of Varela's men crawling toward him from the ditch bank. Behind the American came two Chinese grenading toward Krause. The wounded man was about 20 yards away when Krause rolled to escape the first grenade, then rolled the other way to clear the second. The leading Chinese got to within five yards when, having dodged two more grenades, Krause triggered his weapon and shot down both Chinese. One of them had already blasted toward Krause with a submachine gun and was less than 10 yards away when Krause killed him.

Having started, Krause maintained fire until he had spent half a magazine. He couldn't be sure of friend or foe. But wherever he saw an unhelmeted head, that was his target.

Twenty-five yards away from Robbins, on the extreme left of the defensive crescent, lay Cpl. Richard E. Murdock, rifleman. So far, he had been a bystander, doing nothing. It had seemed to him that when Monier gave the order, "Don't shoot!" the Chinese grenadiers had arisen and moved via their right flank, so that they bore directly down on him. For a few seconds, he watched, certain he would be overrun, yet holding his hand because of Monier's order.

That changed when a Chinese stood almost directly over him firing a burp gun toward Monier's end of the line. Murdock didn't have to aim his M1 to kill the man; there was no way to miss. A second Chinese came right behind him and was dropped by one round. Then from 15 yards out, two Chinese rushed him, grenading as they ran. Both grenades missed and the two Chinese ran right over Murdock. Turning, he threw a grenade without aiming. By sheer luck, it exploded between the pair, felling both of them.

Murdock yelled, "I did it! I did it!" So intense was his feeling of personal relief that seconds passed before he realized there were no longer any targets in sight. He looked around. The scene had become almost inanimate. The rest of the enemy had vanished into the landscape.

Intrinsically brief as were these two personal stands by private soldiers, Krause and Murdock, they were pivotal in effect. In the end, they saved most of the patrol to fight another day. None other among Monier's men had reacted in the same strong way during the critical minute when it seemed that everything was lost. The others did not shrink from duty. It was simply that they could not see anything to be done.

Privates Linkous, Riddle and Wilson still had not fired. So swift had been the transitions in situation that they could not understand what was going on or distinguish friend from foe. Wilson in particular was looking for a chance to fight and was angry that he had been thus far balked.

Again, Monier had jumped for the telephone, still not realizing that it was dead. He wanted flares put over the scene. Since they could hardly have helped him, and the patrol's scrambled situation was beyond effective intervention by the artillery, it is perhaps just as well that he couldn't get through.

Robbins moved toward Monier to tell him that it was useless to call. Before he could reach him, Cpl. J. B. Craft sprawled between them crying, "I'm hit." Monier said, "We better get out of here," then stopped to feel for the wound in Craft's body.

A grenade exploded between Robbins and Monier. The blast knocked Robbins off his feet and backwards. Some of the fragments cut into Monier who, though Robbins didn't know it, was already carrying five burp-gun bullets in his legs.

Stunned, Robbins momentarily lost his feeling of what was happening. When his brain cleared, he could see some of the men already in motion toward the canal along the path back to Arsenal. He started after them, not knowing that Monier was still down and unconscious.

In this way the two leaders lost contact. Craft also had arisen from beside Monier and started back. From out of the darkness, occasional grenades pitched and exploded onto the ground where the patrol had been. There was no more automatic fire.

Carmela, the strong Puerto Rican, loaded the helpless Devries on his back and started for Charley Company's home on the big ridge. He made it, 1,500 uphill yards, carrying his wounded comrade all the way.

Robbins got only so far as the knob which the support group had occupied. There, seeing a huddle of his men, and hoping to get them reorganized, he called out, "What kind of weapons you got?" Himself so dazed that he could not remember whether he had come the 100 yards walking or crawling, he still had the wholly mistaken impression that only three or four members of the patrol had been hit. That illusion died when he checked the group of nine. Every man was weaponless. All were too badly hit to do much more than stumble along.

Bashaw's body was there, the sniperscope beside it. Murdock felt for his pulse and said, "Dead." Pvt. Jimmy R. Wilson wanted to be sure. He also felt the pulse and said, "You're right; he's very dead."

Sergeant Pratt, the mortar FO, shot in back, hands and chest, was still at his radio working, at last in the act of raising the Baker mortar section. He told them that the patrol was shattered and that a succoring party was needed to get the survivors back to Arsenal.

The people on Erie relayed that message to Lieutenant Coble. He was told that the men under Robbins would mark time at the foot of Arsenal. It was the only message received by anyone in the battalion and it proved to be wrong.

Robbins reckoned that there was still death all around him, and if anyone was to be saved, it was best to get his dependents moving. At first they strove to reach the high ground bringing out their dead and wounded. But it was a vain effort. Then Private Wilson protested that they were uselessly spending the residue of strength which might enable them to save Colvin. There had been no need to check the pulse of the man with the shattered skull; he was screaming high in delirium.

So they left Bashaw's body there and struggled on. Their main enemy was now the slope. Such was the weight of the wounded that they could move upward only a few feet at a time. In the next hour they moved only 150 yards.

During this vulnerable passage the Chinese dogged their footsteps. On both sides enemy flankers moved parallel to the column. There was no fire. But the Americans were mocked by derisive calls and the jangling of cowbells from out of the darkness.

Private Soon, slowed by his wounds, fell into enemy hands. Before dawn he would show up at an outguard post on Erie with a strange story about contriving escape by feigning death.

At 0315 the men in the center of Third Platoon's position on Arsenal heard repeatedly a plaintive call coming from beyond their belt of protective wire.

"Gist! Gist! Come help me."

They were baffled by it because the slope in that sector was supposedly interdicted by a tightly laid minefield. But they passed the word to 2nd Lieut. Roy A. Gist. He crawled through the wire and found Lieutenant Monier flattened on the far side.

Monier was badly dazed and bleeding hard. Consciousness had returned to him shortly after Robbins had left the position. But in his shocked condition he had missed the trail, gone to the wrong ridge finger and kept climbing. His erratic course took him directly through the minefield. When the wire stopped him, he at last got his bearings and called for help.

Even so, he had returned before the patrol. From him, Gist and the others got the first word of how the patrol had been ambushed. Gist got him through the wire and carried him to the CP. Already, Gist had volunteered to lead a rescue mission. He rounded up twelve men and led them through the minefield along a marked path leading to a listening post, approximately reversing Monier's upward journey.

Within a few minutes, they were at the knob where Varela had been hit. Because of Pratt's message to Coble, Gist had expected to find the survivors there. He found no one.

So he called out for the two men in the patrol whom he knew best.

"Craft! Fontaine! Craft! Fontaine!"

From just a short distance up the finger, Craft answered, "I'm here." The party under Robbins had all but foundered. Robbins sent Krause down to guide Gist's group to him. Then the worst wounded were loaded on litters.

They were ready to start climbing when someone said, referring to Bashaw's body, "But we've left a man behind."

Gist answered, "Then we have to get him."

Private Wilson again lost his temper. "Damn it, Lieutenant," he said, "that man is dead."

Said Gist, "We've got to be sure." He then told SFC Kenneth G. Booth of his own party to take along another man and bring back Bashaw.

Young Wilson, nettled to the limit, volunteered for the job, saying, "Damn it, I'll go along to show you that he's dead." He turned back to the valley.

When they reached Bashaw, Wilson again felt for a pulse beat. Then he tried to shoulder the dead weight. The sergeant meantime was covering him, with his rifle pointing downtrail. Bashaw was heavy. The weight was beyond Wilson's strength. As he struggled with it, Booth called, "Chinese coming up the finger!"

Wilson said, "Damn it, we got to leave this man."

Before Booth could give him an argument, they were engaged by rifle and grenade fire. Both men returned it with their M1s and Wilson threw his last two grenades. Still more grenades came in on them.

Wilson yelled, "Damn it, follow me. I'm getting out of here."

They legged it toward Gist. As they rejoined the party, Wilson said to him, "If you want me to bring that man out, you better give me a few hands who can do some fighting."

His complete earnestness won Gist over. He could no longer see any logic in risking additional lives toward recovering a body. He said, "Let's march."

The fifth litter was loaded and the last of the patrol was started uphill.

When they counted heads on reaching Arsenal's first-aid station, six men were still unaccounted for. Four of them showed up later at Erie. They had missed their way in the darkness and wandered until they heard a friendly challenge.

At dawn Lieut. Roberto L. Cordova led another patrol down from Arsenal to recover Bashaw's body. They also salvaged part of the litter left in the patrol's wake—telephone, radio, sniperscope, BAR, three M1s and five carbines, the last all fully loaded.

As they lifted cargo to start the return journey, cowbells jangled among the wild thorn beyond the canal. The morning was delightfully calm but the enemy still lingered in the valley.

The Incredible Patrol

Like Horatius at the bridge or the screaming eagles at Bastogne, it was a classic fight, ending in clean triumph over seemingly impossible odds. But unlike other great tales of war which become legend, it went unsung, though it happened almost under the noses of 163 war correspondents then in Seoul, forty minutes' air flight from the fight. Held spell-bound by the headline values of Operation Little Switch, they had neither time nor space for the reporting of epic courage. Such abberations are common in modern warfare. Homeric happenings go unreported. Sometimes the bravest meet death with their deeds known only to heaven.

If another reason is needed for now unfolding the tale, there is this, that of all troops which fought in Korea, the Ethiopians stood highest in the quality of their officer-man relationships, the evenness of their performance under fire and the mastery of techniques by which they achieved near perfect unity of action in adapting themselves to new weapons during training and in using them to kill efficiently in battle.

They couldn't read maps but they never missed a trail.

Out of dark Africa came these men, thin, keen eyed, agile of mind and 95 per cent illiterate. They could take over U. S. Signal Corps equipment and in combat make it work twice as well as the best-trained American troops. When they engaged, higher headquarters invariably knew exactly what they were doing. The information which they fed back by wire and radio was far greater in volume and much more accurate than anything coming from American actions.

Their capacities excelled also in one diversionary aspect of the soldierly arts. There are no better whisky drinkers under the sun. They take it neat, a full tumbler at a time, without pause or chaser, and seem abashed that Americans can't follow suit. This unexampled skill might properly become a proper object for research by a top-level military mission.

Their one lack was a good press. The Turks, the ROKs, the Commonwealth Division and others in the medley got due notice. But the Ethiopians stood guard along their assigned ridges in a silence unbroken by the questions of the itinerant correspondents. They were eager to welcome strangers and tell how they did it. But no one ever asked.

If to our side, at the end as in the beginning, they were the Unknown Battalion, to the Communists they were a still greater mystery. When the final shot was fired, one significant mark stood to their eternal credit. Of all national groups fighting in Korea, the Ethiopians alone could boast that they had never lost a prisoner or left a dead comrade on the battlefield. Every wounded man, every shattered body, had been returned to the friendly fold.

That uniquely clean sheet was not an accident of numbers only. Knowing how to gamble with death, they treated it lightly as a flower. On night patrol, as he crossed the valley and prowled toward the enemy works, the Ethiopian soldier knew that his chance of death was compounded. It was standing procedure in the battalion that if a patrol became surrounded beyond possibility of extrication, the supporting artillery would be ordered to destroy the patrol to the last man. That terrible alternative was never realized. Many times enveloped, the Ethiopian patrols always succeeded in breaking the fire ring and returning to home base. If there were dead or wounded to be carried, the officer or NCO leader was the first to volunteer. When fog threatened to diffuse a patrol, the Ethiopians moved hand in hand, like children. Even so, though they deny it, these Africans are cat-eyed men with an especial affinity for moving and fighting in the dark. In most of the races of man, superstition unfolds with the night, tricking the imagination and stifling courage. It is not so with the Ethiopians. The dark holds no extra terror. It is their element.

Of this in part came the marked superiority in night operations which transfixed the Chinese. It hexed them as if they were fighting the superhuman. The Ethiopian left no tracks, seemingly shed no blood and spoke always in an unknown tongue. Lack of bodily proof that he was mortal made him seem phantom like and forbiddingly unreal.

That may explain why, toward the close, everything done by the Ethiopians seemed so unbelievably easy, even under full sunlight. We watched them from Observation Point 29 through glasses on a fair afternoon in mid-May, 1953, in as mad an exploit as was ever dared by man. Under full observation from enemy country, eight Ethiopians walked 800 yards across no-man's land and up the slope of T-Bone Hill right into the enemy trenches. When next we looked, the eight had become ten. The patrol was dragging back two Chinese prisoners, having snatched them from the embrace of the Communist battalion. It was only then that the American artillery came awake and threw smoke behind them. They got back to our lines unscratched. So far as I know, this feat is unmatched in war. How account for it? Either the hex was working or the Communists thought the patrol was coming in to surrender.

This brazen piece of effrontery took place only three days after the fight of the Incredible Patrol. These were actions by men who had never previously been under fire. Ethiopia sent a fresh battalion every twelve months. Kagnew Battalion—named after the war charger of King Menelik in the first war with Italy—had just sailed for Africa after little more than a year in line, with its men grousing, as soldiers ever do, because they had been held overtime. They were also piqued because the relief battalion was boasting that it was better before it had ever faced the enemy. Thereafter the war lasted just long enough for the new arrivals to supply a few items in solid proof that they might have cleaned it up, but for the papers signed in Panmunjom.

My part in these things was that I was working over all patrols along our part of the front which had met and fought the Chinese. We were trying to get uniformity into our debriefing system so that all data would be equally reliable and we could see where we were making our mistakes.

My work was to get to the survivors immediately and draw out of them all that had happened. It necessitated ridge-hopping by helicopter through the late dark or early light so that I could interview the patrol at the point where it reentered our lines. By dawn, the front was normally quiet save for the singing of larks, thrushes, thrashers and cardinals. It was a wonderful front for bird watchers.

There were fifteen men in the Incredible Patrol under the command of 22-year-old 2nd Lieut. Zeneke Asfaw. They were of the Third Company of the new Battalion Kagnew, and the First Company of that command, under Capt. Behanu Tariau, was garrisoning two outpost hillocks flanking the narrow draw via which Asfaw's party moved toward enemy country.

The plan and scene were typical of many such operations during the last two years of the Korean war. Forming the right flank of the United States 7th Infantry Division along the Eighth Army's main resistance line, the battalion held the crest line of a great ridge which rose about 300 meters above the valley floor. Forward of the great ridge approximately 750 meters were the outpost hillocks, Yoke and Uncle, each entrenched all around its summit, and with slopes well covered by wire entanglements.

Yoke was just large enough to accommodate a platoon. As with a hundred other such small hill positions forward of the Eighth Army's main line, the twofold object in garrisoning Yoke was to parry any attack before the Chinese could reach the big trench, and, also, to lure the enemy into the open where he could be blasted by the markedly superior American

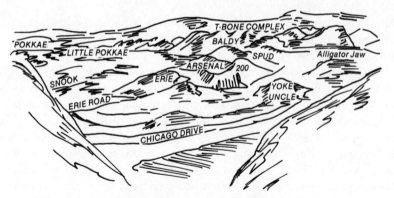

The front along the Yokkokchon as seen from the crest of Hill 327. This sketch was made by a tank gunner and used by him to assist his firing.

artillery. It was wearing duty, for it made troops feel like the bait in a trap. So the garrisons were rotated every five days.

Lieutenant Asfaw's mission on the night of 19 May was to descend into the main valley about 800 yards to the right front of Yoke and in this disputed ground attempt to ambush a Chinese patrol and return with prisoners. This was the more or less routine object in all patrolling. He started his march at eleven o'clock, with his second in command, 21-year-old Cpl. Arage Affere, leading the column. In exactly thirty-five minutes, they reached the bottom. The actual trail distance had been one and one-half miles, partway uphill, where the route traversed two ridge fingers. But they had done most of it at a running walk.

At twenty minutes before midnight, having seen nothing of the enemy, Asfaw decided to halt. The patrol had come to a concrete-walled irrigation ditch. Where Asfaw stood, the ditch did a 90-degree turn, with the elbow pointing directly at T-Bone Hill. To the youngster came the flash inspiration that here was the tailor-made deadfall. Three trails crossed within a few yards of the bend in the ditch. He could deploy his men within the protecting walls and await the enemy. Within the next five minutes he distributed his men evenly around the angle with one Browning automatic rifle on each flank.

It was done in the nick of time. There was the briefest wait. At ten minutes before midnight, Asfaw, straining to catch any movement in the darkness, saw standing in the clear, 300 yards to his front, a lone Chinese. While he looked, approximately one platoon built up on the motionless scout and simply stood there, as if waiting a signal. It was a tempting target; though too distant for his automatic weapons to have more than a

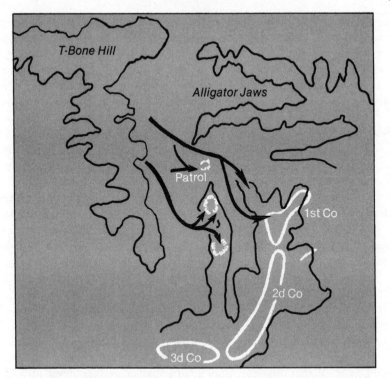

The attack on Yoke and Uncle. By the time the outposts were invaded, the patrol was fully enveloped.

scattering effect upon the enemy force, it was still vulnerable to the American artillery fires which could be massed at his call.

Asfaw switched on his radio to call Battalion. By some fluke in those first minutes as the game opened, it wouldn't cut through. He spat in disgust at a technical failure which, seen in retrospect, was clearly a blessing in disguise. The whole pattern of this strange fight developed out of the accidental circumstance that during the next half-hour, the Chinese felt free to extend their maneuver, and Asfaw, being without radio contact, had to keep telling himself that he had been sent forth to capture prisoners.

In that time, the body confronting him rapidly swelled to two platoons, but still did not move. That meant that close to 100 men would be opposing his group of 15. That was fair enough. So he crawled along the ditch cautioning his men to maintain silence and retain fire until he gave the word. It was done.

When at last the Chinese moved toward him, it was not in columns, but in V-shape like a flight of wild geese, with the point marching directly toward the apex of the ditch. All of this time Asfaw had been concentrating attention on the enemy directly to his front. Now as he turned his gaze toward the files at the far ends of the V, he caught what all along his eyes had missed. Five hundred yards to his left, another Chinese company, marching single file, had passed his flanks and was advancing directly on Outpost Yoke. He looked to his right. Another body of the same size had outflanked him and was marching against the ridge seating First Company. With that, he saw the problem as a whole. He was in the middle of a Communist battalion launched in a general attack. Its grand deployment was in the shape of an M and the V-shaped body advancing on his ditch was simply a sweep which tied together the two assault columns.

By now they were within 200 yards of him and the column on his left was almost at the foot of Yoke. His radio was still out. To his immediate rear was an earth mound perhaps 10 feet high. Thinking that the mound might cause interdiction, he moved leftward along the ditch, whispering to his men to stand steady and testing his radio every few feet.

The eight Chinese forming the point of the V were within 10 yards of the ditch when Asfaw yelled, "Tekuse!" (fire). He already had arranged it that the fire from his two flanks would cross so that both sides of the V would be taken in enfilade. The eight-man point was cut down as by a scythe. It was a rifle job. The two wings which followed at a distance of 15 yards lost another dozen men to the BARs before the surprised Chinese could recoil and go flat. At that moment Asfaw's radio sparked and he raised a friendly answer. This was his message as entered in the journal, "The enemy came. I stopped them. Now they surround me. I want artillery on White Right."

"White Right" meant the ground to Asfaw's left and rear. Their ranks being unable to use map coordinates, the Ethiopians achieved artillery fire control by blocking out in colors the map areas where they were likely to need help. Thus, they simply called for fire on "Blue Left" or "Red Right," etc. In his own hour of emergency, Asfaw was ignoring the force to his front, hoping that he would still be in time to shatter the columns moving against Yoke and Uncle.

No sooner had he given the direction than he saw the flattened company in his foreground start skirmishers around his left flank. He felt this was the beginning of an envelopment. Still, he did not amend his fire request. Instead, he shifted more of his men leftward in the ditch, figuring that with grazing fire he could slow the movement. As he said, "By then I had steadied and was enjoying it."

In three minutes, the American barrage fell right where Asfaw had wanted it. Illuminating shells from the 155s began to floodlight the valley. By their glare, Asfaw could see the killing rounds biting into the column, killing some Chinese, scattering others. But he could also see figures in silhouette moving against Yoke's skyline and he guessed that the enemy had penetrated the works, which he reported on radio.

So he was just a bit too late for a perfect score. The small-arms fire all about him had made imperceptible to him that the Chinese artillery had massed fires against Yoke and the big ridge almost coincidentally with the opening of his own engagement. It was a real clobber. Within the space it takes to tell it, all wires were cut and the men were forced back into their bunkers.

On Yoke, 2nd Lieut. Bezabib Ayela and his 56 men had heard the first volley of Asfaw's skirmish. But it sounded far away. The impression it made was swiftly erased when the enemy artillery deluged their own hill. Both of Ayela's radios were hit and his field phone went dead. Ayela moved from post to post crying "Berta!" (standby), but for all the noise, he had no forewarning of what was coming.

Realization came when three red flares cut the night above Yoke's rear slope. Ayela ran that way along the trench, knowing they had been hand-fired by the enemy. At the rear parapet, he could hear voices chattering from downslope. Yoke's rear was lighted by a searchlight beamed from the battalion ridge. Raising himself to the embankment, Ayela could see at least a squad of Chinese working up through the rocks not more than 30 yards away.

Cpl. Ayelow Shivishe was with him and survived to tell about it. Within call of Ayela were thirteen riflemen and one machine gunner, covering the backslope, but all in the wrong spot to see the approach. Before Ayela could either fire or cry out, he was drawn back the way he had come by the sounds of shooting and a piercing scream right behind him. Two squads of Chinese had come up the side of Yoke, killed a BAR man, and jumped into the main trench.

Ayela ran for them rifle in hand. In full stride he was blown up by a bomb—an ordinary grenade with TNT shaped around it, used by the Communists to clean out bunkers. Shivishe went flat in the trench and emptied his M1 into the enemy group. He saw three men drop. Then he knew he had been wrong in wasting time that way. The hill was leaderless though no one else knew it. Shivishe ran the other way around the trench to tell Sgt. Maj. Awilachen Moulte that he was in command. As he made the turn, the Chinese at the rear slope came over the parapet and were in the trench. But not unopposed. The machine gunner, Pvt. Kassa Misgina, had heard the noise and rushed to the breach. He cut down the first three men. Then two things happened right together: his gun jammed and an enemy grenade got him through both legs. Deep wounds, they didn't jar his fighting rhythm. Misgina passed the gun back to a rifleman, yelling to him to get it freed. He then grabbed a box of grenades and, returning to the step

where Ayela had been those few seconds, resumed the fight to block the
rear portal. Reasoning that if he kept them ducking for cover they couldn't
rush, he stood on the parapet and let fly.

None of this ordeal was known to Asfaw down in the valley or to the
higher commands tucked away among the high ridges. But unlike every
other actor in the drama, Asfaw alone could see all parts of the big picture.
From his place in the ditch, he had witnessed the enemy's grand deployment. Also, he knew that the observers on the high ground had no such
advantage, and due to the interposition of the lower ridges, could catch
only fragmentary glimpses of the developing action. When his eyes told
him that the artillery dropped on Yoke's forward slope had effectively shattered the reserves of the Chinese column there, his reason replied that the
hills masked that fact to everyone else.

Having already concluded that his task was to destroy the Chinese battalion by use of artillery, and realizing that he only was in position to
regulate fires so that there would be no "overkilling," Asfaw saw clearly that
a halfway success along either flank must finally doom his patrol. Driven
back, the survivors would converge within the draw which was his escape
route to the rear. There they would re-enforce the company which was
moving around his left flank. From that side, the ditch provided no protection.

For fifteen minutes, he had watched the artillery stonk the Chinese on
the lower slope of Yoke while doing nothing about the enemy column
attacking First Company's ridge. The reason was that the latter force had
made slower progress and was still toiling toward the hill. During the same
interval the Chinese platoons to his front had continued the crawl around
his left flank and were now even with his position. He took another look at
the enemy's solid column on his own right rear: it was just 50 yards short of
the main incline. At that point he gave his direction, calling for the fire to
be placed where it would catch the attack head-on. It was delivered "on the
nose." The column attacking First Company began to dissolve and recoil
toward him.

In this manner, while his withdrawal route was still open, he made his
decision to fight it out on the original line. Here was a youth having his
first experience under fire. But the role he had voluntarily accepted made
requisite a sense of timing rarely found in a division commander. The
Chinese nearest him continued to extend their outflanking maneuver; he
but shifted a few more riflemen to the left to slow them with grazing fire.

On Yoke, Sergeant Major Moulte's first act after taking command was to
run to Ayela's body to make certain he was dead. Two enlisted men had
been felled by the same bomb which killed the lieutenant. Moulte yelled
for stretcher bearers. Then, gathering six men and passing each an armful

Yoke and Uncle were separately fortified knobs along one ridge finger extending into the flat valley floor.

of grenades, he swung along the trench toward the front of Yoke on the heels of the Chinese group that had entered the works after killing Ayela. It was a sneak movement, the men moving silently and in a crouch, with one scout five yards to the front. Surprise was complete. Perhaps 35 to 40 yards beyond, the scout gave an arm signal, hand out, pointing the direction for the grenade shower. The explosions came dead center amid the enemy group. Some Chinese were killed. Others scrambled for the parapet or tried to hide next to the sandbag superstructure of the bunkers. Moulte saw at least six Chinese in clear silhouette as they climbed up from the trench wall. He was carrying a BAR. But he didn't fire a shot. He said later, "I don't know why; I just didn't think of it." (This same aberration occurs much too frequently among GI fighters.) Ordering others in his party to carry on and hunt down the invaders in detail, Moulte doubled back to see how things were going at the rear slope. By then, the wounded Misgina's machine gun had become freed, and with that weapon, he was still holding the portal, supported by one BAR man. Looking downslope, Moulte counted ten dead Chinese in front of Misgina's gun. Beyond them, he could count at least thirty of the enemy among the rocks. They became revealed momentarily as they grenaded upward. But the distance was too great and the bombs exploded among their own dead.

At that point the action was taken out of Moulte's hands for reasons requiring a brief recapitulation. Because of broken communications, Asfaw's fight had been underway thirty minutes before Battalion knew the patrol was in serious trouble. Asfaw's first radio message had gone to the platoon of First Company on Uncle and his call for artillery on Yoke had perforce bypassed Battalion because First Company's radio went temperamental at the wrong moment. As relayed from Outpost Uncle, the message taken by Capt. Addis Aleu, the battalion S2, was merely a brief warning, "Main movement against Yoke . . . fire White Right." Then the Uncle radio cut out and Battalion CP could only guess about developments.

But from his hilltop on OP 29, First Company's commander, Capt. Behanu Tariau could eyewitness the skirmishing on Yoke's rear slope. He had received the relayed message that the patrol had engaged; it came to him from Uncle during the period when First Company could no longer raise Battalion. Then for fifteen minutes—the critical period when Moulte was rallying his men to repel boarders—his own radio cut out. His anxieties mounted because of his helplessness. By the searchlight's glare he could see Chinese massing against Yoke's back door but he was in touch with no one. When quite suddenly his radio cut through again, he told 2nd Lieut. William W. DeWitt, his artillery forward observer, to hit Yoke directly with VT (proximity fuse) fire and illuminating shell. The order was passed upward to Lieut. Col. Joseph S. Kimmitt: "Fire Flash Yoke Three." Five minutes later Yoke was under a fierce rain of hot steel. The effect of the fire was to drive Moulte's men back to their bunkers for protection while transfixing the Chinese in the open. There was thirty minutes of this. Then Tariau asked for a curtain barrage on both sides of Yoke to box in the enemy survivors. He pondered extending the barrage to across the forward slope, then rejected the idea, apprehensive that Asfaw's men might be falling back on Yoke.

On that score, he might have spared himself worry. Asfaw was still sitting steady in the ditch and enjoying it. By now the Chinese who had been to his front had completed the half-circle and were spread across his rear. Their skirmish line, a lean 100 yards from him, had already been joined by the first stragglers retreating from the fires on Yoke, Uncle and First Company's hill. His big moment was at hand, when having nailed his flag to the mast, he would now win or lose it all. To Uncle, he gave the message, relayed from there to Captain Tariau and from him to the artillery, "Fire Blue Right!"

If his guess was right and the fire was accurate, Blue Right would crush the Chinese to his rear and fall just short of his own position. There was a suspense of two minutes. Then the barrage dropped dead on target, braying the enemy line from end to end. He kept the artillery on Blue Right for ten minutes; when it lifted, there was no more fire from his foreground or immediate rear.

But it had been, and still remained, the closest kind of thing. At the moment when Asfaw asked for Blue Right, his own patrol was wholly out of ammunition, save for the cartridges in the magazines of three M1s. The fragments of the two main enemy columns continued to drift back toward him. He knew that the patrol's survival from that point on would pivot on the radio and the accuracy of his call to the artillery.

At last fortune rode wholly with him. The fight continued on these terms for the next two hours, with no firing from the patrol. There were times when the Chinese, rebounding from the two outposts, then regrouping, got within 50 yards of the ditch. Blue Right never failed him. There were also times when he asked and got barrage fire on all four sides of his patrol, thereby to close the enemy escape routes leading to T-Bone Hill.

By four o'clock in the morning the battlefield was at last quiet and Asfaw could see no sign of a live enemy. The patrol arose and stretched, satisfied that it had done a good night's work. Asfaw radioed the message, "Enemy destroyed. My men are still unhurt. We have spent our last bullet." Being now unarmed, the patrol expected a recall.

What came back proved with finality that Ethiopians prefer to fight the hard way. This was Captain Aleu's message to Asfaw: "Since you have won and are unhurt and the enemy is finished, you are given the further mission of screening the battlefield, examining bodies for documents and seeking to capture any enemy wounded."

That task, which entailed another four to five miles of marching, preoccupied the patrol for the next two hours. The light was already full and the bird chorus was in full song when I met them as they re-entered the main line. Asfaw went briefly into the statistics of the fight. On the ground within 150 yards of the ditch he had counted 73 dead Chinese. On the slopes of Yoke and within the trenches were 37 more enemy bodies. There were other bodies among the paddies forward of Uncle, still not counted. But assuming the usual battle ratio of four men wounded for every one mortally hit, the score said that he had effectively eliminated one Chinese battalion.

As a feat of arms by a small body of men, it was matchless. No other entry in the book of war more clearly attests that miracles are made when a leader whose coolness of head is balanced by his reckless daring becomes attended by a few steady men. Victory came not because of the artillery but because Asfaw believed in it, willed it, then planned it.

But as the story unfolded, its significance transcended the importance of this one small field. On a vastly reduced scale, we had witnessed the prevue of great battle in the future, as it must be staged, and as its risks, decisions and movements must become regulated, if the field army is to endure against, and with the use of, atomic weapons.

What we heard fired the imagination. Asfaw's patrol became a combat team riding armored into enemy country, too small and elusive to be a profitable atomic target, large enough to block and compel the enemy to extend his deployment. So doing, it would perforce make use of the most advantageous earth cover possible. Then, having developed the situation, from the vortex of action, it would call on the big lighting to strike all around. At no point would its force be any better than its nerve and its command of communications.

Done by an Ethiopian second lieutenant, it is a case study for generals pondering the possibilities of the war of tomorrow.

Hexed Patrol

From the mass of hill 172, which was part of the main line at the extreme left of the division sector, three hogbacks ran roughly parallel toward the river. Hill 172 was generously proportioned and a full infantry battalion could stand guard there.

The hogbacks were called "fingers" because they directly abutted the big hill. But they were in fact transverse subridges set perpendicularly to the American fire front. The banks of the river and the extreme ends of the hogbacks were no-man's country though the outposts from both sides pressed close enough to oversee the river trench in daylight. Deep-scored valleys, each having its small stream and complex of paddy fields, separated the hogbacks.

The graduated descent of the hogbacks, their fairly smooth and reasonably straight-running crests marked by well-beaten paths leading to the disputed ground, invited vigorous patrol action. They were like so many staircases permitting a comfortable approach to the danger zone where the Communist enemy was most likely to be found after dark. The terrain features on his side of the river having an almost identical character, his patrolling was not less vigorous.

With the river serving as a kind of neutral buffer, the game played by both sides was to maneuver down to its embankments, set up a deadfall and then wait hopefully. It was like animal trapping, with man as the trapper, the bait and the prey.

The bottoms of the feeder valleys had a well-scrubbed look, but the untended slopes of the hogbacks were matted with thicket, flowering shrubs and stunted pine. When this growth was in full leaf, it limited observation from the crest line and was a great advantage to the side which could move most stealthily.

In mid-May, 1953, the river rose to near-flood stage after three day-long rains. In front of the hogback on the right was a ford where the water ran

King-Queen-Jack Finger, which extended almost to the river, was the scene of two patrol disasters.

not more than knee-deep. It was a logical deduction that if the enemy came at all, he would advance via the ford.

Second Battalion of 31st Regiment, which had been sitting comfortably on Hill 172, thought long and hard about the ford, and worked up a tentative plan. It called for sending a strong patrol to the valley bottom and rigging an ambush which directly covered the water passage. The shore on the American side next the ford was thick with dead cedar stumps. Riflemen could use them for concealment. Machine guns from the heights directly above the ford could protect the rear of the patrol. This reasoning disposed of the argument against setting an ambush on low ground.

Second Battalion moved from Hill 172 before it could make the experiment. On taking over Hill 172, First Battalion inherited the plan and decided to modify it. To Maj. William M. Calnan it seemed that the rigid ambush over the ford put too many eggs in one basket. He favored sending a patrol down the hogback to the left of the ford, and after the patrol had prowled the nose and base of the hogback to make certain that its flank was clear, it would then shift rightward and go into position at the ford.

At that stage of planning, Regiment intervened. If Calnan's idea was good, then it was worth amplifying. Two strong patrols should be sent. One out of Charley Company, numbering twenty men, would go to the ford where lay the main chance for action. The supporting patrol out of Baker Company would police the finger where Calnan had intended to make only a brief reconnaissance. By going out earlier and staying later than the Charley patrol, the Baker patrol would serve it as a fortifying backstop during its hours of greatest danger.

Artillery and mortar fires were plotted for both patrols. The Charley patrol would take along two light machine guns and two sniperscopes. Two additional machine guns would be put in the battalion outguard line so sighted that they could give Charley patrol a covering fire should real trouble develop.

As for Baker patrol, its power and protection were made lighter because its mission was reckoned to be safer, simpler. It had conventional strength for Korean operations of this kind—fifteen men under a second lieutenant. Just as conventionally, the patrol was to be split when it reached the far end of the hogback. Three hundred yards short of the river the "support" group of six men under a sergeant would go into a defensive perimeter. The nine men with the lieutenant would advance to the final promontory directly overlooking the river. If either party was attacked, the other could sustain it in less than four minutes.

The last half-mile of the hogback along which Baker patrol was to advance was interrupted by three rather bald and sufficiently spacious limestone knobs, which for operational purposes had been named King, Queen and Jack. The support would tarry at Queen. The "fix" element under the lieutenant would advance to Jack, 300 yards beyond. There was no obstruction to clear observation between the two points. Queen Knob was about 35 feet higher than Jack, which would greatly advantage the two BARs and the light machine gun with the support group in protecting the fix's rear. The peak of Jack rose a good 200 feet above the valley bottom. Its base nudged the river and from there to the cap its densely covered slopes were of such steepness that the climb was difficult even in daylight.

The operation was set for the night of 14 May. That afternoon, Baker Company assembled for a ceremony. Pvt. Randolph Mott was decorated with the Silver Star for gallantry and strong soldierly conduct in the defense of Dale Outpost, one month earlier. Attending the formation was SFC Robert C. Reasor who had already been given his Silver Star for superb personal conduct in the same fight.

Both were going out on the patrol that night, Mott because he had been assigned, Reasor because he had volunteered. These circumstances were in direct contrast with the moods of the two men. Mott was in high spirits and so relaxed that he grinned broadly when the medal was pinned. Reasor was grim-faced and his talk was morbid.

Baker's sixteen men moved out at 2030, hitting the trail in column. All hands were armed with four grenades apiece and carbines with sixty rounds apiece, except for the two BAR men with the support group and the one BAR man with the fix, who carried twelve full magazines. Via the circuit which tied all of the operators together, Battalion, Company and the outguard posts had full knowledge of its progress as the patrol advanced.

The patrol moved along very slowly. That was because Mott, who was serving as point man, also carried the sniperscope. The patrol dressed on Mott, and being a careful operator, he stopped every few feet for an infrared sighting on the bushes and other likely hiding places in his foreground. The sides of the King-Queen-Jack finger were well pocked with small caves of such varying size as to conceal anything from a half-squad to a platoon. Mott stopped at each entrance and tried to screen the interior with his glass. No one had told him that the sniperscope was useless for such a purpose.

The support group reached Queen Knob at 2049 and set up immediately. From there to Jack Knob in daylight would be a short five-minute walk. But because of Mott's excessive caution, the fix group took 69 minutes to get to Jack.

One advantage went with the position. Its crown was already slotted with a circle of shallow rifle pits, dug by the Chinese during one of their forays. The men fitted themselves into these holes, after Ferris had ordered their conventional deployment. Pvt. Alvin A. Bolf was put on the left flank, covering toward the river with his BAR. On the opposite side were Pvt. Sherman Cagle and Sgt. Chester F. Hamilton, armed with carbines. The light machine gun was mounted on the forward slope, Pfc. James F. Cooper handling the gun, with Pvt. Lester LeGuire assisting him. Cpl. Dee Thompson covered the rear with a carbine. In the center was the "reserve," 2nd Lieut. Roland R. Ferris, Pvt. William H. Reed, who was handling the sound power phone for him, and Mott, with his sniperscope.

For three hours, the men maintained a motionless vigil in unevenful silence. The only active figure was Mott who, at five-minute intervals, checked the area through the sniperscope, moving in a circle around the perimeter. During the three hours, he saw and heard nothing. Ferris called the company every fifteen minutes to make the same report: "Negative."

At exactly 0100, Lieut. Ernest Clark O'Steen of Baker Company started to lay down the phone to light a cigaret. He felt sure that the cast had missed and the night would prove routine. Private Reed had just told him, "There's nothing doing and I think we'll soon be coming back." The line was still open as he lowered the instrument. Then he heard Reed's voice screaming, "My God we're hit!" O'Steen asked, "What is it? What is it?" but the line had gone dead.

Surprise had been complete. Not one warning sound had been heard by the men under Ferris. From 20 yards away, a burp gunner lying prone on the slope opened fire on Private Bolf. The burst ripped him through the chest. In falling he cried, "They've killed me."

That opening volley was the signal loosing the attack against the knob by approximately twenty Chinese who had crawled undetected halfway up the slope of Jack. The gunner, obviously the leader, had yelled a command as he fired. Immediately, from three sides of the knob, three or four other burp guns joined fire, and from front and rear of the knob, grenades fell among the defenders. Within one second after Bolf died, his comrades were under full pressure from all around.

Ferris was given time only to empty his carbine down the slope. The men heard him yell to Cooper, "Get the machine gun going!" As the carbine emptied, he reached for his pistol. Then four or five bullets hit him in the upper body, still not killing him. He yelled to Cooper, "Get the gun going!" just as he sagged. A potato masher landed between his legs and exploded. He gave a gurgling sound and died.

Knee to knee with Ferris at that moment, Private Reed picked up the radio and started crawling across the knob, figuring that his place was with Hamilton, who was now in command.

Private Mott threw three grenades toward the river. He saw no targets but he guessed that the bomb that killed Ferris had come from that direction, and he wanted to do something about it.

Yelling, "I can't stand the noise of those God-damned Chinks!" Private Cagle cut loose with his carbine, firing down the rear slope. By chance, and not because he saw the man, his opening burst cut down a Chinese burp gunner who had charged to within 10 yards of him. There were two others behind him and they also went down.

Reed made it to Hamilton, who had engaged with his carbine side by side with Cagle, and had already fired two of his three magazines. Reed asked, "Can I get into your foxhole?" Hamilton said, "Try it." But when he wedged in, the hole was so cramped that it was impossible to work weapons. So Reed got out. As he emerged onto the open, he was hit around the shoulders by several burp-gun bullets. Whether he died then, the others did not know. Within a few seconds, a white phosphorus grenade struck directly on him and exploded. His body was slowly incremented while the fight continued.

Reed had left his radio in the hole. Cagle picked it up and called Sergeant Reasor of the support group, saying, "We're hit hard and Ferris is dead. Please come help us." Reasor replied, "I'll be right there."

Privates Cooper and LeGuire on the LMG weren't doing very well. Cooper had test-fired the gun just before leaving the MLR and it had worked perfectly. Now, whether because the gun had become dirty or anxiety had sapped his fingers of dexterity, he couldn't get the gun started.

On the other side of the knob, Private Thompson, a colored soldier, had first reacted to the situation by standing in the clear and running from one point to another to fire downslope with his carbine. But he quit that quickly because of the bullet swarm around his head and returned to his foxhole. He had heard Ferris cry out to Cooper to get the LMG going. Since the gun was still silent, he thought it was because the crew had been hit.

So Thompson quit his foxhole and crawled across the knob to get to the LMG. Three times during the crawl he was hit by grenades. The fragments cut deep into his neck, chest and limbs, wounding him nigh fatally. Still he dragged himself along. Mott, who watched him make the journey, reckoned that it took Thompson five minutes to get from his foxhole to the gun.

When he made it, Cooper at last had the gun going, and though it never did respond normally, Cooper fired 463 rounds during the fight. Thompson propped himself beside Cooper, swaying back and forth from weakness, but still firing downslope with his carbine, to protect Cooper and LeGuire on their open flank.

Mott had also gone to the LMG. Looking downslope through the sniperscope, he saw five Chinese scrambling upward, not more than 30 yards away. One man in the center carried a box of grenades. Mott yelled, "Fire with me!" and pulled the trigger. Cooper and Thompson turned weapons to the same spot. Through his glass, Mott saw the five Chinese pitch forward and lie still.

For the next twenty minutes, the fight went on that way. The six Americans sat there, working their weapons against the enveloping darkness, seeing no more live targets, but maintaining the fire. Midway, a grenade exploded in Hamilton's foxhole, wounding him around the shoulders and head. He yelled, "I'm hit but I'm still shooting." The effort was just enough to hold the Chinese back. Twice they seemed to come on at a charge, as the defenders judged by the crescendo in their screaming. Both times the assault withered under the blast from the knob. Then they pressed a third time and were again driven back. With that recession, Hamilton cried: "I'm almost out of ammunition; we got to get to hell out of here." It was time.

What meanwhile had happened to the support group? Sergeant Reasor, who was handling communications, got Lieutenant O'Steen on the phone within seconds after the fire fight started. He said to O'Steen, "I think the fix is being directly hit and I'm sure the Chinks have cut in between us and the MLR." At that moment the sound power line went out. Reasor then got on the radio to O'Steen but the contact was maintained by Reasor just long enough for him to say, "Now we're surrounded."

Only O'Steen heard him say it. The other members of the support, noting merely that Reasor was busy talking to the rear, were mystified by his hesitation. They had heard the burp guns open fire on the fix element, but they could also see machine-gun flashes from the far side of the river. The noises, close up and distant, were confusing. The men were not altogether sure that the forward group was being directly pressed and they waited for Reasor, the old hand, to say something. He did not tell them about the call from Cagle nor did he tell O'Steen. Pvt. Paul F. O'Brien grew so concerned about the support's inaction that he started down the forward slope of Queen with the object of reconnoitering Jack. Right then Reasor called him back, spun him back toward his foxhole and said, "We've got to stay compact." But no one in the group had seen any Chinese or heard one suspicious sound, apart from the fire forward. Reasor had told them not to fire until he said so, and he never gave the order. His messages to O'Steen remained as inscrutable as his conduct.

Ten minutes passed. A few "overs" from the fight on Jack had plunked into the dirt of Queen. Other than that, nothing had happened. Then Reasor said, "We'll have to go back to the MLR in the same order that we came." And that was what they did. The other five men fell in, and the support trekked back uphill during the same minutes that the fight on Jack was wearing to its dreary conclusion. It was a fifteen-minute retreat and

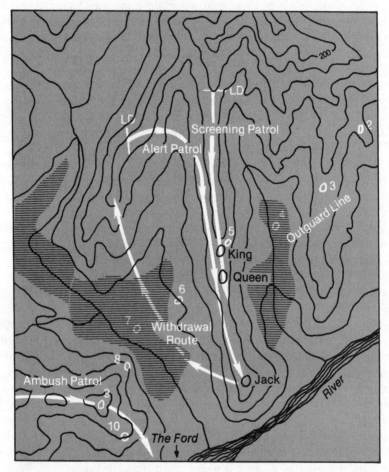

Group movements in the first attempt to rig an ambush along the King-Queen-Jack Finger. The Ambush Patrol did not become engaged.

during the climb neither Sergeant Droney nor any other soldier thought to ask Reasor what he had on his mind. The lack of protest in his comrades is no more explainable than the aberration in Reasor, a brave but worn fighter, so mixed up emotionally from his ordeal on Dale Outpost that he volunteered to stay two extra days in Korea to attend this last patrol.

Instead of returning via the finger, the six survivors on Queen slipped rightward off the knob, reckoning that the Chinese had barred the back door. Cagle and Cooper, carrying Thompson, who was unconscious from loss of blood, went first, with Hamilton limping along. Mott and LeGuire trailed behind, Mott weighted by his sniperscope and the LMG, which he had determined to bring out "because it is such a damned good gun."

Haltingly, pausing every few yards to rest, they started upward through the terraced rice paddies which cover the draw lying northeast of the finger. For perhaps 100 yards, it seemed that they had gotten away clean. Then from the paddy embankment toward which they marched, a .30 machine gun opened fire on them. There were just two bursts.

From the first one, a bullet got Hamilton. Cagle had crawled forward to throwing distance of the bank. His grenade fell short but the Chinese picked up the gun and ran. Hamilton could still walk, though he needed arm support. So he fell back on Mott and LeGuire.

They got to the last paddy where the draw ended and the ridge began. Then from the height above, fire from a .50 machine gun searched the paddy and drove them to the cover of the banks. It was random fire from one of Baker's own guns. No one atop the hill had imagined that the patrol would attempt to exit via the draw.

What stopped the fire was that two lights from the battalion's 60-mm mortars broke suddenly directly over the heads of Mott and his party. They stood up in the clear. Men mounting the outguard posts halfway up the ridge saw them. Back to O'Steen went the message, "Hold all fire! Some of our men are coming in. We see three of them."

Because of doubt about what had happened in the valley, Major Calnan at Battalion had already alerted 2nd Lieut. John J. Tierney of Able Company. He was to take his Second Platoon, advance to Queen and then try to screen Jack. He called his CP, got cut into the hot loop, and heard for the first time that Ferris' party had probably been "beaten up." He asked, "But what happened to the support?" The answer was supplied by his own first squad leader, Sergeant Taylor, who at that moment entered the bunker to report, "I see a group of Americans coming up the finger; I'm sure it's the support from the Baker patrol." It was then 0200.

Reasor arrived breathless. His support group had passed through an outguard on the last leg of the climb. Mott had reached another outguard post almost at the same time. The word had gone over the loop, "three Americans left on Jack," and Reasor had heard it before reaching Tierney.

When he caught his breath, he said, "Will you please call Baker Company and tell them I've got to go back? There are three men left on Jack. It's my job to get them." While Tierney was phoning for authority to include Reasor's party in his own patrol, Reasor spoke to the men he had just led uphill, saying, "Now we've got to go back. We've got to help the fix." Still, such was the high excitement of the night that neither Tierney nor the rest of the patrol was impressed by his irrational behavior. O'Steen might have been inclined to question it, but then O'Steen believed from what he had been told on the phone that Reasor had been caught in the same trap as Ferris and had broken out.

O'Steen agreed by phone that it was all right to send Reasor's party back. But Major Calnan felt there was no longer need for Tierney to move his full strength out immediately. Instead, Tierney was to detach one squad to beef-up Reasor's party, which would go posthaste to Jack Knob, and Tierney would follow as promptly as he could get the platoon in order and the company could make the extra stretch to cover the hole he left behind.

Several hitches developed. Reasor, in departing, picked up Tierney's radio, and, dropping his own useless Peter 6 on Tierney's lap, said, "You can hold onto this damned thing." It is not surprising that this exit left the lieutenant speechless. His remaining two squads had already been routed from the bunkers and were standing at alert in the main trench. Lieut. William D. Hughes called Tierney to say that he could go when ready. Tierney said, "But now I have no radio." Hughes got one from the communications section and started it out by runner. Enroute, both the runner and the box were hit by a mortar burst. It took Hughes forty minutes to learn what had happened and to send another radio. In the interim, two of Tierney's outguards came in to tell him that their phone lines had been cut by mortar fire. Tierney gave the outguards a fresh doughnut of wire from which to make the repair, realizing as he did so that he might be running the patrol short. Ten minutes later the radio arrived and he reassembled his force. In this way one hour was lost. He still had heard nothing from Reasor. It was 0300 before he felt free to start. So he led his platoon down the finger at a run, fearful that he already was too late to help the other patrol.

The column got to King Knob in less than six minutes. The wire was running out, and there was just time to set up the sound power phone before Tierney's worst thoughts were confirmed. From the thicket just in front of them came sounds as of men crashing through heavy foliage. Then a voice screamed, "For Christ's sakes, are you GIs? For Christ's sakes, tell me, are you GIs?" Before anyone could answer, two figures reeled out of the bush, stumbled a few yards and collapsed flat on the trail.

It was Sgt. John H. Droney, of Reasor's patrol, and the medic, Private Naparez. Droney was shot through the wrist, shoulder and buttocks. Naparez bled from a number of superficial grenade wounds. Droney looked up at Tierney and said, "You gave us only green men and they scattered all over hell." Tierney questioned him about what had happened. For the time being it was useless. Droney's teeth were chattering and his effort at speech produced only a mumble.

Had Droney been more articulate, he still could not have explained much to Tierney. He and the others under Reasor had once again followed mechanically a man who moved as if in a trance. The experience had so bewildered them that when crisis overtook the group it had already morally disintegrated.

Reasor had led them only in the sense that he had gone first as the column trotted to its rendezvous. After his outburst at Tierney's CP, he had said not a word. The men knew only that they were going back; they had no idea what they were expected to do. The other fourteen trailed after Reasor silently.

Come to his former position at Queen Knob, Reasor walked on. The group got perhaps another 35 yards. The saddleback just beyond Queen was now thick with smog. Mist rising from the valley bottom had mingled with the smoke from the brush fires atop the higher ridges. The smog had a sharp edge as if a curtain had been lowered on this part of the finger. Reasor pulled up short on seeing it. Then he leaned toward the curtain, pointing with his finger and cupping the other hand to his ear as if listening. He said nothing.

For perhaps two seconds the others stood behind Reasor, motionless and waiting. Four riflemen stood abreast just to his rear. Back of them, Pvt. Paul F. O'Brien, who was just completing his first week at the front, and Pvt. Robert Beaver, a BAR man, dropped to a crouch, not because they heard anything but because they thought it safer. The two files immediately to their rear followed their example. The others remained standing.

Five seconds. From within the smog bank, and not more than 15 yards in front of Reasor, a burp gun opened fire. Whether he was killed by the opening volley is not known. As of that moment he vanished from sight of the patrol. No one heard him cry or noted his fall. He was missed in the early searching of the area and was first carried MIA. Days later his body was found in the brush halfway down the knob. It was too late to determine how he had met his death.

As the gun cracked, O'Brien and Beaver fell sideways and started rolling toward the slope of the saddle to escape the line of fire. But in rolling they saw the four riflemen behind Reasor cut down in a body. The burst had gotten each man through the upper part of the body. The Chinese gunner had gone flat after firing about twenty rounds. Beaver could hear someone yelling, "The damned sons-of-bitches! The damned sons-of-bitches!"

O'Brien whispered to Beaver, "Why don't you fire?"

Beaver answered, "I can't. That pile of bodies is between us and the Chink."

Grenades came in on them from out of the smog. Some exploded lightly; others shook the earth around them. One loosed a rock mass between the two men and sent Beaver careening down the slope. O'Brien wondered whether to follow him or to try to get at the burp gunner. He took out his three grenades and crawled a few yards closer. But he did not trust his arm and he was afraid that if he threw, his bombs would explode among the American bodies.

Sergeant Droney, near the end of the column, had been attempting a hopeless stand. Men were trying to break past him and he was lashing out with hands and feet in an attempt to stop them. O'Brien looked that way. He saw Droney standing there, struggling violently to turn the other men around. O'Brien heard him cry, "Where in hell are you going? Where in hell are you going?" But the bag was already empty. The last two men had just dodged past Droney. Then the Chinese gunner turned his fire in that direction, and the burst hit Droney and the last two runaways. That completed the rout. One submachine gun and not more than twelve grenades had done it. The Americans hadn't fired a shot.

O'Brien rolled downslope to Beaver. They did a semicircle and came back on the trail some 30 yards to rearward. Both men were armed with BARs. For a moment they discussed whether to join the flight or have a go at the enemy gunner. What decided them was the sudden appearance of Pvt. Reynald St. Pierre who had fallen beside the trail. He said, "I'm hit. They got me in the foot. I can't walk."

O'Brien passed his weapon to Beaver. Then he picked up St. Pierre piggyback and started uptrail. Beaver made the climb walking backwards, so as to cover the other two men. This, and the fact that he was trying to handle two BARs in his first experience as a rearguard, gave the three-man retreat a unique flavor.

Of these details, Tierney, having arrived at King Knob and met two survivors, still knew nothing. He judged from Droney's hysteria that the patrol had been hard used. On radio, he told the company to send litters down the finger to pick up Droney and Naparez. Then he relieved Droney of his grenades and the patrol again moved, going warily, with its skirmishers spread well apart on both sides of the trail.

Halfway to Queen, Tierney again heard a movement in the underbrush ahead. Six men staggered into view and then fell flat when they saw Tierney's party. Concluding from their reeling gait that they were all wounded, Tierney again called the company, "Send six more litters." One of the men mumbled over and over, "The sergeant's back there. We left the sergeant. Somebody ought to get the sergeant." This was Pfc. Walter P. Brooner who had been serving Reasor as point man. Later he told a strange story about seeing Reasor cut down by burp-gun fire only to fall on an exploding grenade which blew him apart. But the other men said the Red Chinese did not use grenades at the beginning. They thought Brooner had suffered an hallucination. The failure of the screening patrols to find Reasor's body deepened the mystery.

From that point forward, Tierney proceeded with maximum caution, fearing another ambush. The interval between men was increased. Instead of going at a slow walk, the patrol advanced by individual bounds, each man moving about 15 yards at a time.

But the method slowed their advance to a crawl and the patrol got not more than 50 yards before it was checked by the breaking of 60-mm mortar flares directly overhead. Intended to help Tierney, the lights, through misdirection, nearly ruined him. Able Company had been aiming for the ford down in the valley; it missed by at least 350 yards. The third flare came down directly on Tierney's head; at the last second he threw up his hand to ward the blow. He was just too late. The metal opened his scalp, knocked him cold and broke two of his fingers, though he was not aware of the hand injury until the patrol had ended.

In a few minutes, Tierney regained consciousness. Sergeant Taylor was just saying to some of the other men, "What will we do now that the lieutenant's hit?" Tierney gave the answer by getting to his feet and resuming the march to Queen.

He found nothing at all on the knob. There were no dead men and no signs that an action had taken place. So he called for a flare between Queen and Jack; in these few minutes the smog had vanished and visibility was good. It took a long time and much trying to get the lights where he wanted them. Still, nothing was revealed other than the peaceful-seeming valley.

Since he had not been ordered to prowl Jack Knob, Tierney called Company on radio, asking, "What do you want me to do?" He got the order, "Proceed to Jack and look things over."

Tierney moved to a shallow trench on Queen and stopped the patrol. He had decided to split the patrol, which was still strung out over trail space. With him was the first squad under Sergeant Taylor. Slightly behind him, he thought, was Sergeant First Class Strauss and the second squad.

So he said to Taylor, "Crawl back and tell Strauss to hold this knob and pare off three of his men to serve as rearguard." Taylor returned in ten minutes, saying, "Sir, I'm sorry but there aren't any men back there." It was true. Despite all the care exercised the patrol had broken in half.

So Tierney put it to Taylor to stay on Queen with half of his squad and cover the route to the rear. He took the other half-squad and moved on to Jack. From that point, he radioed Able Company, "I am sitting on Jack with four men. No one is shooting at me. There are dead Americans here but I can't carry them back. Now what do you want me to do?"

That was at 0352. Tierney was told, "Return to the MLR and screen the area as you come back." He did his best to comply, but it was a broad-backed finger and well covered by undergrowth and thicket. The "screening of the area" consisted of five men crawling single file up a poorly marked trail just as fast as they could make it. Halfway to Queen they were stopped by mortar fire coming in three-round salvos two minutes apart and hitting just a few yards beyond them. Getting his men off the trail and onto the slope, Tierney kept them flattened there for twenty minutes until the hill became quiet.

They resumed crawling and got on past Queen Knob. Private Dunlop, who had been serving as point man from the moment of departing the main line, suddenly went flat beside the trail, aimed his carbine and cried, "Are you GI?" Tierney crawled up next him. He could see a helmet projecting above a boulder just a few yards on beyond. Dunlop called again: "Are you GI? Answer, dammit, or I'll shoot."

Back came a voice, "Don't shoot! Me ROK soldier." Then two men got up from behind the boulder. They were two of Tierney's own ROKs, the forward files in Strauss' squad. The rest of the squad was strung out behind them. At the rear was Sergeant Strauss, still unaware that Tierney and his party had moved to Jack and returned. The two ROKs had been told to maintain the contact. On the final bound toward Queen, they had watched Taylor's men move forward, and had deliberately stalled in their tracks, thereby breaking the patrol in half as it maneuvered into the danger zone. Asked why, one of them said, "Me afraid."

First light was just breaking. Tierney marched his platoon back to the MLR as rapidly as the fatigued state of the men would permit. As they closed, he keeled over from loss of blood and was carted to the dispensary to have his head wound dressed. Although the patrol had not made contact, it had been a relatively rough go for a youngster having his first experience under fire after only six days in the company.

At 0515, 2nd Lieut. Laurence Dankel, of Able Company, led still another patrol down the finger. In it were four men from Able and four from Baker. Lieutenant O'Steen, counting heads, reckoned that Baker was still missing seven men, counting the losses on both Jack and Queen. Baker needed Able's help in making a final screening and recovering the bodies.

Daylight was arriving fast, and so the patrol was given a WP smoke screen which in the end did more to confuse than to protect it. When he arrived at Queen, Dankel thought he already was standing on Jack, and so told the men. They acted pooped and several of them sprawled flat and fell asleep while he prowled the vicinity. Then the smoke cleared and he saw that he was on the wrong knob. He started to Jack, not noting that two of his men failed to follow.

Enemy machine-gun fire from the far side of the river raked the forward knob as the patrol approached it. They crawled the last 40 yards. Dankel quickly found Private Bolf's body, and a second corpse, burned beyond recognition. (This was Private Reed.) The carrying party moved out, three men to each litter. That left Dankel alone on Jack in the moment when he found Ferris' body lying in the shallow trench. Still under fire, he lifted Ferris and made the portage back to Queen unassisted, where the burden was shifted to the pair who had slept. They were another hour in getting to the top of the ridge. Dankel said, "I'll never do anything like this again."

During that night, the strong patrol out of Charley Company which had moved out on the right, with the object of rigging a deadfall at the ford, was left in peace. Its members saw the lights and heard the sounds of fire on their left. But such was the quiet in their immediate neighborhood that they felt no alarm.

Yet the Chinese had contrived to maneuver around this main ambush to twice ambush the smaller forces intended only to backstop it.

Doomed Patrol

As FIRST LIGHT BROKE, WE GATHERED IN A COMMAND BUNKER ON A high ridge near the ruined village of Sokkagae, Korea.

It was 19 May, 1953. Except for the division commander, all others present were members of the 31st Infantry Regiment, which has a unique record: it has never served so much as one day inside the United States. Our purpose was to hold an inquest. We wished to learn, if possible, how and why an entire patrol of Americans had been killed with every man dying in an identical manner.

Begun as a more or less routine debriefing of forces in an operation which had gone badly for our side, it developed into a hearing on a plain case of mass murder. Where death at the hands of the enemy is a not unexpected incident in war, it is still something new on the battlefield to engage an enemy with a plot and purpose as diabolically conceived and as terribly executed as was the St. Valentine's massacre in Chicago.

Two American patrols had been sent out the night before. It was my task to determine, through living witnesses, and by physical proof, why one of them had not returned.

The patrol which had been annihilated had expected to operate in relative safety. The patrol which had survived unscathed had intentionally been given a mission of great danger. Here was the paradox which from the beginning suggested that the results came of a deliberate design by the Red Chinese.

First Battalion of the 31st Regiment, like other infantry along the main line, nightly patrolled down into the valley which separated its ridge from enemy country. The object in all such patrolling was to take prisoners and to keep check on enemy movements.

To descend to the valley, the patrols normally moved via the trails winding down the ridge fingers which projected into the valley like so many flying buttresses. Arrived at the bottom, the patrol would usually set up a defensive perimeter on a likely knob to ambush or intercept any Communist party moving toward the main line.

For control purposes, the knobs along the descending ridge fingers were given names. Able Company of the 31st Regiment sat astride the ridge from which the finger marked by Ace, King, Queen and Jack knobs tapered to the valley.

Four nights earlier a patrol from Able had descended all the way to Jack Knob and there set up a defensive circle to await the enemy. But the Red Chinese had proved too clever. The American ambush had been counterambushed, caught in a crossfire and almost destroyed, only three men escaping unhurt.

That is why there happened to be two patrols on this particular night. The Americans were anxious to avoid being caught once again in the same trap. And perhaps they reflected a bit too wishfully that their own side was just as capable of playing the devious Red Chinese game.

Both the problem and the American resolve to whip it were well put by Lieut. Jack L. Conn of Pasadena, Texas. This tall, mild-mannered Longhorn was a veteran of seven months' experience in the warfare of the stabilized front. Conn speaking: "I like to have a patrol leader on the line ten days before I send him on patrol. But right now I haven't got one who's been here that long. So with the green lieutenant, I try to send along an old sergeant. That means a veteran of at least one patrol.

"Sometimes they act like footpads out there—the Red Chinese. They latch onto our patrol when it leaves our lines and just shadow it. They birddog it right into their own works and out again. But they do nothing. Our men can't see or hear them. They just sense that they're being shadowed. It's sort of ghostly. At other times, they get in early, rig an ambush and just sit there waiting for our men to make the return journey. So we have to get smart after we hear that whistle or birdcall a few times and are then showered with hand grenades from both sides of the path. We get to going out one path and returning by another. That's not a highly original thought, but it's the best we can do when we're bushers in the ambush league."

So changing pace, the Americans decided that a half-strength patrol would be sent down the Ace-to-Jack finger. Only this time it would stop at Queen Knob, two-thirds along the way to the bottom of the valley. It would have simply an "alert" mission, meaning that it would not deliberately engage or seek the enemy, but would stand by ready to help if needed.

At the same time a full-strength patrol would move down the parallel finger fronting Baker Company. The patrol would go all the way to the bottom, set up a defensive perimeter and remain quiet. The Baker finger was rightward of Able's position and its terminus was closer to enemy country. If the Red Chinese were drawn back to the Ace-to-Jack finger because of their earlier success, not only would they find the lower knob unoccupied, but in transit, they would have to cross Baker patrol's front.

This was the plan, and the movement into the valley by the two patrols precisely followed it.

From Baker Company went a patrol of twenty men under Lieut. Benjamin L. Collins. Because the prospect for the Able patrol was that it would sweat out nothing worse than a night's exercise in ridge-climbing, it was cut to ten men under command of a 21-year-old corporal, Otis Alford.

Thus the preliminary moves toward the setting of the stage. The drama itself is composed from the lines spoken by the men who fought that night.

There are many Korean nights like this one during the late spring. Along the crests of the higher ridges the air is clean and the stars shine bright. As the sun goes down, mist rises from the paddies in the bottoms and shortly thickens into fog. From the top view, the scene is not formidable. The valley below is a place of lost horizon.

Collins led his patrol out at ninety minutes before midnight. The march route was straight down the ridge finger, and they did it single file. So that progress could be measured accurately in the CP, the path of descent had been divided into five check points, named in order, Champagne, Beer, Rye, Scotch and Gin. It took forty minutes to reach Champagne. Collins knew by then that he would be bucking the weather no less than the enemy. Visibility and the patrol were together reaching bottom.

At Point Champagne, the patrol split, Collins leading half the party forward to Beer, while the other half tarried at Champagne so as to put 150 yards' distance between the two parties during the move into enemy country. With Collins was the "fix" element. The "support" element was under Pvt. Loy J. Bearchild, an Indian who had volunteered for the night's task because he had accidentally shot a sergeant that afternoon and wished to square things.

Point Beer was marked by a tall pine, lone and conspicuous amid the belt of scrub oak, sumac and jack pine which covered the lower abutments of the big ridge. As Collins came abreast the tree, quite suddenly the fog curtain split, as if taken by an updraft from the valley. Standing about 75 yards away, forward and to his left, at the bottom of the draw between the two ridge fingers, he saw two men.

Before he could take a second look, or call anyone else's attention, the fog closed again. He called his commander, Lieut. E. H. Pedrick, by telephone, saying, "I think I saw two men; I think they're enemy." Pedrick answered, "You must be wrong; they must be from the other patrol." Asked Collins, "Why not call LP6 and find out?" Pedrick did. The men on LP6 said they had seen nothing. Corporal Alford answered that his men were on their assigned knob and hadn't moved. As for signs of the enemy, Alford said, "Negative, no sweat, all quiet."

Whether Collins was being tricked by his imagination, at least his sensing of the night was in whole contrast to Alford's. His ear was tuned to the sound of gravel slipping under his men's feet and to the whisper of the breeze through the undergrowth. But there were other slight, unaccountable noises all about him—the breaking of twigs or the rustle of garments. He felt the presence of an enemy almost close enough to him to be touched.

Behind him, Bearchild was harboring the same thought, but for different reasons. He leaned into the mist, sniffing; later, he said, "I smelled them."

But again the fog played tricks. A clear shaft opened for a few seconds between the two ridge fingers, giving Alford a fleeting glance of Collins' men in silhouette. He so reported by radio to Pedrick who concluded that if Alford had seen Collins, then Collins earlier must have been looking at Alford. Highly logical, but still wrong.

When this information was relayed by Pedrick, Collins stood still for an indecisive five minutes. It bothered him badly that the danger he felt could still not be clearly expressed and that Pedrick was giving him too little credit. Finally, he said to his men, "We'll move on to Rye."

On getting to that check point, he called Pedrick, asking "Does LP6 see us now?" After a minute or so, Pedrick answered, "No, so get yourself a drink of Gin." By that time, the two young officers were of opposite minds about the meaning of the same piece of information. Collins' safe arrival at Rye spelled to Pedrick that Collins had been wrong in reporting the presence of Chinese off his flank. To the man on the spot, it meant that he was being ordered arbitrarily to go on to the object, leaving an enemy force on his rear.

Collins believed that at that moment he should have been told to move flankward and beat the bushes for an enemy whose presence he had reported. In moving on to Gin, he would have to bring Bearchild's group to Scotch, thus completing the movement according to the original plan. That would put the patrol as a whole about 75 yards beyond where the Chinese had first been sighted.

In their final positions, the fix was about 70 yards forward of the support. The two knobs, Gin and Scotch, were at equal elevation, possibly 200 feet above the valley floor. Figuring that no conventional disposition suited the extraordinary hazards of the night, Collins arranged the patrol in two V's with points toward each other. He and Bearchild would occupy the pivots within shouting distance of each other. If the Chinese tried to rush the saddle between them, both flanks of the two V's could provide mutually supporting fires. A spur-of-the-moment arrangement, it is perhaps just as well that it was never tested.

For almost forty minutes Collins listened and sweated, while the flattened patrol went silent. It was drizzling now, and though the breeze quickened, the fog hung thicker than ever. He could see not more than 10 yards. But again his ear caught a fugue of almost imperceptible sound. His anxieties were mainly for what was happening on his left, not that he thought of Alford's group, but because it was on that side he had first seen

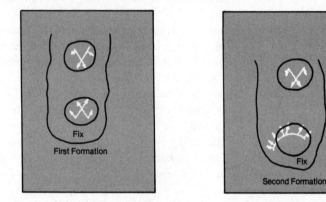

the Chinese. So he went that way, moving perhaps thirty paces down from the knob. His ear caught—he felt quite sure of it—the restrained breathing of a body of men out beyond the fog. Then for a third time a corridor was wafted briefly in the fog and in the clear, as if spotlighted, he saw and counted six men. The impression of a split second, it was gone as quickly, and the swiftness of the transition made him doubt that he had seen anything at all.

He sprang back toward the summit, aware even as he moved that his men were not favorably deployed toward the point of danger, and concerned not to lose time and energy in turning them that way. At his own position was a 60-mm mortar tube and two rounds which he had brought down from the hill. It took him perhaps one-half minute to fire the weapon. As the round got away, he yelled, "Keep lookout to left!" The shell fell and exploded right where he thought he had seen the six Chinese. But the flash and roar revealed nothing. Now the silence became oppressive as he halfway decided that all along he had been tricked by his imagination.

For the next few minutes, he played it cool. He didn't bother to tell the men what he thought he had seen, nor did he radio Pedrick that he had fired a mortar round hoping to scare an unknown number of the enemy.

However, Pedrick had watched the round explode from his post on the hilltop and, baffled by it, had murmured, "Now, what the hell!"

At last suspicion overcame reticence. Collins asked his runner, Pvt. Walter E. Busch, Jr., "Tell me, am I nuts, or are you hearing anything?" Busch answered very solemnly, "I sure do. I been hearing it for an hour. There's something very funny out there." That one word of assurance, coming from an enlisted man, was all that was needed to get Collins back in balance, confirming his worst thoughts about the situation and clearing his recurrent doubt of self. At last he felt sure that most of the night's noise was man-made. It built higher as he listened. His main worry—the fear of envelopment—was partly relieved only because, now that he knew he was dealing with something real, his ear told him that the noise came from the low ground between him and Alford's patrol.

Collins sent Busch crawling back to Bearchild to give him the picture and warn him of the need for full alert. Busch carried along two communications wires, so that Collins and Bearchild could signal each other by jerks on the wire if they sighted the enemy or needed fire. Collins then altered his formation as shown in the diagram on page 194.

In this way, his party faced about toward its own main line and concentered its weapons in the direction of the noise. Collins decided to tell the others what he thought he was up against. The men showed no nervousness and proceeded silently to reorganize. It was now near midnight.

Of these forebodings in the Collins patrol, Corporal Alford and his nine men knew nothing, though they were but 230 yards distant. That can be charged off to greenness and lack of knowledge of each other. Alford, the most experienced man, was making only his second patrol. Four of his men were non-English-speaking Katusas. Of his five Americans, three had been assigned only that day to Able Company and had not yet met their comrades. The other two had been with the unit ten days and had seen no action. In this not-dry-behind-the-ears look, it differed not greatly from Collins' patrol, only two members of which had been with Baker Company longer than six days. It was an evil that was characteristic of Korean operations in that period, imposed on the fighting line by the rotation system.

Alford had marched his men straight down the ridge finger, insensible to the night noises which were disquieting Collins. Passing through King Knob, and then arriving at Queen, he had deployed his men in a circle around the knob. It was already worked with half-dug foxholes and the men simply fitted into them. There they sat, resting and relaxed, while Collins was hesitantly moving down from the ridge top. They did not expect a fight, because the other patrol was moving into the forward ground and their own mission was to assure it extra defensive protection. Whether that outlook made them less wary, it is at least clear that Alford

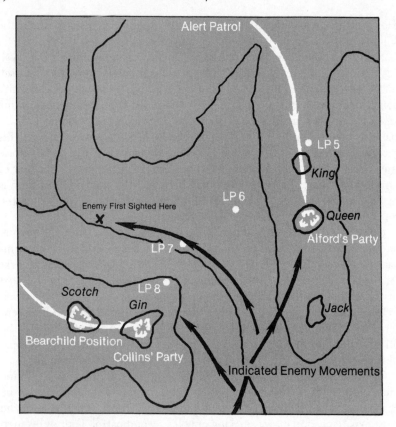

Movement in the second attempt to spring an ambush at the King-Queen-Jack Finger.

said nothing to his men to alarm them and he reported nothing to Pedrick indicating a belief that he was in the presence of the enemy.

So at their station the fog simply worsened the monotony. Time moved routinely until just past midnight. A few of the men dozed and Alford did not bother to prod them into wakefulness.

The new day was just two minutes old when Collins heard several bursts of fire off to his left. The fog muffled the sound; still, he thought it came from the direction of the Able Patrol. Pedrick called him immediately, "What's happening?" Said Collins, with pardonable exaggeration, "All hell has broken loose on my left rear." Pedrick asked whether the fire came from friend or enemy, and Collins gave him his best judgment: "I think it's Chinese."

Exactly eight minutes later, Pedrick called again. The time interval is important because, till the moment when this second conversation opened, Collins had been listening to automatic fire in heavy volume over on his left. As he began to talk, the automatic fire died; thereafter, he heard nothing but what he described as "scattered rifle fire." Asked Pedrick, "What's happening now?" Collins started to say that the fight was still going. Then corrected himself and reported, "Negative. There's no fire except what my people are giving in support, and we're pouring it on heavy."

The line and radio links with Alford's patrol on Queen Knob had gone dead, Pedrick having heard nothing from it since the fire opened. He guessed, or hoped, that Alford's men by now were scrambling back up the ridge finger. So he said to Collins, "Fall back on your support, move toward Queen and be ready to assault if the Chinese have it." But a bell already rang in Collins' brain telling him that he was too late. Dropping all caution, he shouted at top voice, "Join me at the rally point!" and without waiting to organize the fix group, started for Point Rye. They trailed after; Bearchild and his men were already ahead of him. The Indian, too, was filled with a terrible premonition. What he had heard through the fog lacked the dynamic and rhythm of a normal fire exchange followed by disengagement. A BAR had fired prolongedly amid a crackling of carbines and rifles. That noise was swiftly drowned by the rattle of burp guns fired in large number. Then as the automatic volume suddenly cut off, there was a diminuendo of rifle shots. Afterwards, only silence. It was a senseless pattern for a skirmish between sides fighting for ground.

Collins got his men to the base of Queen in ten minutes, moving in squad column on the double. Only then did he bother to form a skirmish line for the upward sweep. It was a useless precaution; the scene was utterly quiet. Without interruption, they got to the top of the knob. There they found eight dead men in American uniform. Alford's patrol was still formed in a circle around the top of the knob. Each man seemingly had met death where he had been stationed. Their weapons lay beside or under them. "It was," said Collins, "a perfect execution." And he spoke better than he knew. It was much too perfect for war.

Collins called Pedrick. On hearing that the alert patrol had been massacred, Pedrick told him to bring the bodies out. Collins' men tried, but it was no go. Clean spent from the emotion and exertion of the night, climaxed by the shock of their discovery on Queen Knob, they had lost all lifting power. They dragged several of the bodies a few yards, then gave it up.

When Collins explained this to Pedrick, he relayed the information to Able Company. Its commander, Lieut. R. F. Rasch, thereon told 2nd Lieut. John J. Tierney to take a patrol of fourteen men down to Queen, get the

ground under control and give such help to the Americans as proved necessary. The exact order given shows that Rasch had no clear idea of the
situation and was unaware that his alert patrol had met disaster. He said to
Tierney, "Go down the chogi trail to Queen. There's a disorganized enemy
force holding it. You are to form an assault line and recapture Queen."

So Tierney started down the ridge, falsely assuming that his main job
was to move into a fighting situation and get it under control. Tierney told
his men to fire at anything moving off the trail. They moved along at a
running walk. There were eight Americans and seven Koreans in the party.

During that half-hour Collins' men simply lay down and rested alongside
the chogi trail above Queen Knob. They were still flattened when they
heard Tierney's patrol come clattering along and forthwith challenged it.
That circumstance possibly averted a collision between the two parties as
Tierney was wholly surprised to meet friends in the neighborhood.

When Collins gave him the news that his task was to porterage a dead
patrol, Tierney immediately had heavy trouble with his seven Koreans.
They refused to touch the bodies. So Tierney pointed his carbine and said
he would fire unless they obeyed the order. When they still didn't move
and he failed to fire, he lost his point. Only one Korean, Pvt. Chim Sa Soo,
changed his mind, shouldered a body and carried it to the company lines
under his own power.

The other seven bodies had to be handled by Tierney's eight Americans,
since Collins' men had but sufficient energy left to pull themselves along
up the trail. Thus the carrying had to be done in relays, while Tierney, to
help his men, moved along under a load of three rifles and four carbines.
The combined party was two hours and 35 minutes in reaching the main
trench atop the ridge.

As stated, there were eight men in the killed patrol. But in the beginning, ten men of Able Company had been sent to Queen. The discrepancy
comes of what happened to two Katusa (Koreans serving with American
units) soldiers.

Cpl. Pak Si Jong and Pvt. Im Ben Gun ran from the perimeter shortly
after the beginning of the fire exchange, before any hurt had been done the
patrol. They bolted blindly from sheer panic and were already well up the
ridge finger by the time Collins' patrol got to Queen Knob. By their own
statements, and according to all of the facts developed in the official inquiry, it was an act of inexcusable cowardice.

But they were not the only weak vessels present. Three hundred yards up
the chogi trail, their line of flight carried them through an outguard post
manned by Pvt. Gerald Costello of Able Company. A draftee, he had
joined the company just that day.

His job in the outguard post was to serve as contact between the patrol and the company and sound warning of any untoward development. He had heard the fire below. Still, it did not impress him as anything which should be reported; no one in the Army had ever told him how a fight sounded.

The two fleeing Katusas literally overran him and knocked him down. He had made no effort to stop them, and had they halted, he would have asked them no questions. That there was any connection between the sounds of the fire and their precipitate flight didn't occur to him. He thought it mildly interesting that two men should be running so hard through the fog on a black night. But he didn't bother to report this or anything else to the company.

Costello was simply a lost soul wholly surrounded by a meaningless wilderness. Given a number, a rifle and a responsible soldierly task to do by Uncle Sam, this hapless nephew was utterly incapable of understanding his relationship to anything about him.

So at dawn atop the big hill we met with the living and the dead of the three patrols. All of the actors were there, including the company and battalion leaders who had participated only as voices from the wings, Collins' men who had survived, Costello the vacuous outguard, the two Katusas who had fled the fight and their comrades who would never speak again.

Yet from these mute witnesses came the most eloquent and damning testimony of all. It was supplied by the look of their broken bodies. Even the barest examination of them raised the question: "How did this unbelievable thing happen?" Eight men had been killed; all had died in the same way. In that lay the great riddle of the night. And even as the nature of their wounds prompted the question, in the end, it proved the key to the answer.

Tierney had been instructed by radio to bring the bodies out exactly as he found them and had been faithful to his mission. So they lay there, eight dead men, each wearing a bulletproof vest, zippered from the lower belly to the neck.

The vests were unscratched. The heads of the victims were also clean. Each man had died from a single bullet. Each bullet had entered at the groin, just below the edge of vest. Thereafter, in each case, the bullet had ranged upward through the body and lodged there. All eight men had died from internal hemorrhage.

The mathematical chance of that having happened in a straight-on fire fight would be one in ten million. Every bullet would have to be a ricochet. Yet these men had died while deployed in a circle with backs turned toward each other.

Something clicked. In years of covering the courts in West Texas, I had run into not a few self-defense cases in which the victims had died from a bullet coursing almost directly upward. And I had heard counsel and the experts say, "He had to be shot from the floor."

So we went into the debriefing and heard from the living witnesses.

Pedrick, Collins, Bearchild and the others who were identified with the big patrol described their experience as it has been related here. Again and again their feeling came out, supported by what Collins had seen, that from the beginning of the movement into the forward ground, there had been Chinese all around them, a feeling obviously not shared by Alford's men.

"I am sure they knew we were there," said Collins. "After I fired the mortar round, they had no reason to doubt it. Then when we fired in support of Alford, our position became cleanly outlined. But for some purpose of their own, they let us alone."

We continued, developing the big patrol's story by routine questions and answers. At last we reached the point where Collins told about the outbreak of small-arms fire on his left.

I asked him, "Was it friend or enemy? Who fired first?"

Answer: "The Chinese."

"Are you certain about it?"

"I think so."

"Think about it! You say the sounds were muffled because of the fog. You knew there were Chinese between you and Alford. Isn't it therefore possible that, expecting enemy fire, you are mistaken about the sound and source?"

Answer: "My impression was quite definite."

At that point, I asked the same main question of Private Bearchild, who had been about 50 or 60 yards farther from the fire. The Indian shook his head, and answered, "It came so suddenly that for the first minute or so, my brain was confused. I have no idea who fired first. Then I cooled and could hear the BAR going and later the burp guns. Afterward I heard scattered rifle fire."

That was how we left it as we went on with the debriefing of the big patrol.

Cpl. Pak Si Jong, the Korean who had fled the fight, stood about 5 feet in his socks.

His commander, Lieutenant Rasch, cut him down to yet smaller size as he walked before us. "The boys call him Easy Ed," said Rasch. "That's because he's slick and a first-class liar."

I looked the little man over. He could speak no English, so he stood mute, waiting for the interpreter's questions. But one thing about him was thoroughly impressive. He was shaking like an aspen and he had the dread of death in his eyes. There was no question what Easy Ed was thinking. A tribunal was passing on his dereliction and the end of it would be a post and a firing squad.

The tension was terrific. Yet I had to avoid smiling at the runt lest it give him assurance. It was necessary to keep him pitched to the terrible solemnity of the occasion, if we were to draw the truth from him.

His story came forth, one jerk at a time.

"We ten men set up on top of Queen about eight o'clock. There were half-dug foxholes there, more long than deep, so that we lie down in them.

"We hear nothing. We see nothing. Corporal Alford makes the rounds, but with everything quiet, it is hard to keep the men from sleeping.

"Then right after midnight, we have trouble. Alford sees two Chinese walking up the forward slope toward his position. He fires his carbine, maybe six rounds.

"That's all, right then. Maybe thirty seconds later, I think I see an enemy moving about 10 yards downslope from me. I can't be sure. No noise from them yet. But I fire my carbine, four bullets. My position is on the other side of Queen from Alford. When I fire, he gets excited and yells, 'Everyone fire.' So we all fire, a few rounds each. Nothing happens. We see no one. We hear no enemy. Everything gets quiet and we guess we have made a mistake.

"Eight, maybe nine minutes pass. Then the big noise. Up the forward slope toward Alford come many Chinese, maybe twelve or fifteen, all firing burp guns. That's when I run and Pvt. Im Ben Gun follows me out. I couldn't stand. I do not wait to see how any of our men are killed."

I stopped him then to take a double check on the one important thing he had said, asking, "And you are sure absolutely that you, Alford and the others all fired your pieces from your prone positions some minutes before you heard any enemy fire?"

He answered, "Yes, sir, sure, there can be no doubt."

I grinned at Easy Ed, and I guessed he realized for the first time that he was not going to be shot. His body relaxed and he slumped onto a wooden bench. Then I turned to the division commander, Maj. Gen. Arthur Trudeau, and said, "The boy's story wraps it up. It is now possible to say with absolute certainty how these men died."

Trudeau's first question was, "How can you be certain that his account is true and that Collins is wrong in his impression that the Chinese fired first?"

I answered, "There are three reasons. To begin, Collins was too distant to be a reliable witness, and moreover he was expecting enemy fire. But the man on the spot must certainly know how the fire started, who started it and probably why. Therefore the only question is whether Easy Ed is lying. And there the answer must be 'no.' For he would be lying against interest. Had he been startled and driven out by a sudden burst of enemy fire, there would be an excuse for his flight. But by his admission, his own comrades started the fight, held their ground and were still facing enemy fire when he made off. So he tells the truth only to convict himself. He must be telling the truth. That leads to the final point, that with his story, all the parts now fit into place and we at last get blueprint clarity out of what has been a wholly confused action."

So with all hands listening, the general asked for the rationalization, and it was given to them this way.

The Chinese had known all along that both patrols were there. But they had decided earlier that on the next go-round, when the weather favored such a design, they would plan toward not simply ambushing an American patrol but murdering it. That called for an extremely devious arrangement.

When the Americans decided to send two patrols down the separate fingers on one night, it put an extra complication in their plan. But counting on the insulating effect of the heavy weather, they must have reckoned that if they ignored Collins' patrol, and did not even harass it, Collins would stay placed in isolation. The approved plan was intended for execution upon a smaller group.

Alford's unawareness of the enemy presence played into the Chinese hands. The first two skirmishers who advanced up the forward slope toward him were a diversion, sent to draw American fire and then fall back. But at the same time, a ring of Chinese skirmishers had been sent wriggling up the slope of Queen to get right under its rim next the fire pits, under cover of the fog.

The pair advancing openly had exposed the position of only one weapon—Alford's. So another man had stood up to draw more fire—Pak Si Jong's. Then all the Americans fired briefly. That put the final touch on the enemy arrangements. The executioners who had deployed under the rim of the knob simply moved a foot or so one way or the other to get directly under the intended victim. They made that adjustment during the eight-minute silence.

Now all was ready for the *coup de grâce*. The wave of Chinese armed with burp guns advanced up the forward slope to flush out the game and force members of the patrol to their feet, in the first act of withdrawal. As the silhouettes rose, the circle of executioners simply canted rifles upward toward the lower half of the looming figures and fired.

Yes, it was "shooting from the floor." There were powder burns on four of these dead men. Their killers must have been less than rifle's length from the victims when the rounds went off.

The debriefing was over. The general and I walked back to the choppers for the flight back to Division Headquarters.

He asked, "But what's the object?"

I said, "As in most patrolling, to prove that you're top dog, to demoralize the other fellow as much as possible and to make his patrols feel weak in the stomach before they ever start."

Then he thought a moment, and popped the real question: "What can we do about it?"

I answered, "Nothing. They sit here year after year. The longer they stay, the smarter they get. Our youngsters keep moving in and out. They're smart and they've got guts, but they don't stay long enough to learn. You can't beat Davy Crockett with a boy scout."

The Fight at Snook

Even the name of the place had a blessed appropriateness. According to Webster's, "snook" means to smell, to nose about, to lurk and to lie in ambush. It can also mean "a thumbing of the nose."

Either or both definitions could have been in the mind of the unknown but scholarly GI who first looked at the outpost and said, "Let's call it Snook." The tiny knob interrupted the otherwise flat bottom of the Yokkokchon Valley in awesome isolation. It was an act of deliberate defiance by the Americans that they insisted on garrisoning it.

Yet there was something about Outpost Snook which charmed the eye and soothed the senses. The other outpost hills all appeared melancholy. Snook alone looked chipper. It was if God had made this funny little place just to provide special care for the watchmen of the night.

Snook was joined to the big ridge of the main line by an attenuated and sharply descending ridge finger of such tapering narrowness that from the high ground it looked like a dinosaur's tail stretching into enemy country. The last knob on the tail was Outpost Snook. From the main line of resistance, a communications trench ran 1,100 yards down the spine of the animal to serve the peewee fortress. The trench was of such depth as to prohibit supporting weapons being fired from it. So steep were the slopes of the finger and so sharp-edged its crest that the trench embankments did well to withstand a pounding by mortar fire. Except by entering the trench itself, the enemy could not use the upper heights of the finger to take Outpost Snook from the rear. But because the finger ran straight and true from the hilltop, fires from behind the big ridge could beat upon the sides of the extension while re-enforcing infantrymen descended to Snook via the deep trench.

Atop the knob there was room for just one bunker, which was called the CP, and a straight-running, 30-foot sandbagged trench which could accommodate not more than ten men. To cover and strengthen the battalion

From the fortified height which anchored the main line, little Outpost Snook was almost lost to sight and only one squad guarded it.

position, eight outguard (listening) posts were mounted in an arc around the base of Snook, closer to the enemy than was the CP by an average distance of 200 yards. Outguard No. 14 was almost directly to the front of Snook. Outguards No. 15, 16 and 17 were echeloned to its left and rear so that they curved upward along the lower slope. Outguards No. 13, 12, 11 and 10 stretched rightward across the paddy fields and therefore had maximum exposure. There were two or three men in each outguard post.

By reason of its extreme isolation, limited means and extraordinary terrain, Snook had therefore more the nature of a stationary patrol than of a fortified redoubt. The knob was not either wired in or protected by minefields, as the position was too cramped and the slope too steep to permit it. If hit, the garrison would survive mainly by its own power.

For the greater part of two years, the Chinese Communists had looked hungrily at Snook, knowing that if they could grab it, they had a sally port to the main ridge. But while they continued to probe and hit every other outpost position, Snook they left very much alone.

On the night of 15-16 May, 1953, Snook was defended by eight men from Third Platoon, Able Company, 17th Infantry Regiment. Sgt. George Transeau, who was in command, had seen Snook for the first time late that afternoon. The others already had spent one night on the ground. Including Transeau, the average length of service along the fighting front by the members of the garrison and outguard was thirteen days. Of the eight men atop the knob, four were newly arrived replacements.

All of the outguards were tied in with the CP by a telephone hot loop. The same open circuit kept Battalion in continuing touch with developments at Snook. If, for example, one outguard got on the loop and cried warning to Transeau, all other outguards heard it, as did the CP people on the company hill, and Major Acuff at Battalion.

At exactly 2304, Transeau heard a rattle of fire from somewhere along his immediate front. The sounds were muffled and at first they conveyed to Transeau's mind nothing of great importance, though he immediately reported what he had heard to Acuff at Battalion.

While he was talking to Acuff, a number of the outguards cut in and sounded off on the wire. They had heard the firing, but they had seen nothing; they wanted to know what the shooting was about. Transeau counted them off, one by one. There was a conspicuous blank: Outguard No. 14 hadn't reported. Quickly, the other outguards were calling it to his attention: "We're hearing nothing from 14; what's happening?"

There was good reason for the silence. At Outguard No. 14, Privates First Class Robart, Holmen and Gothier had met sudden death. Afterward, the look of their bodies indicated that they had all been killed where they sat by one submachine gunner and, after that, grenaded for good measure. But

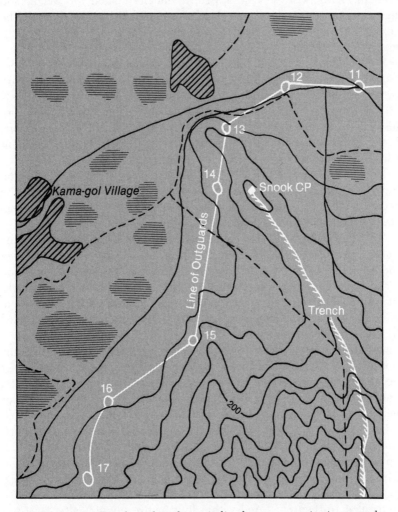

Isolated Outpost Snook, tied to the main line by a communications trench.

the men on Snook did not then know it. Transeau reported to Acuff only this, "We are hearing nothing from 14."

Acuff told him, "Use the other outguards and re-enforce toward the vacuum." Otherwise sensible advice, it underestimated the weight and speed of the threat. Time and developments had already closed off the chance for any such maneuver, as Transeau realized before he had time to repeat Acuff's order.

Pvt. Harold Gardner was on the hot loop now, talking to Transeau from Outguard No. 15: "We see them. There are fifty to sixty of them. They have overrun 14 and are now heading straight toward us. We've got to get out."

Transeau said, "O.K., run for the hill as fast as you can!" Acuff heard him say it, and realized that his own present task was to alert the supporting heavy fires that would save Snook, leaving it to Transeau's judgment whether the other outguards should be withdrawn.

Private Gardner and Pvt. Bae Yon Bee started for Snook on a dead run. But the main body of Chinese was already across their line to the CP. So they ran diagonally upward intending to get into the commo trench between Snook and the main hill.

Wholly occupied with his communications which kept him inside the bunker, Transeau didn't have time to spell out the situation to the seven men behind him who were in the trench garrisoning the knob. They had to play out the show by instinct and according to what they had been taught in basic training; so did the men in the outguard posts on the low ground.

The truly remarkable thing is that, with no exception, all hands decided to remain right where they were, fire if they saw anything that looked like a target and move only when ordered. The voices they had heard over the hot loop were steady, and that fact steadied them. They had made their personal decisions even before Transeau said over the phone, "We've got a fight on Snook; stay where you are and give it all you can." The outguards heard that message; the seven men in the trench behind Transeau didn't.

To Pvts. Roy L. Howell and Robert A. Cayo, who were having their first time under fire in the Snook trench, it was momentarily disconcerting that no warning had come and that no one said, "Look here! You are in a fight. There is the enemy. Now fire!" That was more or less how they had expected it would be. But the noise of "two or three burp guns" had sounded unfamiliar to their ears. And within four or five minutes after they had heard the first shots, enemy mortar shells, arriving ten or twelve to the minute, began to shake the earth near them. They decided, on their own, that Snook and their personal fortunes were in jeopardy and that they had best do something about it.

Howell heard a Browning automatic rifle (fired by one of the outguards) go into action. He said, "When I heard the friendly fire, I came out of my trance. Until then, though I had heard enemy fire, my reaction was still as if I were watching a movie of which I was not a part."

Howell was within arm's length of the CP. He walked five or six yards and looked down the slope. At a distance of about 40 yards he could see "from twenty-five to thirty men" climbing the shale bank toward him. They were in "gang formation" and were moving obliquely across his front as if their purpose was to gain a slightly defiladed saddle and enter the trench on the rear of Snook. As fast as he could load and pull trigger, he fired four clips from his M1 and saw "several" of the Chinese fall. Others changed direction when he opened fire and, dropping to their bellies, crawled toward him. They yelled, "Cease fire!" as they came on. Others among them cried, "Spread out! Spread out!" Though they spoke clear English, it did not disconcert him. He dropped his rifle and put his three grenades on the rampart. When the leading Chinese got to within 20 yards of him, he unpinned his grenades and threw. He heard screams and saw two of the Chinese go limp and lie still while the others scrambled downslope and were lost in the dark. That ended the assault on his personal position. When the targets vanished, Howell quit firing.

Pvt. Robert A. Cayo was about 10 yards from Howell. He was lying in the trench and trying to rest when the first shots were fired. After Howell opened fire, Cayo arose and tried to look over the trench wall. The Chinese whom Howell was fighting were closer still to Cayo. But the trench had been dug unevenly. Where Cayo stood, it was deeper, and Cayo was a shorter man than Howell; on tiptoe, he still could not see beyond the revetment. So he dropped to a squatting position and waddled a few yards, still wondering what he should do. That brought him within a couple of paces of Howell who was still firing downslope. So far, Cayo had seen no sign of the enemy. Cayo looked up. He saw a man's head bob up above the trench wall not six feet away. As he looked, two more heads appeared behind it, and then a fourth and fifth head. But since the embankment covered the prone figures, Cayo saw only the heads and not the bodies, and was reminded of objects in a shooting gallery. He said to himself, "They must be Chinese." The heads didn't stir and Cayo remained as motionless as possible. Still on his haunches, he unpinned and flipped a grenade over the bank, the toss carrying not more than six feet. There was a loud explosion. He heard men screaming. He said, "Got 'em! Got 'em!" and felt enormously satisfied, though as far as he knew, there was no one to hear him. He threw another grenade. Then a hand pulled at his elbow. It was his buddy, Pvt. John Alcott. Alcott said, "I've got three grenades," and handed one to Cayo. Keeping low, they put their three grenades over the bank and heard more screaming after the bombs exploded. Then they crouched back-to-back, carbines in hand, facing in opposite directions along the trench line, awaiting the enemy. But there was no need to fire.

Transeau, for just one minute, stepped outside the CP bunker. He could hear the noise of fighting along the Snook trench but could see none of his men. He judged that his position was already in the process of being over-run. On the other hand, he dared not leave the telephone. The supporting fires from the mortars and artillery had not yet come in. Moreover, the men on the outguards were still in full jeopardy and would not likely stay steadfast if he quit talking and they concluded that Snook was gone. So he could do little more than take a quick look and then duck back. With his carbine, he fired several rounds downslope, then returned to the phone. Without knowing it, he had aimed the right way in the right moment.

The enemy plan had been quite simple. The main body—between forty and fifty men—went for the big prize, charging up the left slope of Snook to get on its rear. But a smaller party—perhaps ten men or so—had come right up the nose of Snook, aiming to grab the CP bunker and polish off the garrison.

Pvt. Freddie Sakai was not more than 20 feet from Transeau, guarding the entrance to the CP passageway. He had heard a crackling noise from somewhere down the right-hand embankment. (Howell and Cayo had become engaged from the left.) Sakai leaned toward the noise. Standing not more than 10 yards from him were five Chinese, pausing for breath after their hard run up the nose of Snook. That was Sakai's first sight of the enemy. Three of them sprang toward the trench. Sakai emptied his carbine into them. A fourth Chinese jumped on top of the CP bunker, firing a burp gun at Sakai, range five yards. Sakai dodged to one side, then hugged the sandbag wall of the bunker, reloaded, stepped back into the open and fired upward. Though he saw the gunner go down, he felt certain that he had missed him. But it was impossible to put a grazing fire over the bunker roof. The fifth Chinese was still standing uncertainly outside the trench; Sakai fired and the man dropped. That ended his action. He said later, "It was too bad; I didn't get a chance to do any real fighting."

Pvt. George Sakasegawa was at the upper entrance to Snook, his job being to hold the fort if the enemy got into the commo trench. He had heard the burp-gun fire from the valley; it bothered him that no one came to say what it meant. About five minutes passed. Sakasegawa had been straining to catch any sign of movement down the commo trench. Quite suddenly he looked over his left shoulder toward the rampart. Six Chinese stood on the earthbank directly above his head, gazing down at him. From behind Sakasegawa someone (it was probably Transeau) opened fire with a carbine. The sound animated Sakasegawa. He cut loose with his M1, firing three clips in less than one minute. He thought he saw three of the six

Chinese fall to his fire, but in his excitement he could not be sure. The others ducked out of sight downslope. Sakasegawa leaned over the trench wall and fired a fourth clipload that way. He could hear "many voices" chattering Chinese, broken repeatedly by a sharp command in English: "Spread out! Spread out!" It sounded to him then as if the enemy was trying to move around him and enter the commo trench farther up the finger. Rifle resting on the parapet, he leaned far over. But beyond 20 feet he could see nothing because an earth hummock masked the lower slope. Close at hand he could hear burp guns clattering and grenades popping. But he could not tell the direction of the sounds.

Sakasegawa waited for about five minutes, wondering what to do, fearful that if he fired more, he would run out of ammunition. There was plenty of it in the bunker, 35 feet away, but he felt rooted to the spot. Then two grenades thumped on the earthbank within a few feet of his head, rebounded down the slope and exploded; that meant that the Chinese grenadiers were not more than 10 yards below him. Pvt. Andy Amadelo joined Sakasegawa. Another grenade came in, landed right next to Amadelo's feet and, exploding, spent its force in air, not even scratching him. He said to Sakasegawa, "I think we better give them something." So both men grenaded the outer sides of the trench wall upslope, throwing four bombs apiece. They saw no positive sign that the Chinese were moving in that direction. But that was their open flank and the point of main danger. The grenading was just a precaution. They heard nothing more of the enemy.

Privates Gardner and Bee, who had been bounced hard out of Outgard No. 15, blocked by the advance of the enemy main body and diverted toward the company hill, didn't get very far. Unintentionally, they collided with the enemy group which was recoiling from Sakasegawa's fire. There were about twelve Chinese. Gardner and Bee tried to run on. Several potato mashers exploded at their heels. As the steel bit into their legs, they stumbled and fell. Gardner yelled, "Throw!" They jumped up and grenaded back, each man throwing twice. In the action they became split. For a time they hid in the grass. They were not certain they had hit any Chinese but they had seen the group scatter and run. After the field was clear, they separately found their way back to the Snook CP.

Apart from the action by Gardner and Bee and the killing of the three men on No. 14, the outguards did not get into the fire fight. They sat steady with weapons ready, awaiting the chance to use them effectively. The chance never came.

Sakai continued to worry about the enemy gunner he had seen and attempted to wing atop the CP roof. The man had disappeared into shadow and Sakai, who is a very small soldier, couldn't sight across the roof top. Transeau again emerged from the bunker. The Chinese rose out of the sandbags, fired once with the burp gun and hit Transeau in the shoulder. Then he jumped clear and was lost in the darkness before Sakai could fire.

That was the last shot in the in-fighting.

Transeau returned to his phone to tell Acuff, "Sir, I think we've got it made. We've been going for twenty minutes and I haven't yet heard one yell from my crew." He had not had time to check the squad. He was playing it by ear. But the guess was right.

The fight had started at 2304. At 2327 the Chinese attackers put up two red flares over Snook. It must have been a distress signal, since they made no further effort to close against the garrison.

Acuff meanwhile had put his supporting fires along the flanks of the finger and on the valley floor ahead of Snook. It was a gradual crescendo, begun in the first three minutes by two Quad-50s, joined later by one platoon of 4.2 mortars, four 60-mm mortars and one battery of 105s. When the two Chinese flares were fired, Acuff called for "Flash Snook" and within one minute the curtain of fire closed around the front of the knob. That interdicted the escape route and provided just enough light to put a glow over the finish. One large group of the enemy was seen by Transeau as it attempted a getaway; in midflight, it was hit by a salvo of 4.2 shells, and when the smoke cleared, no sign of life remained.

At 2400 two answering flares were fired from the Chinese hill named Pokkae. If it was a signal to withdraw, it was already too late. Those for whom the signal was intended were already either destroyed or in full flight, due to the more or less random efforts of seven willing American riflemen.

Transeau sat down to make his final accounting, totaling his wins and losses before reporting to Acuff. His bookkeeping completed, he called for first aid.

INDEX